Finding My Way

A Memoir

Jerry Morton

This book is a memoir. It reflects the author's present recollections of experiences over time. Some names and characteristics have been changed, some events have been compressed, and some dialogue has been recreated.

Printed in the United States of America
First Printing 2022
All rights reserved.

ISBN: 978-1-948894-34-0

For reproduction permission, contact the author or publisher:

Tree Shadow Press

www.treeshadowpress.com

DEDICATION

*This book is dedicated to my wife for her patience,
her many re-reads as I wrote the stories
and the sharing of our adventures
since the winter of 1960.*

ACKNOWLEDGMENTS

Without the dedicated teachers, fellow professionals, former interns, parents, dear friends and complete strangers with whom I have had the privilege of interacting I could not have reached the understandings that currently serve as my compass in life. Some of my most insightful teachers have been the young children who have spontaneously demonstrated their inner wisdom to me in remarkable ways. Thank you all for these gifts.

EDITOR'S NOTE

The stories in this book are from the author's podcast. In order to keep them true to their episodes, the reader will find that some stories repeat some details and general information. These repetitions serve as reminders and make it possible to read the stories in any order without missing any vital background information.

TABLE OF CONTENTS

INTRODUCTION

You are about to read true stories I have written relating to events from my early childhood, my adolescence and my adulthood into my senior years. I think you will find them interesting as they reflect many of the diverse sub-cultures within the United States I have experienced. What I think you'll find in these stories is a reaffirmation of the sense of fairness that exists within all of us regardless of our backgrounds or current life situations.

As I reflect on my life, I realize how fortunate I have been to experience so many different belief systems throughout my childhood and into my adult years. In 1942, I was born into a career U. S. Coast Guard family that moved rather frequently. Into my teenage years I had the opportunity to live in six different states and attend at least eight different public schools. During my junior and senior high school years, I worked at a variety of part time jobs like picking up towels in a YMCA weight room, counseling at a summer Boy Scout camp, and cutting up whole chickens and clerking for a retail poultry store.

My college years found me living in a new state, Kentucky. While completing my four years of undergraduate studies in psychology and English, I was employed as the director of student

1

employment in the Centre College dining hall. During the summer between my freshman and sophomore years, I worked as a lifeguard in Pittsburgh, Pennsylvania. My family had moved there in the middle of my tenth grade and remained there for a year after I graduated from high school. The next two summers I worked as a deckhand on an ocean-going dredge boat out of Port Lavaca, Texas. Most of my fellow deckhands were Hispanic or from the Louisiana bayou country.

After graduating from college in 1964, I went to Miami University of Ohio for two years to earn a master's degree in school psychology. Immediately upon graduating from that university in August 1966, I was forced by circumstances to enter the U. S. Army. A book I wrote in 2004, *Reluctant Lieutenant: From Basic to OCS in the Sixties,* describes my year of Army training. Texas A & M University Press published it as a military history book. After completing the year of training, I was unexpectedly assigned to the Psychological Warfare School at the Special Warfare Center, Ft. Bragg, North Carolina. I spent two years there as a psychology instructor assisting those assigned to my classes in understanding and relating to a variety of cultures in other countries. This experience prepared me extremely well for my first job upon leaving the Army in 1969. I was a master's level school psychologist serving seven inner city schools in St. Petersburg, Florida, as those schools were being integrated for the first time.

After two years in St. Petersburg, I entered the University of Tennessee in Knoxville, Tennessee, as a doctoral student in psychology. I specialized in school psychology. Two years later I had obtained my Ph.D. and was employed as the director of psychological and special education services for the Little Tennessee Valley Educational Cooperative (LTVEC). The year I began working, 1973, was the first year Tennessee began implementing its new special education laws, which were followed in 1975 by the first comprehensive federal special education laws. Due to the tragic death of the educational cooperative's director in December of 1975, I became the director of the cooperative and remained in that role until 2014.

While maintaining my role as the director of LTVEC during those years I was engaged in other activities that revolved around providing services to children. For example, for ten years I was a due process hearing officer in special education law for the Tennessee Department of Education. From 1986 to August of 1991, I was the director of an alternative school serving seventh through twelfth graders who had been suspended from their public schools for long periods of time. Rosa Kennedy and I wrote a book about the focus of that school, *A School for Healing: Alternative Strategies for Teaching At-Risk Students.* It was published by Peter Lang Publishing. I served as the director of a doctoral internship program in school psychology through the Tennessee Internship Consortium from 1999 until my retirement.

During my off-duty time in Tennessee, I began exploring claims of psychic experiences. This exploration has taken me to belief systems I would never have considered before and caused me to alter many heretofore unrecognized beliefs of my own. While all of this was taking place, I have continued to live the life of a person who works to value all of the remarkable people with whom I have had the privilege of interacting.

The first story, "Bully," is one from my adolescent years. This book starts with a series of stories from my teenage years followed by ones from my early childhood. It continues with stories from my college years and beyond. All of the stories are copyrighted. You can follow me at Authorsguildoftn.org on my author's page. Now for the first story, "Bully."

CHAPTER ONE

Bully

It happened in first period English. He hadn't bothered me all that much this year. September was almost over without his trying to touch me, mess up my hair or attempt to push my books off my desk as he'd done off and on in ninth-grade homeroom most of last year. I sat in the middle of the row of seats beside the windows. He sat three rows over and about four desks back from the front.

I was talking to a classmate in the seat next to mine. We were excited about the first graded paper that would be returned to us as soon as the bell rang for the class to begin.

I didn't see him coming. In the middle of my saying something to my new friend, a wet finger rammed into my ear. As I instinctively swatted my hand at the withdrawing finger and turned my head to see what was going on, the guy rushed on down the row, going to his seat with a big grin that stayed directed my way until he sat in his desk chair.

This had to stop now! I had learned a lot since last year. No longer was I naïve about bullying or about whom the bullies were or what the victims had to do to prevent their lives from being a living hell.

Good View subdivision was located on Root River in the northwest corner of Racine County, Wisconsin. It was about a forty-five-minute ride by school bus to get to Washington Junior High School in Racine. That's where I began ninth grade after finishing eighth grade in Kenosha, Wisconsin. I had just completed seventh and eighth grade at Kenosha's Washington Junior High School. As soon as the eighth-grade school year was over, we moved to Good View.

I was a little sad to be moving from Kenosha. The people there were cordial to my family and me. At the end of eighth grade, I had been awarded the Good Citizenship Award from a community organization that presented it each year to the student selected by the teachers and students from the eighth grade. I was pleased to have been so honored. In addition, I was going to attend Kenosha's Camp O-Da-Cho-Ta Boy Scout summer camp for a month. Yes, it was a little sad to leave Kenosha; but I had summer camp coming up. I'd see a lot of old friends there. Besides, my family was always moving to a new location. The adventure of meeting new kids and doing new things was by now usually an eagerly anticipated event.

The actual move to Good View didn't seem like much. We had spent many weekends before the move in the little one-level slab house throughout the spring. The houses were being sold at bargain prices because they were in different stages of completion. My dad spent several weekends laying down the asphalt tiles on the cement floor of the house, completing the attic insulation and installing some of the missing doors. He'd work hard and long into the night to get the house ready to live in. I helped where I could. My primary task was helping my mother care for my two brothers. The youngest was just a baby, and the other one was nine.

When we moved into the house, it finally dawned on me just how isolated the subdivision really was. In Kenosha we lived within walking distance of the movie theatre, the stores and the schools. In Good View, there was nothing. There were no stores, no movies, no parks, no playgrounds and not much of anything else. Well, the exception was a lot of little houses on brown dirt lots.

I take that back. There was Root River. It ran behind our house and was bordered by woods that varied in thickness. I loved the water, and I loved being in the woods. The river was more like a big creek. The other side of the river was Milwaukee County. The city of Milwaukee was further from the subdivision than Racine was. That wasn't much help as it took a long time to get to Racine. The only way to get there was by car. Being a one-car family put a real damper on going anywhere besides the subdivision and school.

The first two weeks of living in the new house were filled with unpacking boxes, putting things away and settling in. Not much time remained to get to know any of the kids living in the subdivision before I left for the Boy Scout camp. When I returned from that month-long adventure, not much time remained to get to know anyone to hang out with. I did learn a few things about the students I'd be going to school with. The subdivision had about fifty boys in it who were attending the junior high school or the high school. I was soon to find out that I was one of approximately five guys who had not served a significant period of time in prison.

Amazingly, none of the kids from the subdivision were ever in any of my classes. Part of that was that I had always done well in school. That was not the case for most of the neighborhood kids.

The mornings provided me with the bulk of my learning experiences concerning how things worked in the subdivision among us kids. It was while we waited for the school bus that my social education took place. The two dominant games played were "hockers" and "hurtum." Sometimes "wedgies" was played but not that often. Wedgies was used by someone who considered himself to be physically overpowering when compared to the victim. He would quietly come up behind the target and violently grab the back of his pants, yank the back of the pants, almost completely lifting the target off the ground and driving the crotch of his pants into his testicles. Another game was grabbing the front of a guy's shirt in the hopes of getting a grip on a nipple and twisting. That really hurt. You needed to be constantly on guard for that one. Naturally, those initiating these games indicated that it was done all in fun to amuse and impress the other bystanders.

The goal of hockers was to snuff up big gobs of snot and spit it as close as you dared at the back of someone's coat. If the person spit at didn't retaliate or become aggressive in some effective way, the spitter, the hocker, would spit it closer and closer to the person's coat. Without an aggressive response or a particularly weak response from the victim, the spitter felt free to actually hit the coat. Sometimes as many as six to ten gobs of slime would cling to the back of a guy's coat as he finally boarded the morning bus.

Hurtum was a pretty straightforward attempt to hurt another guy. It began by someone walking up to you and punching you firmly in the shoulder. The punch had to be hard enough to hurt, but not your hardest punch by a long shot. The receiver of the punch was not to display any sign that he was in pain. He also had a free punch. He was expected to turn around and punch his assailant in the shoulder with a little bit harder punch than he had received. This series of ever-increasing power punches continued until one guy stopped. Now, the way that person chose to stop was important. It had to be done with style. If you didn't do it right, it would be a signal to all the other guys to start using your arm as a punching bag.

Late in the fall of ninth grade, I was still trying to master the best way of ending the hurtum game. It was a favorite of John's. John was really big for his age although I was never sure of his actual age. He was in the same grade as I was but was bigger than anyone else. He was at least six feet, three inches tall and weighed around 220 pounds. He was full of muscle. For comparison purposes, back then I was about five feet, ten inches tall and weighed around 130 pounds. Some of the things I had going for me were that I had a good sense of humor with a touch of a sarcastic bite. I knew that I knew how to fight and I was far stronger than I looked.

Anyway, on this one fall day there had been an early snow. There was an inch or two of it on the ground. It was nothing to slow traffic down but just enough to make the cold a little colder. As we were getting off the school bus, John decided to punch me in the shoulder. It hurt. I instinctively punched his arm hard, really hard. I didn't need this stuff at that moment. He took offense and started at me with his fists up just as the bus pulled away.

"Hold off," I screamed in his face. "Let me drop these books off at the house. I can't pay for damages. Then I'll clean your clock."

"OK, you shit, I'll take mine home and come back and kick your ass."

"That's just fine. See you in half an hour. Behind my house."

Damn, I had a way of getting my-self into fixes. Fighting was all right in the heat of the moment, but given time to think before the fight, I always found myself reflecting on the mess I had gotten myself into. John was going to really hurt me. There was no way around it. He was so much bigger and stronger than I was. This was bad. This was very bad.

He knocked on the back door. I opened it and stepped outside without putting my coat on. I needed as much freedom of movement as I could get.

"You little turd. I've come to smash your face in," he said as he slapped me on the side of my head.

That was it. Nobody slaps me. Just as he was pulling back his fist to land a solid blow to my head, I let go with a right hook that was as fast and as strong as I could make it in my rage. It landed solidly on the side of his nose. He fell to his knees, holding his damaged appendage as the blood gushed through the cupped fingers of his hands.

"I can't breathe. I can't breathe," he shouted, spitting blood on the front of my shirt. Without thinking, I scooped up a double handful of snow and pressed it to the back of his neck.

"Hold the snow on your neck. I'll get some more for you to hold on your nose. Tip your head back."

He obeyed. The second helping of snow went into his outstretched free hand and then to the base of his nose while I grabbed another handful of snow and placed it with the melting snow he was still holding at the back of his neck. We stood together in this strange embrace for a minute or two.

It worked. His nose stopped bleeding. He thanked me as he wiped his hands in the snow and brought more snow to his upper lip to wipe smeared blood off. He didn't do a particularly good job. His face and shirt were a mess.

"How'd you know what to do?"

"I learned it in Boy Scouts."

"Oh, lucky me, hey?"

Actually, I learned it from my mother. She had used that technique on me more than once to stop the various bloody noses I would acquire from being naturally adventuresome. It just didn't seem to be the right moment to tell your newly vanquished foe that your mother taught you how to stop his nose from bleeding as a result of a punch you had thrown just seconds before.

After he had assured me that he was OK, we shook hands and parted as friends. Now, this didn't mean that he never started the hockers game or the hurtum game with me again, far from it. However, when I returned a hocker near his coat or gave him a harder punch in the shoulder than I had received, he would just laugh and turn to someone else to begin the games again.

There were some really strange and often violent things that took place during the year and a half I lived there. For example, in the spring, the county sent some social workers to Good View. I guess the county felt that we needed some professional guidance with so many guys going in and out of jail. Our little subdivision had acquired a reputation in the relatively short time of its existence. One encounter that made this point occurred in a suburb of Milwaukee.

I was waiting one night for my mother to pick me up from a meeting I attended at this Presbyterian missionary church in South Milwaukee. It was dark out. Everyone else had left. My mother was late. It was understandable as the church was at least an hour away from our house. While I was waiting on the steps, some guys on motorcycles drove slowly by. They gave me a good look-over as they passed. Towards the end of the street they turned and came back up. They stopped in front of the steps I was sitting on. These guys were men. They looked mean. They quizzed me aggressively and asked if I had any money on me. I was scared. The whole thing was looking to end badly.

"Where you from, kid?"

"Good View, off of Root River."

"No, you're not!"

"I am."

"Who do you know there that we might know?"

"Well, there's Frog and Sims."

"You know them! Ok, kid. You're all right. Tell them Phil and the guys said hey!"

With that, they all started their motorcycles and drove off in a lot of smoke and the fading roar of their cycles.

The county social workers were clearly do-gooders sent to save us kids was the word going around. That produced laughter and curiosity. From our collective perspective, we didn't need saving. Those people didn't have a clue about what was really going on here. Even if they did, there was nothing they could do about it. This one social worker had to have been a weightlifter. He was all sculpted muscle. I mean he had developed an awful lot of muscle just about everywhere. If you had told me that his ears had big muscles, I might have believed you. Clearly, you just did not want this guy mad at you. He could dominate any fighter we of the Good View could produce with the exception maybe of one guy who was not here at the time. The social worker knew that he physically dominated us guys. His swagger, his muscled arms held slightly away from his torso as if about to repel an assault and his haughty stare told anyone thinking of starting trouble that this guy just knew he could pound you into the dirt without breaking into a sweat.

This strong man social worker calls all of us guys fooling around the Teen Center to gather around him. The Teen Center was one of the unfinished houses near the center of the subdivision that had been donated somehow for the use of the community. Anyway, this guy calls all of us around him and says he wants to play a game with anyone willing to play it with him. Taking a large bandana from his back pocket and tying a huge knot in the end of it as he spoke, making sure that the knot was rock solid, he says that he will lean against the house wall and wait for someone to pick the bandana up from the ground behind him and swat him on the butt as hard as they can. Then the hitter is to throw the bandana back on the ground. As soon as the man is hit, he will turn around to see if he can catch the person who has hit him. If he can correctly identify that person, then that person has to stand with his back to the crowd and be hit. He will have to stand there and be hit until he can be quick enough to turn around and correctly identify the hitter. Thus the game would continue for a while.

We all looked at each other. This guy looked fast enough to catch the hitter after the first time to me. I sure would not want to be hit by a swing of the knotted end of the bandana from this guy. Why was he doing this? We all were amused that this adult would want to engage us guys in this way. The girls seemed to think it was really funny. What was he trying to prove? He didn't need to prove anything to me.

There had to be thirty or forty of us standing behind the fellow as he stood with his back to us resting his eyes on his forearm pressed against the wall. The crowd murmured as eyes swung around to see if someone would rise to the challenge.

Quick as a mountain lion springs on its prey, Frog bent down, grabbed the long end of the bandana and swung it. Its contact on the man's butt sounded like a rifle shot. Before you could blink an eye, Frog had thrown the bandana on the ground to assume a relaxed stance in the first row of kids.

Instantaneously, the guy shot around. He pointed to Sims, "You did it, didn't you!"

The crowd hooted and hollered. He knew he was wrong. Smiling, he turned to assume the position for punishment again.

Again, Frog picked the bandana up and administered an astoundingly punishing blow. As he threw the bandana down, he switched places with Sims. Even faster than the first time, the social worker twisted around to face the crowd. He pointed at the guy I had seen Frog knock unconscious with one blow last winter. The crowd booed this supposed savior of us wayward youth.

The poor social worked allowed his butt to be hit by Frog several more times before he called an end to the game. I think he was a little wiser than when he had started. In any event we were all proud to have seen a cocky, adult muscle-man meet his match. We were proud of us as a group. You had just better watch out if you messed with the guys from Good View.

When I returned from being away for the entire summer season as a camp counselor at Camp Oh-Da-Cot-Ta, the summer between my ninth and tenth grades, all of the kids were busting to tell me the story of Frog and Sims. The story was told with great humor and pride.

We all knew that Frog and Sims hung out together most of the time. They had spent some hard time in prison together in the past, I'd been told. They were pretty much inseparable, it seemed. All I knew was that it was good to stay away from them although both of them seemed to respect me. They never tried to hassle me or engage in the teasing games with me. In that regard, I was a rarity.

As the story went, a few weeks before I had returned to Good View, Frog and Sims stole a car from someone's driveway in the subdivision. Apparently, they didn't want to sell it or anything like that. It was just a fast car. They wanted to drive it as fast as they could up and down the highway at the far end of the subdivision, the highway that went to Milwaukee. They tore up the highway driving the car back and forth with the wheels screaming on the curves, the motor roaring on the straight-a-ways and the wind whipping in their faces. They did this many times until the engine blew. They ditched the car off the side of the road, right where it had died.

Well, it didn't take the highway patrol long to come pounding on Frog's and Sims's front doors. A lot of highway patrol cars showed up for the arrest. They surrounded the two nearby houses Frog and Sims lived in as if a major shoot-out was going to take place. Well, of course, everyone turned out to watch the show. The street in front of the two wild riders' houses was full of on-lookers. Frog and Sims opened their doors, raised their hands and calmly walked up to the state cops amidst the cheers of the crowd. The state troopers had them put their hands behind their backs and cuffed them. They were escorted to a highway patrol car and put in the back seat. The back doors of the police car remained open as the officers talked among themselves, and the on-lookers shouted words of encouragement to their beloved criminals.

Frog and Sims shouted out humorous comments to the crowd, which pleased everyone. Even the police officers laughed. They weren't particularly concerned about their two prisoners, it seemed.

Suddenly, Frog and Sims exited the police cruiser and took off running into the nearby woods. They didn't run particularly fast as they were hampered by the cuffed hands behind their backs. The crowd roared with laughter. The two of them couldn't get far.

Reportedly, the police didn't fully understand what was happening until the guys had just about reached the tree line. The officers formed a firing line and began walking into the woods after them as they shouted for the two fugitives to surrender.

Once in the woods, the officers held up their pistols and shot into the air, trying to flush the guys out. It was understood that they were shooting straight up into the air so as not to accidentally shoot either Frog or Sims.

All of a sudden, Frog and Sims started walking from the tree line. They got to the police car they were originally in and calmly sat down in it. What a cool move it was, and the crowd roared its approval of this gutsy finesse. It took the troopers a while to realize that the adventurers had passed through their lines and returned to the car. Everyone admired the audacity of the two guys. They were definitely stupid but had somehow demonstrated that they were momentarily smarter than the state troopers. The consensus of those telling me the story was that once again Frog and Sims showed everyone that they were good guys. They had approached folk-hero status.

# # #

So, this bully had given me a Wet Willy. I could not let this stand. If I did not do something, make some kind of statement, my life in this school would be hell!

The bell rang. The English class had begun. Everyone was seated as the teacher told the class that she would hand back the graded essay papers and proceed to discuss some of the good points she had observed in them and some of the issues we could improve upon for the next paper we would write. She went to the head of the first row of chairs by the hallway door, picked out the right number of papers to be passed back down the row and then started to repeat the process on the second row.

With clear determination, I quietly maneuvered myself out of the desk-chair without scooting it as I squeezed past the armrest-writing-table part of the chair. I determinedly walked to the back of my row over to his row, up to his chair. He never saw me coming. He sat in his chair looking at the teacher as she gave the first person in his row the papers to hand back. Pulling back my fist, I let fly a downward punch into his jaw. It was a solid, hard punch, not as hard as I could have thrown but definitely one that would really hurt.

He was stunned. He tried to get out of his chair but was held back by the armrest-writing station part of it and his inability to untangle his feet from under it. I pulled back to lay another one on him if it looked as if he was actually going to get out of the chair when the teacher began pushing me back. She had both her arms spread out, holding us apart. He stopped struggling to get out of the chair.

"Boys, boys, you stop this right now," she shouted in alarm. "Jerry, you go back to your seat."

I did.

Periodically, the guy shot mean glances at me. That was OK. I hadn't finished with him. It was OK if he wanted this to continue. Oh, I had gotten an "A" on my paper.

The bell rang. The class was over. He waited for me at the door. When we were face to face, he spat out, "This isn't over. I'm going to get you."

"That's just fine. I'll meet you in front of the football stadium

16

right after school. We'll fight, all right."

"I'll be there, and I'll smash you to pieces."

With that we parted. By the end of second period all of the guys from Good View seemed to have heard of the confrontation. They wanted to know what was going to happen. I told them.

John was particularly excited about it all as he asked, "Do you want a couple of us to just knock the shit out of him as he's leaving the last class? He's a hell of a lot bigger than you are. We can take care of him for you."

"No, no, I can fight my own fights. It would be good if some of the guys could show up with me just in case some of his guys decide to jump into the fight. I just need for his people to be kept off of me. It would mean you'd miss the bus."

"It's done. We'll be there. We'll take care of you!"

By the end of third period, it seemed that the whole school knew that there was going to be a rumble between the Good View guys and the bully's guys. The more I thought about it, the more I thought that having the guys there was a bad idea. Why, half the school might turn out to watch the fight. The whole thing was a bad idea. First of all, this guy was so much bigger than I was, and he had a hell of a lot more muscle. I was probably going to get the shit kicked out of me. Then there was the issue of our guys. Some of them were not going to stand by while I got slaughtered. This could end up being a large-scale free-for-all. Some of the Good View guys just might pick up sticks, boards or rocks to use if it got really bad. The whole thing could get extremely violent. People would be seriously injured. There would be blood. The police would show up. People would be arrested. I could be arrested. I would be the one who assaulted the guy in the first place. No, this was bad. This was very bad.

At lunch, I put out the word that the fight had been called off.

I was not going to fight the guy. No one needed to miss the bus. For the rest of that day and through the night, I dreaded the thought of showing up at school the next morning. The bully was going to make my life hell.

No one had much to say to me during the bus ride home nor in the morning going back to school. I walked into English class ready to receive my medicine. Fortunately, the bully hadn't arrived yet. I sat in my usual seat by the windows waiting for my nemesis. I saw him in the hallway as he approached the door. He entered without a glance my way. Quickly, he went straight to his seat. He never looked towards the window. That was the way it was. He would never look in my direction. The classroom hour passed without a glance my way. When the bell to change classes rang, he was one of the very first to leave the room. That was the way that first semester of school at Horlick High passed. The bully never looked at me directly, he never approached me and he appeared to go to great lengths to stay as far away from me as possible.

His behavior was a puzzle to me. I did not understand why he didn't confront me as a coward, why he didn't take my failure to show up for the fight as an incentive to bully me even more. Years had to pass before I finally felt that I had figured it out.

CHAPTER TWO

Off the Bus

Right off, she started out on the wrong foot. As the ten or so of us boarded the Racine County school bus that cold October morning in 1957, there was the usual horseplay among the boys. We were a mix of junior high school and senior high school students isolated by an hour drive from Good View Subdivision to our destination, Horlick High School in Racine, Wisconsin. Mark had a few snot gobs hanging on the back of his coat that he didn't know about. Susie screamed that someone had just tried to goose her and then burst into laughter. You know, it was just another of those typical Good View, getting on the bus, mornings.

"You people had better start behaving," she shouted at us with an angry stare flowing from the large rearview mirror hanging over her head.

"I've had it with your smart-alecky sassiness. You're going to behave like young adults or you're not going to be on this bus much longer."

"Oooohwhooooo,"

"What a bitch."

"Your days are numbered on this bus, lady."

These were just a few of the catcalls I could hear from the crowded bus. The uproar was massive. She had just stirred up a hornet's nest the likes of which she could not imagine, was my take of the situation.

Our collection of kids from Good View was not one that responded favorably to angry words from an adult telling them to act like ladies and gentlemen. The group pride ran in the direction of being the baddist of the bad. There was a collective pride in the fact that almost all of the guys had spent time in prison. The word was that there were only about three or four of us who had never even been arrested. I was one of those three or four as was poor Mark, the guy with snot gobs on the back of his coat.

Several of us felt bad that Mark was picked on that way. He was a quiet enough guy who always smiled when anyone spoke to him. Where there was a gathering, you'd usually find Mark. He never participated in any bad behavior or caused anyone grief. He was just there with that pleasant, puppy-dog smile. He'd help you out if you dropped some books or needed someone to go back to the makeshift baseball field to get a glove that had been forgotten. He was an all-around nice guy. Everyone agreed on that point. When you could, you looked out for him. Waiting at the bus stop in the morning was not a time to look out for anyone but yourself. You had to be on guard to respond just as soon as someone began to reach for your chest to twist your shirtfront to cause it to look as if you had a nipple pushing out. They'd actually grab your nipple under your shirt and twist it as well if they were lucky enough to get a good hold through your coat, your shirt and your tee shirt.

Naturally, you had to be on the lookout for someone spitting a big hocker close to your coat. To let that go unchallenged instead of a return hocker closer to your assailant's coat than he was to yours was an open invitation for the back or your coat to end up like Mark's. Those mornings at the bus stop required so much alertness on my part to protect myself that looking out for Mark then was just out of the question.

My first year as a member of the fifty or so boys riding the school buses from Good View to my ninth-grade school had taught me how to maintain my own space from all of the bullying that took place. Good View was not a happy place for someone who did not stand up for himself. This first semester as a tenth grader, my first year in a real high school, my fellow occupants on the bus didn't intimidate me. I had established that I could and would stand up for myself. I was respected by my peers. Not because I'd been in jail, I hadn't; not because I was the best fighter or the best athlete, I wasn't; but because I had grit. I would stand up for myself even when I and everyone else knew I would lose. I never picked on anyone. I always tried to be kind when the opportunity presented itself, and I was often a loner. My chief entertainment was being in the woods and attending Boy Scout activities. I knew that to spend much time with these guys was to get into trouble. I had no desire to rob a grocery store, break out someone's windows because they had made me mad or to become overly committed to winning some group game. Now, that's how I saw myself with these guys. I'm not really sure how they actually saw me. I doubt that I will ever know that.

She just stopped the bus in the middle of the two-lane road, "You are all out of control. You just stop this. You just stop this right now. You will not insult me one more time. I've had it with you. Every one of you!"

For a few seconds, there was silence on the bus. With a slight smirk, as if she thought she had won, the lady driver sat back in her seat and started the bus.

Just past my ear, flying up the aisle went a balled-up

sandwich. It smacked onto the front windshield just to the right of her face. It seemed to have been a grape jelly sandwich. A huge burst of laughter and anger erupted from the two thirds of the bus to my rear. The gates of the dam had been opened.

Bananas, water-soaked napkins, cookies and a host of other objects flew to the front of the bus. It was clear that there was a collective objective: it was not to hit the lady bus driver but to come as close to hitting her as the assailants could. They were successful.

Her terrified face in the rearview mirror served as all the reinforcement the kids needed to continue the barrage. The laughter filled the bus as missile after missile was launched towards the front.

I did not participate, of course, but I did openly chuckle at the absurdity of it all. Looking back at the guys, there were several who paralleled my response to the outlandish eruption of rebellion. We were not participants in this assault. We didn't throw anything or shout insults at the lady. No one on the bus expected me or the other non-combatants to join in. It was just that the aggressive ones were predictably being themselves. They were having fun, and those that were having the fun didn't mind if other fun lovers wanted to join in; that was all. Clearly, from their perspective it was getting a little revenge, while having fun, on the adult, the lady bus driver, who had unjustly treated them. After all, she had provoked them; she had asked for it.

Yes, she had used the wrong way of trying to calm this group down. I could have told her that yelling at the group and telling them to behave would not work. Not only would it not work, but it would produce the opposite behavior she wanted the kids to display. However, like most adults of our day, she didn't want to hear what kids had to say. She just wanted us kids to obey and follow her orders the way she wanted them to be followed. Maybe that worked with the good children of Racine, but it would never work with those from Good View.

The onslaught of food thrown towards the lady fairly quickly came to an end. She had been silent after those last confrontational words. Her silence enabled her to stop reinforcing the behavior. The fact that there probably wasn't much more ammunition available had to have been a contributing factor.

The ride back from the high school to our bus stop in Good View had to be hell for the lady bus driver. She glared at each of us as we boarded the bus at the end of the school day. Several of the guys and some of the girls mumbled curses at her as they passed by her seat.

"Bitch."

"Ugly cow."

"Whore."

The bus driver didn't respond; she just glared at all of us. Once we were a few minutes down the road, it seemed the kids finally forgot about her. There was the usual horseplay going on between John and Lance. Some girls were flirting with a couple of the guys. Henry was starting to do his homework. He always did that on the trip back. I was engaged in talking with an acquaintance about something that had happened during the rehearsal for the play I was in. My English teacher was having me be a reporter giving made-up news broadcasts to anyone who would listen during lunch hour in the school cafeteria. I was the co-star. It was a funny show. I hoped the high school kids liked it.

As my group was getting off the bus, the driver said, "You're going to be sorry for your behavior! I've called the police!"

"Whoo-hoo," was the cry from several in our collection of students.

It took a while for all of us to get off the bus at this particular spot. A lot of us lived on this street or on nearby ones. As I was walking by the back of the bus, I noticed someone on the other side of it wedge a metal spike between one of the double rear tires and the asphalt. When the bus pulled out, that spike would puncture the tire. I looked away. I knew not to be a part of this act of revenge.

Well, I thought I'd hear a loud explosion as the tire was punctured. Nothing happened. The bus just drove on. I didn't see the tire go suddenly flat. A few of the boys and girls walking my way had seen this event unfold. We all looked at one another and shrugged. Nothing happens as you expect it to.

The next morning found us all together at the bus stop as usual. It was like all the other cold dark mornings with shoulders being punched, snot being spit and laughter mixed into conversations. The bus pulled up. There was a new bus driver and some man standing at the door of the bus with his hand held up to stop us.

"Only the girls are allowed on the bus."

"What, how are we going to get to school?"

"That's your problem. Only the girls. Come on girls, get on."

They filed in.

All the guys were left by the side of the road; there was nowhere for us to go but back to our houses.

I told my mom what had happened. She tried to call the school. All of the lines were busy. She was mad. She drove me to school. I was one of the few guys from Good View subdivision attending school that day. Nothing was said to me about not being able to ride the bus to school. It seemed to be a normal day of classes.

When my mom picked me up from school that afternoon, she

asked me what I had heard about the bus situation. I hadn't heard anything. No one brought it up. She said the school had called her. They told her about the boys assaulting the bus driver and destroying something on the bus. The boys from the subdivision were not allowed to ride the school bus again. There was supposed to be an announcement about it on the TV that evening.

Before supper, the two sisters from the end of our street were walking by. I went outside and asked them what they had heard. They said all the guys were banned from riding the bus because of what had happened the day before. It wasn't fair, they said because most of the guys didn't do anything. Well, I could have argued that at least half of them did throw something even though I hadn't seen more than a couple of guys tossing things because I was seated so close to the front of the bus. I let the point pass without contradiction. No one knew when we would ever be allowed back on the bus. The girls said they had gotten back at the system for being so unfair. Between riding to school in the morning on the bus and riding back home that afternoon, they had removed all of the screws they could from inside the bus. They had used their fingernail files as screwdrivers. At some point, someone would discover that all of the seats wouldn't stay on their metal frames, lots of the windows wouldn't work and the side panels would fall off. They were pretty proud of their handiwork.

I didn't see the governor tell the state of Wisconsin about us. I was doing homework in my room. The two sisters told me that he said that all of the boys from Good View subdivision were juvenile hoodlums who were all failing in school, destroyed school property, cut out of school more often than they attended and were a disgrace to the state. Well, John and Lance were the only two guys I knew of who had destroyed school property. A few weeks ago, John pointed out to me where he had carved, "Fuck you Horlick" into the beautiful wood planks that divided the marble walls from the higher stucco wall that went to the ceiling. John was one of the few people in the school, if not the only one, tall enough to have reached that high to do the damage. Both John and Lance thought that what he had done was really funny. Lance went on to tell me that while John was doing that, he stuffed a bunch of paper towels and stuff in a trash can in the bathroom and set it on fire. They both laughed at that one. I just shook my head at them and said they were crazy. They thought that was funny, too.

While driving me to school for the second morning, my Mom told me that next week there was going to be a big meeting for the parents of all us boys. I could come to the meeting with her if I wanted. I declined the offer. It would be embarrassing to sit there while Mother vented her anger at this unjust act. There was no telling what she would say.

Well, the whole process was really upsetting. It was a big bother for my mother to drive me to school. She had to deal with the babysitter for my baby brother, get my other brother off to elementary school, drive my dad to work when he was in town and then go to her work after dropping me off. I was sorry for all of this trouble. There was nothing I could do about it.

One of those no-bus bad mornings, my biology teacher asked me to stay in the classroom after the other students had left. It was the class just before lunch, so it was OK for me to stay.

"I'm concerned about your homework. It seems to have gone down some over the last few days. What's going on?"

This is terribly embarrassing. I had straight "A"s in all of my assignments and on all of my test papers for biology so far. This was my best year in school ever. I had "A"s in all of my classes except algebra. I mean, there was nothing to do but study in the evenings at home. It was so boring. There was just one TV station we could pick up in the isolated Good View subdivision of Wisconsin. At night the only radio signal that got through was some country music station out of Nashville, Tennessee of all places. It played something called "The Grand Ol' Opree." There was no rock and roll music to be heard. You couldn't hang out with the kids of the neighborhood. That would get you in jail. All there was to do was to study. That's what I had been doing. As I said, it was boring.

"I got kicked off the bus. They won't let us boys ride the bus," I said looking hard at the floor.

"I didn't realize you were involved in that. I'm sorry to hear that. It must be hard for you and your family."

I burst into tears. It was hard. I didn't know what to do to make it better. I was embarrassed. A guy wasn't to cry in front of a teacher. My tears wouldn't stop. I began to sob. She leaned over and gave me an awkward hug, patting me on the back. Oh, this was terrible.

As quickly as I could, I regained a degree of self-control. She handed me a Kleenex to wipe my face. Thanking her, I used it.

"You know," she said in a soft voice, "The administration wants to know who the ring leaders were. It would help the situation be resolved if they knew who the leaders were. You could tell them."

"I can't do that," I shouted through a new flow of tears. "You don't understand what would happen to my family. My younger brother would be beaten up. The windows in our house would be busted, our car windows too, the garbage cans would be thrown all over the yard. That would be just the beginning. I can't tell on anybody. There's no protection; there's no protection from what they would do."

"All right then, just think about it. Just know that I'm here for you."

As I walked to the cafeteria, I thought, *She doesn't have a clue about what life is like in the subdivision, none of them do. Anyway, I really don't know who the ringleaders were. I seriously doubt that there was a ringleader. It was just a happening. It just happened, that's all.* One thing was for sure; I wasn't about to tell my parents what the biology teacher had said. They would be angry. I certainly couldn't tell any of the kids. This just didn't happen.

"Hey, your mom really gave them an earful at that meeting last night. She said a lot of good things about you. Is it true, you have just about straight "A's"?

"Yeah,"

I was embarrassed.

"She said you had won awards and things at other schools you went to and all. I didn't know that," the sister from down the street said, as if a question kind of rolled around in the back of her head.

I wasn't going to verify her comments; I wanted to change the conversation.

"What'd they say about getting back on the bus?"

They said they would have to go back and check the school records on you and some other kids before they made a decision."

A few days more of this painful transportation situation passed when I got word from one of the sisters, "Hey, did you hear?"

"Hear what?"

"They kept questioning everyone about who the ringleader was. They called Mark in and questioned him. Mark confessed. He said he was the one who started it all. They've arrested him already. He's in jail."

"What? That's crazy! He didn't do anything. He's not a leader of anything."

"Yeah, that's what we all said too. It's crazy. Why would he want to confess? He never did anything bad like that. It's crazy isn't it?"

Poor Mark, I felt so sorry for him. It just didn't make sense. He was the one who collected hockers on the back of his coat. I've thought a lot about that confession. It's so hard to understand.

A few days later, we were allowed back on the bus. Not much was said about it. Someone said that someone from the governor's office got on TV and apologized to the community. I don't know if that was true. If an apology was made, I don't know what was said in it. My dad was being transferred. During Christmas break, we moved to Pittsburgh, Pennsylvania.

CHAPTER THREE

Missing Money

It was so nerve-racking to apply for a job. I hadn't applied for many. The last two summers I'd been a camp counselor for a Boy Scout summer camp in Kenosha, Wisconsin. In the middle of my sophomore year of high school, my family moved from outside Racine, Wisconsin to a suburb of Pittsburgh, Pennsylvania. I really liked being a camp counselor. However, the travel expenses of returning to Kenosha and then coming back made the adventure out of reach. The pay I would receive was about the same as the cost of the traveling involved.

That's why I was applying for a job that spring of 1959. I could use a job now but I really wanted to set things up for a summer job. My hope was to land one with a poultry store. Jim, a classmate, had a job with Ray and Bob's Poultry and Delicatessen. He liked it and it paid a dollar an hour. That was great money for a junior in high school about to become a senior. Of course, I'd have to quit the job when school started in the fall maybe even a little earlier in the summer when football practice started in earnest.

"We don't usually consider someone as young as you," the director of the YMCA branch for our Pittsburgh borough stated matter-of-factly.

"I understand that. I believe I was the youngest camp counselor to be in charge of a complete section of campers. It was called Pioneer Village. It was isolated from the other camping areas. I had two assistant counselors with me. There were around fifty or sixty campers and their adult leaders in the cabins every two-week cycle. I can give you the professional Boy Scout camp director's phone number if you want. He will give me a good reference."

"That's OK. I'm going to hire you. I think you'll do a good job. You'll work on Saturdays. I'll have you assist Ernie in the exercise room, assist Mike in the recreational area and maybe assist at the Saturday night dance. Be here next Saturday at 8:00 a.m. Someone will be here to tell you what to do."

That first Saturday was confusing. First of all, the recreation room coordinator wasn't scheduled to come to work until 9:00 a.m.

Ernie, the exercise area director, started his Saturday work schedule at 7:00 a.m. He didn't know anyone had been assigned to assist him on Saturdays. My arrival was a surprise to him. He said he'd been asking for assistance on Saturdays for several months. He seemed to appreciate that I was there.

Ernie was a middle-aged man of phenomenal strength. He was not as tall as I was, but his body was huge. He was all conditioned muscle. His arms had to be as large around as my thighs were, if not larger. Not an ounce of fat seemed to be squeezed between those developed strands of muscles.

By 8:30 a.m. the weight room was almost full. Bar bells were clanking, men were grunting and Ernie was providing words of encouragement along with helpful hints for proper conditioning. I was sitting in the caged towel room handling the electronic door release. It allowed people into the exercise area once they flashed me the proper ID. Then I pressed the electric button that caused a magnet in the metal mesh door to release the lock. Ernie also had me be responsible for handing out towels to those that wanted them. The task of periodically collecting the towels left on the benches by those who didn't put them in the re-wash bin was a natural part of my keeping the area neat.

Ernie always helped pick up the towels when he was walking through the area. He was like that. He just naturally did things to make my work a little easier. I enjoyed talking to him, as did others. He always seemed interested in what I was doing in school or with my friends. It was nice to have a real adult to talk to that wasn't a member of your family.

All of the weightlifters clearly valued Ernie. They would ask him for tips on how to stay in good condition and things like that. I guessed that anyone who knew Ernie simply had nothing but respect for him. I looked forward to the Saturdays at the Y because I got to spend time with Ernie.

Around noon the exercise room would be pretty clear of participants. Ernie would release me to go upstairs and help out in the recreation room. He'd have me check in with him every-once-in-a-while during the afternoons to see if there was any other cleaning up to do. Usually there wasn't. Ernie had already taken care of whatever had to be done.

The guy in charge of the recreation room was not all that much older than I was. He seemed to be more interested in watching a new TV show that came on around noon than in selling candy or keeping the place neat. I never watched television on Saturdays at home. In the morning there were the weekly chores to complete. The afternoons were for being out of the house doing fun things. The evenings were for gatherings at someone's house with your dates and watching the so-called "adult western" Paladin on television. All of us would stop the Saturday night party activities to watch Paladin. Well, all of us guys and some of the girls watched it. The *Have Gun, Will Travel* show was just a half hour long. It was a great half hour in our minds.

The recreation room guy's noontime show was hosted by some new DJ called Dick Clark. He played the popular rock and roll music of the day and teenagers danced to the music. It was out of Philadelphia. There were some really pretty girls on the dance floor. All of the dancers were really good. It was hard to understand how Philadelphia could produce so many beautiful girls and have so many excellent dancers when our Pittsburgh kids, my friends and classmates, were just plain old nice people. Oh, we had some pretty girls all right; but not all of them were super pretty and most of us were just getting by on the dance floor. There was no doubt about it; Philadelphia was the place to be if you were a teenager.

When the recreation room guy wanted to take a break, he would have me manage the candy store. It was a simple enough task. Everyone knew the price of a candy bar, five cents; you took the nickel and let the buyer keep the candy bar. My primary task was to assist Ernie, so I didn't stay long in the rec room at any one time.

After I had worked for the Y a couple of Saturdays, the bookkeeper asked me to come to her office. She wanted me to work with her on the Saturday nights when the Y held its Dance Night. I would get paid the same hourly rate for working during the day. This was really nice. I could use the money. It was my primary source for having money to spend on recreational activities.

The bookkeeper spent most of that first Dance Night showing me how to take in the money for each ticket and how to keep track of the ticket numbers so that we would know exactly how much money we should have taken in. Then there was the task of counting the total amount of money at the end of the evening and recording both the money and the ticket numbers to prove that the money collected matched the number of tickets sold. Once that had been done, I was instructed to slip the money, the ticket stubs and the records through the mail slot in her office door. When she would unlock the office door on Monday morning, she would have the money and the records. That was it. After that first night of instruction, I was in charge of the finances for Dance Night from then on. My friends were impressed with seeing me at the dance. I was a person of importance. I liked that.

After several Dance Nights, Saturday nights, of my fulfilling these obligations, the bookkeeper sent word through Ernie that she wanted to see me in her office.

"Sit down," she said from behind her desk.

"I don't want you to be concerned about this; it has been handled. You were accused of stealing money from the Dance Night revenues. I thought you ought to know."

I was in a state of shock. How could this be true?

"What, no, I didn't..."

"Now calm down. I took care of it. Everyone knows you didn't take the money. The board of directors called me in to meet with them. They had discovered that money was missing from the Dance Night fund. The director was quite upset about this. At the time, he seemed to be surprised and angry. He declared that you must have been the thief as my bookkeeping records were beyond reproach. I told them that you kept impeccable records. I checked your records every Monday morning and they were 100% correct. You were totally honest. Anyway, they continued investigating. The director of the Y had stolen the money. You didn't. We were able to prove it. He's been fired. They're looking for a new director."

"Thank you for standing up for me," I stated in a subdued voice. It was so shattering to have been accused of stealing. I prided myself on being honest, and to be accused of something like this was simply unimaginable.

After the meeting, I went to talk to Ernie about it. My eyes watered over as I told him. I needed his support, and he gave it to me. I felt better.

"Hey, you can be the new director. You'd be great!"

"They'll not hire me. I've gone as high in the Y as I'll go."

"That's not true. You'll get it. I know you will."

"I'm black. They'll not appoint me. That's just the way it is."

They hired a new director. I never met him.

Ray and Tom's Poultry had an opening for a chicken cutter at the store they had just opened in a shopping mall. It was their second store. I'd work 20 hours a week at a dollar an hour. This was a really good paying job.

CHAPTER FOUR

The Con

Getting a job at Ray and Tom's Poultry as my junior year of high school in Pittsburgh, Pennsylvania, was coming to an end in 1959 made me feel very lucky. I'd get to work at least 20 hours a week at a dollar an hour. This paid better than the thirty-five cents an hour the local movie theatre paid last fall and better than the YMCA paid earlier in the spring. Saturdays would be an eight-hour day with the other twelve hours spread out during the week, as they needed me.

I'd have some real pocket money for dates and to get a Pig-in-a-Poke at Petrocelle's with the guys after football games next fall. It was just good to have some spending money.

The downside of the job was that the store where I'd work was in a shopping mall some distance away. I'd need my folks to drive me over there and pick me up. When they could, they'd let me drive the family car. That was sometimes difficult for them since our family was a one-car family. Hey, that's the way it was for almost all of the families in the area.

Ray had opened a poultry store in our borough. That's

where I was hoping to get a job, but my classmate and friend, Jim, was working there. It was a major business venture for Ray to open a second store, the store where I would be. His younger brother Tom was the manager of it and had interviewed me for the job. I liked him. The younger brother hardly looked older than a lot of seniors in high school. He had short blond hair, an ever-ready smile, a lean body and lots of energy. Tom was married with two young children. I think they were both toddlers.

The first day on the job was a Saturday. The shop sold whole chickens, chicken parts, whole cooked chickens covered in a secret sauce, potato salad and other various side dishes that went well with the rotisserie-grilled chicken. The rotisserie had three prongs. Each prong held four chickens. It cooked twelve chickens at a time.

Tom told me that my basic job was to cut up whole chickens and put the various parts in the display case the way he had designed them to be placed, to keep the display case iced down throughout the day, to keep the place clean during the day and then to do a deep cleaning after the shop closed on Saturdays. When the shop was really busy with customers, I was to stop what I was doing and assist with the sales. When I helped out with the sales, I was to be sure that my hands and my clothes were clean. That included changing my white butcher's apron before serving the customers. He would teach me how to do all of the tasks. Tom said that he was really happy that I was joining him at the shop. Since he was both the manager of the shop and its only employee, the workload had really been hard on him. He was glad to have my help, he said. I was glad to be there and wanted to do the best I could. Tom said that as the business grew over the summer, I would probably get to work more hours. That was great although I was careful to explain that when football practice started in the late summer I might have to cut back depending on when the coach had us practice. Once school started, I'd probably only be able to work on Saturdays, if at all. Tom was all right with that.

There is an art to cutting up whole chickens. They would arrive in an iced-down wooden crate of twenty-four chickens. Both Tom and I were proud of the fact that I could cut up 24 chickens in less than hour after I had fully mastered the art.

Laying the whole chicken on its back with its neck away from you, you'd pull back the chicken leg and cut the loose skin and meat holding the leg to the side and backbone of the chicken down to the joint section of the thigh bone and the backbone. Rotating the chicken so that the neck is now facing you and locking the leg down to the cutting board by holding the end of the drumstick with your left hand, you cut through the joint connecting the leg and thigh bone to the backbone. Next, you pull the leg back and down with force, which frees the joint from the back and strips the small connecting muscle below the joint from the flat plate of the backbone. Tom pointed out that getting this small muscle to stay with the thigh was important as it added to the weight of the thigh. The per pound price for the thigh was considerably higher than the per pound price of the backbone. It might be necessary to use the knife in your right hand to cut through some of the clinging muscle to fully separate the leg and thigh from the back. If the maneuver were followed correctly, there would be no need to use the knife at all. It took a lot of practice to do it correctly every time.

The wing on the legless side was then removed by holding it up at a right angle to the side of the chicken and cutting straight down the inside of the wing. This movement allowed you to cut through the joint and pull the wing free. Then you turn the chicken over to its other side to repeat the leg/thigh and wing removal process.

The hard part for me was separating the backbone from the breast of the chicken. Tom showed me how it could be done in two quick sweeps of the knife. Developing the skill to pull it off took a lot of practice. Once mastered, the process was quite efficient. Inserting the index and middle fingers of your left hand into the inside indentations of the backbone at the rear cavity, you hold the chicken on end with the neck section resting on the cutting board and the back of the chicken to your front. Placing the knife just below the joint socket of the leg with the blade at a 45 degree angle to the flat section at the back of the backbone, you cut into it, twist the knife causing the blade to be parallel to the backbone and forcefully cut down the side of the backbone separating the ribs from the back. This is done in one smooth and continuous movement of the knife. You need both strength and a sharp, sturdy knife to complete this task. Of course, you repeat the movement on the other side of the backbone. It is important to keep the knife blade as close to the side of the backbone as possible without cutting into the backbone itself. If you let the knife blade wander from the backbone towards the end of the downward cut you won't separate the wishbone extensions from the backbone. This makes a mess of the cut and wastes time as you go back to re-cut the backbone from the breast. Once completed correctly on both sides of the backbone, you have freed it from the chicken breast.

All that remains is to remove the breastbone and free the two sides of the breast from each other. Placing the backside of the breast, the skin side, on the cutting board with the wide section to your front, you cut through the breastbone. Then you press both sides of the breast down flat and insert your fingers under the top of the cartilage section that joins the two halves of the breast and yank the cartilage out. If you do this procedure correctly, you have nothing but meat connecting the two sides of the breast. One quick stroke of the knife separates the breast into the two halves that are ready to be placed in the display case.

All that is left of the chicken cutting is to separate the thigh from the drumstick. That's an easy one-stroke task. You just cut where the little line of connecting fat is that naturally creates a division between thigh and leg. Following that thin yellow line puts the knife blade in the correct spot for easily cutting through the cartilage of the joint connecting the leg and the thigh.

It took me a while to get up to speed to be able to cut up a crate of chickens, twenty-four chickens, in less than an hour, but I did. That was as fast as Tom could do it, too. I was proud of the accomplishment.

By the time school was out and summer was a reality, Tom had increased my time. I was working almost every afternoon until closing and all day Saturday, plus staying late on Saturday to do the deep cleaning needed after the store had closed for the day. Tom used me as his front counter assistant often. He liked the way I greeted the customers and how I served them. We would both do the cash register close-out at the end of each day especially on the days that I had provided service to customers. It was a simple process of going over the cash register receipts and then counting the money in the cash register at the end of the day. Both figures had to match. That was all.

It would take me long into the night on Saturdays to do all the deep cleaning chores that Tom had assigned. He began to express concern that it was taking me too long. Of course, he was paying me a dollar an hour for the hours I clocked in. I explained to him that I was working as fast as I could. It would take until 10:30 to

11:30 at night to get them done. It was OK with me if he didn't want to pay me for some of that time, I told him. I really appreciated working there. A dollar or two wouldn't make any difference to me, I explained. Tom just wouldn't hear of doing that. I really liked him.

After expressing his concern for the time it took to do the cleaning for several weeks, Tom said that he was going to come the next Saturday night and watch me work. He wanted to see if he could come up with ways that I could save time. The night of the observations proceeded as all the other Saturday nights of deep cleaning did. I cleared the display cases of the remaining chicken and placed them in the walk-in cooler the way that Tom had directed me to do. Then I turned the refrigerating system for the display cases off to allow most of the ice to melt while I completed the other cleaning tasks. This included cleaning out the rotisserie. That was a tedious task. The cooked-in chicken grease mixed with the Walkers' secret barbeque sauce covered the insides and glassed-in area for viewing the cooking chickens. That viewing display area was the entire front of the rotisserie. Tom wanted that to be cleaned to spotless clarity. Then taking the trash out, wiping down all of the counters tops and sides with disinfectants, doing the same with all of the serving utensils and cutting knifes, sweeping and mopping the floors, removing the un-melted ice from the display cases, removing the coverings for the wooden slats that served as the raised platform for the display cases, draining out the accumulated water in the bottom of the display cases, sanitizing the complete insides of the display cases, cleaning the windows of the display cases on both the inside and outside consumed a lot of time. Finally, there was the scraping of the wooden slats to remove the slimy stuff that had accumulated on them. That took a lot of time as well. Then it was putting everything back into the display cases, correctly covering the slats to hold the ice and products in the cases that Tom would put in them the next Monday morning.

I had worked up a good sweat that night as was true for every other Saturday night. I just didn't waste any time and worked as fast and as hard as I could to get it all done. When I had finished, it was 11:30 p.m. Tom agreed that I could not have worked harder or faster or more efficiently than I had. He never questioned me about the time it took after that.

Going to work Saturday morning was always a treat for me. Tom was so nice to work for. He was full of a great sense of humor. We would laugh and joke between ourselves. Tom often joked with the regular customers. I refrained from that. I was pleasant but retained a professional distance from them. No question about it, I felt important to be serving customers. That was the best part of the job.

Sometimes a customer would come in and ask to talk to Tom. When this happened, I knew to keep my distance from the two of them. The big steel strike in Pittsburgh was in full force that summer. They couldn't even finish the bridge downtown that went over the Monongahela River and the Allegheny River at the very point that they came together to become the Ohio River. The customers were asking Tom to allow them to get some chicken for their families even though they couldn't pay for it. Tom always let them have some. I had already deduced that the store's profits were not as high as Tom hoped they would be. I knew he was a little stressed for money. Even with that pressure, he would quietly see to it that everyone who asked got some chicken to take home. I just thought that he was a good man.

This one Saturday morning everything was going perfectly. There had been a lot of customer action that morning. By 11:00

a.m. it was clear that the cash intake for the day would make this one of the best, if not the best, money day for the shop of the summer. Tom was particularly pleased. It showed in his overflowing humor and good will toward anyone who entered the shop. We were both busy serving customers almost constantly that morning.

A lull in the hectic pace arrived around 11:45 a.m. or noontime. Only Tom and I were in the shop. Tom was restocking the potato salad and related sides in the back display case that faced the front door while I was by the cash register near the front door making the money drawer neater when the pair walked in.

The woman was stunningly beautiful. Her blond hair was full of curls that framed her glowingly pleasant face in a golden hue of summer light. Her dress hugged her upper body in a most attractive manner and tapered down to her wonderfully trim waist only to fully spread out around her legs the way it was highlighted in all the fashion magazines of the day. Her high heels clicked rhythmically on the tile floor as she rushed to the back display case.

As she approached Tom, she seemed to be singing to her partner as she turned her head towards him just as he was entering the shop, "Oh, honey, look at this wonderfully quaint shop. Isn't it simply lovely?"

The man, dressed in a coat and tie, just as handsome as the woman was beautiful, replied, "It is just as you described it, dear." He stopped in front of the cash register.

"Are you the marvelous creator owner of this shop?" she questioned Tom while providing him with a big, gorgeous smile.

"Well, yes, this is my shop. Can I get you anything? I'd be glad to give you a sample of anything you'd want to taste."

"Did you hear that honey? He is so gracious. I told you, we

just had to stop at your shop. This is so wonderful."

The man addressed me, "Are you his son?"

"No sir. I just help out on the weekend and then some during the week."

"No doubt, he relies on you, and his trust in you is well placed."

I blushed, "Thank you."

The woman kept talking to Tom. He was really taken by her. I could not clearly make out what was being said. Whatever it was produced a lot of smiles from Tom as he handed this vision of womanhood in full bloom a small sample of potato salad.

During this interaction, the man kept asking me questions. He wanted to know where I went to high school and if I played sports there. He bet I was a really good football player.

"Honey, oh, honey," she called to him in that melodious voice of hers, "Now don't quarrel at me, but I just have to have a little of this potato salad for lunch."

Turning to Tom, she stated, "I'm on a diet, but I just can't help myself. Please just give me the smallest amount of the potato salad."

Tom, beaming with pride, put a little into a serving cup and placed it on the scales.

"What do we owe you?" the handsome man standing in front of me asked Tom.

"It's just sixty-four cents," came Tom's pleasant reply as he handed it to the woman.

She began to go into great and extensive detail as to why she found the potato salad to have such an exquisite taste.

"Here, let me pay for it," the man stated as he pulled a twenty-dollar bill from his wallet.

As I started to make change he asked, "Where do you plan to

go to college?"

With great pride I stated, "I hope to go to the Coast Guard Academy."

"Oh, that's an outstanding school. What caused you to want to go there? Oh, wait; did I give you a twenty?

"Yes sir," I said still counting out the small change.

"Forgive me. A twenty-dollar bill for sixty-four cents of potato salad, what am I thinking? Here, I've got a five and fifteen ones I can give you."

As I was taking those bills and starting to count them before placing them in the cash register, he exclaimed, "Wait, wait, I've got three fives. Let me have ten of those ones back, you don't need to be fooling around with all of those ones."

"Ok, sir," I replied, trying to be courteous but getting a little confused about the exchange.

"Hey, could you give me a ten, one five and five one-dollar bills while you're at it? I need that change for this afternoon."

Still not having completed my counting from the last exchange, I confusedly replied, "Yes sir."

He kept it up. He kept producing money. I was totally stressed. I started counting out the last exchange he had requested very deliberately and slowly. I didn't want any more money to change hands. Something was wrong.

Turning to his beautiful companion, the man exclaimed excitedly, "Oh, Honey, we're going to be late. We have to leave right now, right this minute. Hurry, hurry we must go now."

Parting from Tom, she said, "What a wonderful treat to have had the opportunity to be in your very quaint, very sweet shop. Thank you so very, very much."

Tom just beamed at her wonderful parting statement. As they left through the front door, she turned to Tom and gave him one last wave goodbye. He returned the wave. He was really pleased.

"Tom, come here. Something has happened. We have to count the money. We have to clear the cash register. Something funny was going on; it just wasn't right."

He rushed to the cash register. We counted the money. We were exactly twenty dollars short.

"We've been conned. They were professionals. It's partly my fault, I let her get me off in a corner and keep me distracted while he pulled his quickie cash changing trick on you."

"I'm so sorry, Tom. It just went too fast for me. I'll pay back the money."

"No, no," he paused for a second and then said, "We'll split the cost. I was as responsible as you were. I let her take me out of the picture. You put in ten dollars, and I'll put in ten dollars."

"OK," I said feeling very depressed. That was ten hours of work with no pay. That was a lot.

Later that afternoon, Tom learned that the con artists had hit just about every shop in the mall. One dress shop got conned out of more than three hundred and twenty-five dollars. They were still checking their funds to determine the exact amount they had lost. As the news trickled in, our shop had the least reported amount taken from them of any of the shops conned by the couple.

I took a small degree of pride from that fact. Tom never mentioned the event after that day.

I liked Tom a lot.

EARLY YEARS

CHAPTER FIVE

Orders

The summer of 1945 was one of fun and discovery for me as a two-year-old about to turn three. It was near the beginning of July, somewhere on the outskirts of St. Louis, Missouri. My Uncle Jim and Aunt Millie along with my two cousins, Timmy and Morning were staying with us, that is, Daddy, Mommy and me. Timmy was just a month younger than me and Morning was a year and a half older than us two boys. The three of us loved to play together. I had stayed with Aunt Millie and the cousins at their place in northern Minnesota, on the shore of the lake, when Mommy was gone. Timmy and I didn't like going to the barbershop there. The barber would always yank ticks out of your head before cutting your hair. It hurt. Of course, Daddy and Uncle Jim were off at the war then. We didn't see them until after it was over.

Daddy and Uncle Jim were just back from the war. We stayed at a motel of sorts that summer. Mommy said it was hard to find a place to live in right then because all of the men were coming back from the war. The motel had lots of little house-like places. We stayed in one of them. When it was time for bed, Daddy or Uncle Jim would set up the army cot for all the cousins to sleep in. Timmy and I slept at one end of the cot and Morning slept at the other end. Once we were in bed, I could almost touch the wall on my side of the cot. Timmy said he could almost touch the wall on his side too. I don't remember where Mommy and Daddy or Uncle Jim and Aunt Millie slept. Daddy kept saying how great it was that it hadn't rained. Everyone would agree.

There were lots of children living in the little houses just like ours. We would play with them most of the day. The games were mostly playing catch, playing hide-and-go-seek and things of that sort. We ran and laughed and played most of the day. Mommy or Aunt Millie would call out our names when it was time to come to lunch or supper. We always came when we were called. If it started to get dark, we had to go to the little house. It was bedtime. If we got back after it was dark, we might get spanked. It hurt. I never liked getting spanked: neither did my cousins. They got spanked more than I did, especially Timmy. I felt sorry for him. He was so kind. If someone took something from him, he wouldn't do anything about it. I would not let someone be unfair to me. I'd fight to get my stuff back. Mostly, I'd get it back. Daddy said I shouldn't fight so much.

One play day all the other kids and we cousins were playing behind the little houses. Most of us were afraid to climb over the fence and get into the large pasture. It went a long way back to a fence that had a wooden gate. The gate had a lot of green on it and stringy things hanging down from its boards. At that distance, the gate looked small. It also looked scary. The big trees went on and on beyond that gate. The forest got darker in color the deeper you looked into it until it almost looked black. On the ground near the fence and on some of the trunks of the big trees was the color green. Green was supposed to be just for the leaves of trees and the grass, not for the ground and the sides of trees. It looked scary.

Some of the big boys said they had gone across the field and into the forest behind the gate. They said that it made them feel funny to be in that forest. An old man lived in the forest. The last time the big boys were there, the man, the man in the forest, had tried to catch them. He yelled at them as he ran towards them trying to catch them. He was old and mean. The big boys ran back to the fence, climbed over it, and ran across the open field right back to the back of these little houses. The man stayed down there at the end of the field, by the wooden gate. He just looked at them. The big boys said that we might actually see the man in the forest if we kept watch long enough.

I looked and looked, as did a lot of the other kids. Before long, the little kids started playing and running around as we always did. I continued to look at that gate to see if the man in the woods would appear. All of a sudden, I saw him. He slowly walked out of the woods to the wooden gate. He started to crawl between two of the widely spaced gate boards. He looked to be dull green in color. I was petrified with fear. He got through the gate and stood there looking at us with one arm resting on it.

"I see him! I see him!" I screamed at the top of my lungs. "He just got through the gate."

All of the children began screaming and running. I continued my screams of alarm and joined the runners. We all ran to our individual little houses in deep fear of this unknown. He was real. I saw him move under the wooden boards of the gate and stand up looking at us. Later that evening, Timmy asked me if I really, really saw the man. I did! To this day, I believe I saw the man or something like a man. No one else was sure that the man was there. I saw him. I was sure. Today, as an adult, I'm not so sure as to what I saw. It may have been my imagination. I'll tell you this: I saw something strange at that gate. I really did.

Daddy called me to him. "I want to show you where we put the fireworks. It's in the back section of our motel cabin," he said as he guided me inside and to the rear of the structure. Wow, there were sparklers, firecrackers, roman candles and rockets, real rockets that went up into the air.

"I wanted you to know that they are here. You are not to touch them. You are not allowed to touch them. Do you understand?"

I shook my head vigorously, "Yes, sir."

"They are for all of us to use for the Fourth of July fireworks. Only the adults are allowed to touch them. Do you understand?"

"Yes, sir. I do."

"Ok, that's good. Now go on outside and play."

"Yes, sir."

I was so proud of my daddy. We had the fireworks that everyone had helped buy. That was my dad. He was a leader. That's what my daddy was.

"Your dad has all the fireworks in your cabin, doesn't he?" one of the three or four big boys surrounding me asked.

"Yes," I spoke with great pride.

"Well, we want to see them. I hear that there are rockets, too. We want to make a launch ramp for the rockets."

"No, no, I'm not allowed to touch them. You're not either."

"Who said so?"

"My daddy said so."

"Well, did he say we couldn't look at them?"

"Well...no, but..."

"There, you see, he didn't say we couldn't look at them. We don't want them. We just want to make a ramp for the rockets. Without a ramp, they won't get high enough. We just want to help."

"Well…OK…but don't touch them."

It was agreed. I took them to the back of our cabin.

"Holy cow, there must be at least ten or more rockets," one of the big boys said in a hushed voice.

"Listen, I have to take one of the rockets and make sure I build the launch pad right."

"No, no, no," I whined, "you can't touch them. My daddy said so."

"We just want to help. Why won't you let us help? We'll just take one. After we put the ramp together, we'll bring it right back. We'll put it right back in the same spot it was. He'll never know it was touched, and we will have it perfect for the Fourth."

It made sense. They were trying to help everyone. Daddy said it was good to help people. I wanted to help. I wanted everything to go right for the Fourth of July.

"Ok, but please, please bring it right back."

"We will. We'll be right back."

They weren't gone long. When they got back, they said it was perfect: the ramp was perfect for the rockets. They put the rocket right back against the others, right where it had been.

"Son, come here," my daddy said in a firm voice. "You moved the rockets. You were back here and moved some of these," he stated grimly as he pointed at the stacks of fireworks.

I started crying. "It wasn't me, honest it wasn't me. The big boys said they needed to make a ramp." I had to pause for a breath as my sobbing was making it hard to breathe and talk at the same time. "A ramp to launch the rockets. They only took one and brought it right back. I told them you said not to touch anything. They said," sob, snuffle, sob, "that they were sure you would want it to be perfect. Honest, Daddy." My sobs were beyond my control.

"I understand that you were trying to help. I gave you an order, and you disobeyed. I will have to spank you for it."

"No, Daddy, no! Please! No!" I screamed through my tears.

He led me outside. Holding one of my arms in the air, he bent over and gave me several hard slaps on the bottom. I cried and cried. Then it was over. I have no recall of the fireworks display.

CHAPTER SIX

A Little Bit of Love

To a three-year-old, the world is a little bit confusing. So it was for me. I was sick. My mommy had taken my temperature. She said I had a fever. Once again, she had used the mouth thermometer. I opened my mouth and allowed her to put it under my tongue. It proved that I was a big boy. You didn't have to stick it in my bottom. That's what you did to take a baby's temperature. I was a big boy. I could hold it under my tongue.

She decided to take me to daycare anyway. She had to go to work. I don't know if we still lived in East St. Louis, Missouri, or if we had moved across the river to Granite City, Illinois. If we were in Granite City, we hadn't lived there long. The year was about 1945.

Hand in hand, we entered the building that seemed to be a street-long building amidst a series of street-long buildings. The door opened into a narrow stairwell. We climbed a long way up the stairs. At the top of the stairs was a little landing. It had a small table on it beside an entrance door and a metal hand railing all around the platform except where the stairs were. A small overhead light tried to hide the darkness in the stairwell.

Mother knocked on the door of the landing as she had always done. The door opened. Laughter and chatter from children playing spilled out of the large open space beyond the door.

A lady was holding the door partially open as she spoke to my mother. Mother told her that I might be a little sick. She had taken my temperature at home. The lady said I was to stay outside on the landing while she talked to someone inside. We waited.

Two ladies came out of the door. They said I could stay. Mommy left me on the landing. One of the ladies said that they would have to take my temperature. She went back inside the room. The other lady picked me up and sat me on the table.

The missing lady returned. She had a thermometer in her hand. She told me she was going to take my temperature. I was directed to lie down on my stomach. I didn't know why. Mother took my temperature under my tongue. I was a big boy. That's how big boys did it.

As I moved to lie down so that I faced the ladies, they grabbed me, rolled me over. One of them began pulling my pants down while the other one pressed my chest to the table. Realization hit me; they were going to stick the thermometer up my bottom. No, no, no, this was not right. I was a big boy. I tried to tell them that I was a big boy. My mommy put it under my tongue. They weren't listening. They strengthened their grip on me and pressed me more firmly to the table. I started crying and twisting and screaming. They couldn't hold me still even though they had finally succeeded in pulling my pants down and keeping me face down to the table. Another lady came out of the room to help the others hold me down. This was terribly wrong. Strange ladies were not supposed to pull boys' pants down. This was wrong. This was humiliating. I cried and screamed. It did no good. They stuck the thing up my bottom. All six hands pressed me tight to the table. I continued to scream. No one would listen. I was a big boy. I was embarrassed. This was wrong. I wanted to get away from them. It didn't matter. I could hardly move. All I could do on my own was to sob and sob. This was so wrong.

Pulling the thing out of my bottom, one lady said that I had a temperature. What should they do, asked another lady? I couldn't be with the other children was the decision. They told me to wait on the table. They would be back. All three ladies went into the room.

I was not going to wait. I was going to run away. I hated it here. Slipping off of the table, I began to run down the stairs as fast as I could. I ran and I ran until the stairs stopped. My intention was to run down the stairs until I got to the door that went to the street. There was no door at the bottom of the stairs. It was all different. The stairs had taken me to this large, whitish room that had hallways going from it. I could smell food cooking somewhere. The walls of the stairwell were different too. They were made of some kind of stone that had been painted over. The lights down here made it bright, much brighter than the stairwell that I had climbed up with Mommy.

This was most frightening. I was totally lost. I had no idea where I was or how to get back to the door to the street. Tears rolled down my cheek. I was having trouble breathing between my sobs. I didn't know where I was or what to do. I just stood there sobbing.

Footsteps were coming from a hallway off to one side. This large fat lady in an all-white work dress appeared before me.

"What's the matter, honey?" she asked as she held out her arms to me.

I rushed into those embracing arms. She picked me up and

hugged me tightly as she carried me back to the steps and sat down. Holding me in her lap, she rocked back and forth saying, "It's all right, honey. Everything's going to be all right. Don't you worry now. Everything's going to be all right."

Clasped into that loving embrace, I leaned against her body. She was going to take care of me. It was going to be all right.

"What happened? What happened to you?"

"I ran away. I ran down the stairs but they didn't stop. I don't know where I am. They took my temperature. They stuck it up my bottom. I'm a big boy. I'm a big boy. Mommy puts it in my mouth. I'm a big boy. I can hold it under my tongue," I blurted out between my subsiding sobs and sniffles.

That's all I can recall. I have always remembered that wonderful woman. Some have asked me if she was a cook, a janitor or maybe a black lady. I don't know. All I know is that she loved me. She made everything all right.

CHAPTER SEVEN

Needles

It was a long line even if you weren't about to turn four. Mommy said they were going to give all the little children their immunization shots. The little children were going to get several shots at once because they couldn't get any of them until after the war. The shots were needed for the soldiers until the war was over, she said.

The temperature was just right that late spring day in 1946. The sun was peeking around clouds every once in a while. That was a good thing because the line was really long outside the Granite City, Illinois, high school's gymnasium. There were lots and lots of little children like me holding their mothers' hands waiting to get their shots. The line seemed to move slowly.

"Now remember honey, you're going to be brave. You don't have to be afraid." She kept repeating every so often.

In the past, when I got really sick, they would give me a shot. They hurt. The longer the needle was the more it hurt. They would stick the needle all the way in up to the big part that had the medicine in it. The needle hurt when it first went in and it hurt as they stuck it all the way in. When they squirted the medicine in it really, really hurt. If they stuck it in your bottom, which they always did with the really long needles, the medicine felt like a big ball of hurt inside where the needle was deepest. The hurt stayed for a long time. I didn't like it.

As my experience with the needles grew, I wanted the shots less and less. I would fuss and cry and hold back from the doctor's office. Mommy didn't like it when I did that. She would pull or carry me into the office no matter how much I protested.

"You're not going to be afraid, darling. You're going to be a big boy. Aren't you?"

Being a big boy was what I wanted to be. Yes, of course., I was going to be a good boy. A big boy. I was brave. Little tiny baby kids cried about shots. I was a big boy. I was brave.

When we got inside the gymnasium the line was still long. Way up ahead, the line seemed to split into two lines. There was a lot of noise in the building. Children were crying. Adults were talking. Some children would start to scream all of a sudden. I began to become afraid. I stood as close to Mommy as I could as the line moved closer and closer to a table. At the table they talked to each mother about something. Then you went to one of the two lines that started just beyond the table.

The noise kept getting louder. A lot of people in white coats were up ahead. They were kind of around this big doorframe without a door. Peeking around my Mommy's leg I could see a boy and his mother walk up to the doorframe. All of a sudden the little boy began screaming as he tried to run away from the people in white coats, his mother and everyone else in the line.

As quick as you could blink, the white-coated people grabbed both his arms and pinned them to his sides. Instantly, he fell to the ground kicking, screaming, squirming and crying. But the white coats had him. They stood him up while keeping both arms pinned to his sides. Other white coats began shoving needles into the round parts at the top of his arms, on both sides, at the same time. The little boy screamed and screamed but they didn't stop. They just kept putting needles into his arms. When they finished, his mother picked him up and carried him off. He just seemed to sob and sob until the screams of another little child in the other line drowned out the boy's cries.

"You're not going to be like that, are you? You're going to be brave!"

"Yes, Mommy, I'm brave. I'm a big boy."

I was brave. I was not afraid. I was not like those others. I was a big boy.

My turn was next. I hugged Mommy's leg. The little girl in front of me hardly cried when she got her last shots. She was brave. I was brave.

Mommy and I started walking towards the doorway without a door. The white coats held up their needles. There were needles on both sides of the doorway. The needles were long. The needles were too long. This was going to really hurt.

Without warning, without understanding how it had begun, without willing one conscious action, I realized I was on the floor screaming and kicking and biting and twisting as white coated arms and hands tried to control me. Several times it seems that they tried to pick me up, but I managed to fall back on the floor where no one seemed to get a firm hold of me.

My shoulders were pinned to the floor with my arms pressed to the sides. I was still able to scream and kick at people with my legs. They stuck the needles into both arms. It seemed to go on forever.

Mother didn't say much in the car. I was ashamed. I wanted to be a big boy. I wanted to be brave. It didn't happen. I didn't know why. It just didn't happen.

After that experience, it seemed harder for me to feel nice about going to a doctor's office. They might give me a shot. You never knew about those things. I did go to see the doctor when Mommy took me. She was always careful to tell me about being brave and all. I got through it. It was difficult for me and Mommy. We got through it. I was mostly brave.

Later that fall I hurt my big front tooth. It kind of turned a dark color. Daddy took me to the dentist to see what the problem might be. At supper that night he told Mommy and me that I needed to have the tooth pulled. It was dying. When it died it would make me sick, so it needed to be pulled. A date had been set for the big event. I'd never had a tooth pulled. It might hurt, but Daddy said they would put it to sleep and then they could pull it without hurting. That was fine with me.

Mommy and Daddy told the people who lived next door about it. Mrs. North was really nice. She told me she knew I'd be very brave about it. I would just climb up into that chair, open my mouth and keep it open and the dentist would just pull that tooth without so much as a tiny little problem. I agreed. This wasn't going to be bad at all. You just opened your mouth, and "pop" went the tooth.

Mr. North was a streetcar driver. Daddy said we would go to the dentist on Mr. North's streetcar. Mr. North would be the one to drive me to the dentist. This was wonderful. I felt so proud that Mr. North would be the very person to drive me to the dentist's office.

It seemed that a lot of the mothers and fathers my parents knew, knew about my tooth. Everywhere I went there were mommies and daddies telling me how brave I was going to be

61

when I got my tooth pulled. Of course I was brave. I was going to be brave and have my tooth pulled.

Daddy and I got on Mr. North's streetcar. There he was sitting in the driver's seat holding the door open for me and Daddy. We sat in the front seat so we could talk with Mr. North.

"Little guy, you are going to be so brave. You are going to march right up to the dentist's chair and sit all still and all while he pulls your tooth, aren't you?"

"Yes sir," I replied, about as proud to be talking to the streetcar driver as a four-year-old could be. I was certainly a big boy now.

"Yes, Bob, we talked about it a lot, haven't we, son?"

Beaming in all of this attention, I was at a loss for words. All I could do was grin from ear to ear and nod in agreement.

"He is a big boy now. He's going to make me proud. He'll get into that chair and do exactly what the dentist tells him to do, won't you, son?"

Of course I would. There was no question about it. I would walk into the dentist's office, climb right up in that chair, open my mouth and do what the dentist told me to do. I was brave.

The lady in the front of the dentist's workplace was very happy to see me. Daddy and I waited just a little bit until the dentist called us in.

I walked right in. Without anyone telling me to, I just climbed up into the big chair. The dentist put a big bib around my neck and turned his back to me as he talked to Daddy. With his back still to me, he told me to open my mouth really wide.

I did just as he said. I opened it as wide as I possibly could. The wide-open mouth kind of forced me to tilt my head back as the dentist turned around with a needle in his hand.

It was the longest needle I had ever seen. Fear struck my heart.

He can't be thinking about putting that big, long needle in my mouth. If he sticks it in my gum, it will go all the way to the back of my head, maybe even be sticking out of the back of my head. This can't be.

In total terror, I closed my mouth like a mousetrap being sprung. The needle would have entered my mouth had it not been for my quick thinking. This was horrible. The needle would hurt so bad going through my cheeks, my gums, my tongue and sticking out of the back of my head. There was no way I was going to endure such pain. It was horrible.

"Now, now don't be afraid. It's only going to sting a little," the dentist stated in a falsely calming voice as he waved the enormously long needle in front of my terrified eyes.

He didn't know what he was talking about. I knew needles. The longer they were, the farther they went in and the more they hurt. You couldn't fool me.

Daddy started pleading with me to open my mouth. I didn't budge. I had my teeth clamped shut. I couldn't allow that needle to go all the way through my head.

After a while both Daddy and the dentist got a little angry. They threatened me. I could get punished when I got home. I would get horribly sick if that tooth wasn't pulled. Nothing could force me to open my mouth. I could not stand the pain such a giant needle would give me. I just couldn't.

It seemed like eternity passed while these two men tried to convince me to open my mouth. Who knows what was said? I certainly didn't. The fear that gripped me blocked out almost all sights and sounds with the exception of the sight of that needle sitting on the shelf behind the dentist.

Finally, the dentist said that all he wanted to do was to take a quick look at the tooth. He wasn't going to do anything to me except to put the tongue depressor in my mouth so that he could get a good look at the tooth. Both he and Daddy urged me to just open my mouth so that he could take a look. That was all.

Unclamping the locked muscles of my jaw, I slowly open the mouth just a little bit. The dentist rammed the flat wooden tongue depressor into my mouth and turned it sideways trying to pry my mouth open and keep it open as the hand behind his back appeared with the needle.

Instantly, I understood. Horror overwhelmed me. Fear gripped my existence. I slammed down my teeth onto the wedged in tongue depressor, splitting it down the center. It collapsed onto itself. The now two pieces of wood firmly clasped between my locked teeth became one. The dentist tried to pull the tongue depressor out of my mouth. He couldn't. I had it locked in. I wasn't about to risk opening my mouth for anything. Daddy and I left his office. The tongue depressor remained between my clenched teeth.

I can't remember a big deal being made about my behavior at the dentist's office. I think they must have understood how afraid I was. I just don't know.

The family was going to Grandmother and Grandfather's house in Wisconsin for Christmas. That would be fun. There would be real snow up there. Daddy said that he wanted me to see the dentist that was his dentist when he was a little boy. Daddy said he was a kind man, a gentle man. All he would do was look at my tooth and give his opinion of it.

We went to the dentist. He was like Grandfather. He was kind. I liked him. He told Daddy and me that the tooth didn't need to be pulled. It would get better with time. It did.

CHAPTER EIGHT

Turn Around

It had been a bad day. I was sad. If, I had known the word then, I'd say I was depressed, but then you can't expect a complete verbalization from a three-year-old or an early four-year-old. It's hard to remember the exact timing of these early memories.

I remember leaving the daycare center and getting on the Granite City bus. I would ride it for what seemed like a long time. It would come to the railroad tracks somewhere near our house. The bus driver would stop the bus, open the door and tell me that this was where I got off. I sat right behind him so it was easy for him to tell me it was time to leave the bus.

Once off the bus, I'd walk a ways down the railroad track until I got to my babysitter's house. The back of her house was right there, right off the railroad tracks to the left. You couldn't miss it. There weren't any houses close by it. Her house just sat there in an open field-like area. It was big, a lot bigger than our house. The lady who babysat me was older than Mommy. She was very nice.

After a while in her house, Mommy would come and pick me up. Then we would go on home and she would make supper for

Daddy and me.

I can't remember what happened at daycare that day that made me so sad. All I know is that I just felt sad like as if something unfair had happened to me and there was nothing I could do about it. It was that kind of sad.

Usually, I would walk down the railroad tracks quickly to get to the nice babysitter's house. Sometimes I would try to walk on one of the rails without falling off. I knew to keep watch for a train that might be coming down the tracks. They had all told me to get far off the tracks if a train came by. Something could fall off of the train and hit me. Sometimes the train wheels would send rocks flying from the rails. That would really hurt. I knew to watch out for trains, but there never seemed to be any running when I was walking on the tracks.

This day was not a usual day. I just looked down at the small pieces of gravel between the rails. The cross-ties were dull and oil stained. I just looked at them as I slowly walked down the center of the tracks. My gloomy feeling was such that I just kept my head down looking at the rocks and walking and walking and looking at the rocks and walking.

When I came to a place in the tracks where the center of the tracks was paved, I was startled. This wasn't right. Never before had I reached a point where the center of the railroad tracks was paved before arriving at the babysitter's house.

Looking up, what confronted my eyes was terrifying. It was a road. A road surrounded by rows and rows of big houses on both sides of the railroad track. As far as you could see were houses and more houses. *I must be lost*. What to do?

I didn't know what to do. Turning around, looking back the way I had come didn't help. There were lots of houses going back down both sides of the railroad tracks. I didn't know what to do.

Getting out of the center of the tracks, I walked towards some houses. There were so many streets going so many different ways with so many houses I had never seen before. It was terrible. I began to cry. I just stood there and cried. There was nothing I could do. I was lost. Would I ever find my way? No, I didn't know what to do.

"Little boy, what's wrong?" the teenage boy asked as he leaned down to talk to me placing his hand gently on my shoulder.

Through my tears I sobbed, "I'm lost. I don't know where I am. Got off the bus. Walked down the tracks like always. I didn't look up. I kept walking. It was a long time. I looked up. Here I was. I'm lost."

"You must be frightened. You can come with me. I'll take you home. My folks can help you."

"No, no," I pleaded through my tears, "I'm not allowed to go with strangers. Just turn me around. I can start walking back down the tracks. I'll see the babysitter's house."

"That's not a good idea. Come on home with me. My mom and dad can help you. Really. They can. My dad's a policeman. He will know what to do. Our house is right there," he said pointing to it.

Policemen helped people. I knew that. Policemen always helped people. Shaking my head in agreement, I accepted the hand he held out to me. We went to his house. They wanted to know the babysitter's phone number. I didn't know it. They wanted to know her address. I didn't know it. They asked what her house looked like and what it looked like around the place where I got off the bus. I knew that.

The policemen daddy told me not to worry. He would find the babysitter's house. They were very nice to me. I got to eat ice cream.

I can't remember how I got home that night, but I did. I don't remember if I ever walked those railroad tracks again. I don't think I did, but it's hard to remember everything from way back then.

CHAPTER NINE

Between Worlds

We definitely lived in Granite City, Illinois. I remember that fact distinctly. Now, I'm not sure about my age. I was probably three or had just turned four. Let's say I was about four. It was around 1946. We lived in a real house made of brick. There were houses on both sides of the street. The streets seemed to go on forever with the same kind of houses. I think they all had little fenced-in back yards. At least ours did, as did the neighbors on both sides of our house. The front yards were adequate. The sidewalk was nice and wide.

I had my own bedroom. It was big. The window to the room was big. The closet with its big, open doorway was deep and dark. That was where the first problem started.

After Mom or Dad had me get into bed, they had me say my prayer, "Now I lay me down to sleep. If I should die before I wake, I ask the Lord my soul to keep. Amen." They would then tuck me into bed, say something like "Sleep tight," and then turn out the light.

I had asked them to keep my door open because it made me

afraid to have it closed. They did that for me. It helped. It didn't solve the problem.

There were monsters in the closet. Just when I was about to fall asleep, they would start stirring. At first, it was just a movement of shadows and light in there. As the movement increased, I could see parts of their form. Sometimes it was a partial arm or a shoulder. It got worse. I could see a leering smile in the slowly undulating movements. Sometimes one or both eyes would be staring at me. Most frightening of all was when an arm would try to reach out of the darkness to grab at me.

I tried to not look at them. I'd look away. I'd stare at the open window, forcing myself not to look into the closet. It seemed like forever when I forced myself not to look. Then I couldn't help myself. I'd look. They were there.

This struggle went on for long periods of time. Somehow, in the beginning, I'd fall asleep. When I would awaken, it was morning. It was getting light outside. The light seemed to force the monsters away.

At first, it didn't happen every night. It took a while for it to be an every night worry. Even then, it wasn't really every night. When it got to be three or four nights of the week, it became a struggle to even get into the bed. I did all I could to avoid going to bed. My parents were insistent. I had to go to bed at bedtime.

It got so bad for me that one night, after saying my prayers to my mother, the tears just rolled down my cheeks. I couldn't hold them back. I was so afraid that the monsters would come out of the closet and get me.

"What's wrong, sweetheart?" Mom asked.

"The monsters. I'm afraid of the monsters."

"Where are the monsters?"

"In the closet."

"Do you see them?"

"Yes."

"When do you see them?"

"After you turn out the lights and leave."

"Do they ever get out of the closet?"

"No. I'm afraid that they will."

"There you have it. They can't get out of the closet. You're safe."

"But they try. I can see them trying."

"Pull the covers over your head. They can't see you then. That's all you have to do. After a while they'll even get tired of coming, OK?"

"OK."

It worked. I couldn't see them and they couldn't see me. Sometimes I could hear them struggling to get out. It didn't matter. Even if they got out, they couldn't see me. I fell asleep early that night. After a while, it was like my mother said, they just got tired of coming. They stayed away forever.

Bedtime was a lot happier. The monsters were gone. I still kept my head under the covers for a while just in case they came back looking for me. They never did. It became safe for me not even to bother to put my head under the covers. I just got into bed, said my nightly prayer and fell asleep.

Some time seemed to pass before something else started to happen. It just started one night. There was no build up to it. It just happened right out of the blue.

I was drifting off to sleep. All of a sudden, my body began to tingle. The way it does when you cross your legs for too long and one of your legs goes numb. The tingling would start right after you uncrossed your legs trying to stand up. That tingling feeling covered my whole body. Then my body would start to swell. It got larger and larger. As it got larger, it filled the room. I was expanding. I was expanding rapidly. As I expanded, I became thinner. Without a moment's thought, I had expanded so much that I was outside the house. It was as if the house was within me, but it was very small as I quickly expanded into the night sky. I rose up and beyond the earth. I was in outer space. By this time I was so thin that I couldn't see me at all. There wasn't an end to me. I knew I was me, but everything was a part of me. It was all in me. My expansion enclosed me but there was no end to me. I was everywhere and everything was me. I was among the stars. They looked so beautiful. They didn't move. They were just there. All of space was just black as black could be. There was no glow around the stars. They just stood out against the blackness. Planets were there too. The planets were somehow closer to me. They were bigger inside me than the stars. The planet with the rings around it stood out clearly in the blackness. It was so strange because nothing moved. I was full of that numb feeling.

It was frightening. I knew that I shouldn't be feeling this. I shouldn't be here. I belonged on earth. I belonged in my bed. I started to struggle to get back. It was so peaceful here. It was so beautiful. It was comforting to be a part of everything. I knew all of this even as I knew my fear. I didn't belong here. I had to get back.

I was shrinking. It happened very fast. Then I was back. My body was its regular size. I was in bed. The numbness was still there but clearly receding.

Lying in bed, I was shaken. What had just happened to me? I couldn't explain it. All I knew was that I belonged on earth right now. I didn't belong everywhere. I didn't belong in the stars. Part of me knew that this experience couldn't have been true, but part of me thought that it had actually happened. All of the feelings were real. I felt them. I just didn't know what to believe.

Several nights later it happened again. It began in the same way. I felt the tingling numbness, the expansion of my skin, the expansion beyond the house into the stars. The expansion of me was so massive that I was nothing but my thoughts. My body had been stretched so massively to encompass all of the stars that it had lost any semblance of form. It was just me, my thoughts, and all of the stars and planets being part of me. I did not exist except for my thoughts. During all of this I was afraid. I knew I did not belong here. I belonged down on earth.

As the frequency of this strange experience increased, I began thinking about it during the day and dreading going to bed at night. I never knew if that night was the night I'd feel the numbness and experience the expansion into the stars. Most nights it didn't happen. I seemed to have no control over when it would start. Once it started, I could not stop it.

The whole experience was so strange. I couldn't tell my parents. How could I put all of the feelings into words they could understand? I couldn't. They would never understand. This was something I had to live with. I tried to figure it out. The planets and the stars didn't twinkle when they were part of me, when they were inside me or when they were within my boundaries even though I had no boundaries. This was so confusing to try to understand exactly what was happening. Clearly the stars did not twinkle when I was with them. That proved it. At night the real stars twinkled. My stars didn't twinkle. It wasn't real, just as the monsters in the closet could not be real. I knew this experience could not be real. Yet it kept happening. I never felt comfortable with it. I always tried to fight it.

The experiences started to diminish in frequency, as I got older. In early elementary school they occurred just a couple of times during a year. Slowly they seemed to disappear altogether until they were gone.

In my late adolescence and into my adulthood I began reflecting on the whole experience. It always seemed real to me. A few times when in bed, I would try to induce the feeling of numbness and experience the expansion of my body's boundaries.

When I would feel it start to happen, I always stopped the experimentation immediately. At this time, I belonged here.

CHAPTER TEN

Walnuts

The neighbor girl was about a year older than I was. She was a lot bigger too. We would often play together. She was the only child close enough to my age to be a playmate. Her family lived just a few doors down from our Granite City, Illinois, house. I liked the nice brick house we lived in so much. We had moved there from the apartment above the bar in East St. Louis. A summer or two before that, around 1945, we had lived in a small, one room motel cabin with Aunt Millie, Uncle Jimmy and my two cousins.

Our family lived above the bar the following winter. I can remember climbing up the stairs that went from the street to the apartment door. The stairwell at the street level was open. You just walked up the stairs from the sidewalk to our door. Sometimes you would have to step around someone who was sleeping on the stairs. Mommy said not to talk to them if they woke up. I never remember any of them waking up.

Once you got to our door at the top of the steps and opened it there were more steps to climb. When you got to the top of those steps you were standing in the middle of our apartment. I can remember the doctor coming up those steps to see me. His head appeared just above the floor of the apartment, then his shoulders and then his legs and then he stepped on the floor, and there all of him was.

The doctor came to see me at Christmas time. I was sick. Mommy and daddy had put blankets on the couch to make a bed for me. The doctor said that until I got better, I had to stay on the couch.

On Christmas morning I got my presents. The special present was a wooden diesel train. It had three passenger cars and the diesel train engine. I couldn't get off the couch to play with it on the floor. Daddy got on his hands and knees in front of the couch and ran the train around on the floor for me. He made the sound of the whistle and everything. I remember thinking that he was so kind to do this for me. I loved him so.

My playmate at the Granite City house would always be telling me what to do and trying to take things from me. I didn't like that. I would hold on to them as best I could. Sometimes my best wasn't good enough. It made me mad.

One day we were playing outside together. It was cold. We walked back to her front porch. Her mother had two rugs rolled up, lying on their sides in front of the front door. The girl and I decided it would be fun to roll the rugs around us. It was warm inside my rug. I fell asleep.

While mother was fixing supper that evening, she asked me if I had hit the girl or stuck my fingers in the girl's mouth when we were in the rugs. Her question surprised me. How could I do that when I was all wrapped up in the rug? Anyway, no, I had not done that. Why would I want to hit her was the question in my mind?

"Why did you ask me?"

"The inside of her mouth was bleeding when she got out of the rug. She told her mother that you had hit her."

"I didn't hit her. It was cold. We thought it would be fun to wrap up in the rugs and get warm. I fell asleep. When I woke up, she was gone. I came home. I never did anything to her, honest, Mommy."

"It's all right. I'm fixing Swedish meatballs tonight. It's your favorite."

Strange things like that happened when I played with this girl.

Another time we were playing on the sidewalk in our backyard, the sidewalk that went to the alley where Mommy put the garbage. The girl had brought a bag of walnuts. She said we could open them and eat them.

I didn't know how to open them. She said it was easy. All you had to do was put a walnut down on the sidewalk, and then, with your foot, you smashed the bottom of your shoe on top of it. She did just that to show me how to do it. The walnut was just one flat massed mess on the cement. She bent down and picked an edible piece of the walnut and put it in her mouth. She said it was good and gave me several walnuts for myself.

With a big lunge of my foot I smashed down on my walnut. Like the girl's, it was pretty flat. All of the hard pieces of the shell were mixed in with the nut part. It was hard to find a piece large enough to pick up and put into my mouth. We continued the smash and eat process through several walnuts. It soon became apparent that you didn't want to use so much force in bringing your foot down if you wanted big pieces of walnut to eat.

I was getting some large pieces of nut to eat by not stamping my foot down so hard. A few times I would hit it so lightly that it just didn't open at all. The girl wanted to know how I got such big pieces to eat, so I explained that you just didn't hit the nut with your foot as hard as you could.

She didn't seem to understand. She just kept flattening her walnuts and scrapping little pieces off of the sidewalk to eat.

"Hey, look at this. It came out perfect," I shouted to her in amazement. There it was on the cement. The shell, split perfectly into two halves, was lying beside the whole undamaged walnut kernel.

"It's mine! It's mine! That's my walnut," she shouted as she ran over to me.

"No, it's not. It's mine. I hit it with my foot, and it's mine."

"It is not. It's mine. I'm taking it," she screamed as she shoved me back from the walnut.

I was stunned. How could it be hers?

Standing over the walnut, I defiantly said, "It's not yours! It's mine."

Suddenly, from behind me a voice said, "I saw the whole thing. It's his. He hit it with his foot, and it opened perfectly. It's his walnut."

I turned around to see a big boy two backyards away. He had a rake in his hand.

The girl just looked at the boy. She didn't say a word. She walked away from me and went back into her house.

CHAPTER ELEVEN

Differences

Mom said I could have anything I wanted for lunch on my first day of going to school in 1948. I was about to enter first grade at a Granite City, Illinois, school behind our trailer park. A big, ripe, red tomato and a peanut butter and jelly sandwich were what I wanted and what she put into my small paper bag. I was definitely a big boy now!

The next day I would take my lunch in my paper bag, some papers mom would give me to give to the school people, walk behind the trailer park through the woods, cross the railroad tracks and walk a few blocks through all of the real houses until I saw the school building. Then I would walk into the school and someone would tell me what to do next. Mom was going to leave her work early that day so she would be home when I got out of school. I didn't have to go to the babysitter's house. I'd come straight home from school and tell mom all about the first day. Being responsible for myself made me so proud. I was a big boy now!

The next morning mom kissed me goodbye as she left for work. Before she left, she made sure I had the important papers and knew the way to school. She knew I would love going to school. I did, too, but I was a little afraid as well.

Arriving at the school, I saw nothing but confusion. More children were there than I had ever seen before in one spot. Many of them had their mothers with them. A big person told me to go to the room on the first floor for first graders. She pointed to the room's door. The room was full of children like me. All of the desk chairs had been taken. I was told to sit with the large group of children already seated on the floor. All morning there were big people coming in and out of the room. They kept talking to each other. Finally, we were told we could go outside for recess and play. Then we were told to come back into the room. There were some more chairs in the room, but there were still more children than chairs. I sat on the floor with my back resting on the wall with some other kids.

They told us it was lunchtime. We could go outside and eat our lunches. Outside, the kids quickly joined their friends to eat lunch together. I didn't see any of the children I knew at the trailer park. Towards the back of the school, by a stairwell that went down to a lower level of the building, were two older boys taking their sandwiches from their sacks. I decided to join them. They said hello. I replied hello back to them.

I had been looking forward to eating my tomato. I loved tomatoes. It was a rare treat to get to have a whole tomato to myself. As I pulled it out of my bag, one of the boys said, "He's got a rotten apple."

This statement caused a giggle to come from the other guy as he replied, "When he bites into it a big worm's head will poke out at him. He'll puke his guts up."

This caused the first boy to laugh loud and hard. I felt totally defeated. I was humiliated beyond belief. That was it. I quit. I was going home. While glaring at the two boys, I threw the tomato to the ground right in front of their feet. I ripped out my peanut butter and jelly sandwich from the sack and flung it into the stairwell. Then I turned my back to the two boys and started walking home.

The trailer door was locked. Mom had made sure that it would lock when I closed it that morning. There wasn't much to do around the trailer with all my toys locked up. I just allowed the time to pass somehow until Mom came home. She was surprised that I was home before she was. Mom asked if they had let school out early.

"No, I quit. Besides, they didn't have any room for me. There were too many children. They didn't have a seat for me."

Mom said she would take me to school the next day. That evening, a lady came by the trailer and gave mom some papers. She told mom that her son had brought them home from school. He had found them on the playground. One of the papers had my baby footprint on it and some writing. I guess I had forgotten all about the papers. I was so humiliated and embarrassed by those two boys; it was all I could do just to leave the school grounds without their seeing me crying. I had no idea as to when or how I dropped the papers. I did not remember them until the moment the lady came to the trailer. Mom thanked her. She did not scold me for losing them. She didn't even mention them.

The next few days of school are not a part of my memory. What I do remember is liking the school and my teacher. I loved playing with the other children. As soon as we left our classroom for morning recess, we would start playing "Come Over Red Rover!" Before long it was what we did all the time when we were outside. The group of us that loved playing the game all laughed and ran as fast as we could when the person who was "it" called out, "Come Over, Red Rover." We ran from the line in the dirt four feet or so in front of the school building wall to touch the wall for safety. As we ran across the open space, the person in the middle would try to catch as many children as he or she could before they reached the wall, the safe place. Then that person, along with the children he had caught, would stand between the wall and the line in the ground, getting to catch more children running from the wall to the safety of the far side of that line in the ground, as she or he again called out, "Come Over, Red Rover!" This continued until there was only one child left that had not been caught. Then that child got to be "it." She or he got to be the one to start the new game of "Come Over, Red Rover." We never tired of playing the game. All of us boys and girls enjoyed playing it. There were never any real disputes about who was really "caught" when we ran across the line. It was just as much fun catching someone as it was trying to avoid being caught.

At the end of second grade, my dad was transferred to Cincinnati, Ohio. That was the late spring of 1950. I had to leave school a few days before the actual end of the school year. Mom and Dad had sold the twenty-eight-foot trailer and bought a brand-new giant of a trailer that was thirty-six feet long. It was made of real airplane quality aluminum, Dad said. He was proud of that fact. Dad would be pulling it with our car all the way to Cincinnati. In the middle of the afternoon on the day we were leaving, Mom and Dad and my little brother and Blackie, our dog, drove up to the school with the trailer behind them. Mom came into the classroom to get me. The teacher asked me to step into the cloakroom where we hung up our coats and put our galoshes when it was raining. In the cloakroom she gave me a paper bag with things in it. She told me it was a gift but not to open it until I got in the car. She was such a nice teacher. I was surprised that she liked me enough to give me a present and thought she was being very kind to me.

When we started down the road to Cincinnati, I opened the bag. It had several pieces of candy in it. The teacher was so kind. It was so thoughtful of her to do that for me. Mom and Dad thought so too.

Starting school in Cincinnati was different. Lots of kids from the trailer park and from the newly built houses that made up the subdivision on the other side of the trailer park went to Kirby Road School. The community was a part of Cincinnati called College Hills. We had to be bused to a school much closer to the downtown area. It was called Kirby Road Elementary School. The trailer park kids filled up more than half of the school bus when it made its stop at my part of the trailer park. Then the bus went into the subdivision of real houses to fill up with kids. I'd be starting third grade at Kirby Road School. There were kids on the bus who were in all of the grades above mine. The school had first through sixth graders. I don't remember if first graders or second graders from our section of College Hills went to Kirby Road School or not.

Lots of buses brought lots of kids to Kirby Road School. All of the boys went to the left side of the building. All of the girls went to the right side. The boys entered a large gym-like room. Everyone had to line up with the boys in their classroom. My classroom had about twenty boys in it. We were to go to a specific spot that was just for our classroom and stand in a single file line. No one was allowed to talk. The principal and three or four men teachers carrying big paddles walked up and down the rows of male students trying to catch someone talking. They would come up behind a talker and swat him hard on the butt with their paddle. Even from a couple of rows away you could hear the hard slap of the paddle on someone's backside. When the bell rang, it signaled that it was time to go to your classroom. Then we all marched single-file to our various classrooms with the fear of being hit if we dared to talk. It was surprising how many boys would talk while standing in line or going to their classrooms. The hit on the butt from the teachers did not seem to bother a lot of people. There was no way of knowing how the girls were treated.

Boys and girls were in the same classrooms, but the asphalted playground behind the school was divided. Girls played on the right half of the playground and boys played on the left side. If any boys were caught on the girls' side of the playground, they would be paddled.

Kirby Road School seemed to like paddling little boys. The school seemed to think that little boys would behave only if they were paddled or frightened into being good out of fear of being paddled. Kirby Road School also believed that little boys were too rough to play with little girls.

As young as I was, I knew that it would cause me nothing but trouble to tell the adults at Kirby Road School that in Granite City, Illinois, they knew little boys and girls could play together with great joy and no one would get hurt or knocked down or anything like that. The school in Granite City also knew that there was no need to paddle little children or threaten them with being paddled. We were good children who wanted to be good and we were. I wanted to ask the Kirby Road School teachers why they thought little boys were bad. I knew that if I did, I would be paddled. I never asked.

My teacher at Kirby Road School was nice. She made us feel happy in her classroom. I liked her. As the school year progressed, she was absent more and more often. We had a lot of substitute teachers. After a while, the same substitute teacher would be the one to fill in for our teacher, who was gone a great deal of the time in the second half of the school year. One morning the constant substitute teacher told our class that if we were good all day, the last half hour we could do whatever we wanted to do as a class.

We were good all that day as I think we were every day. When the last half hour of the school day arrived, the substitute teacher said that we needed to decide what we wanted to do as a class for the rest of the day. Hands went up. The teacher called on one of the kids.

"We want Jerry to read to us."

My classmates all began shouting that they wanted me to read to them from some of the storybooks in the room. I was surprised that they would want me to do that. I liked telling the kids stories about the Granite City School and other places I'd lived. At this point, I don't remember having read stories to anyone there before that request. I guess I must have, or they would not have asked for me to do so then. I loved doing it. I used different voices for the characters in the books I read. My classmates seemed to like my reading to them. That was the only thing they ever asked for as a reward for being good all day, and they were always good.

They would have fit in nicely at that Granite City school.

CHAPTER TWELVE

Hero?

Given the human tendency to see ones' self as the hero of one's life's story, I must confess to being human. This tendency was particularly strong in the summer of 1953. It was a good summer. At the start of the school year I'd be in sixth grade at Kirby Road Elementary School. That was the senior class of the school. I'd be one of the "big kids." I knew my way around the school and in our trailer-park located in College Hills. It was a suburb of Cincinnati, Ohio.

I no longer had to ask my parents for permission to ride my bike over to the Mt. Healthy swimming pool. I just had to tell them that I was leaving for there and when I'd be back. I loved being at the pool. It was great playing tag with the other kids in the water. Arguably, I was one of the best swimmers, if not the best swimmer of the group. I rarely got tagged.

Another good thing about that summer was that I had really gotten excited about reading novels, adventure novels. They were all about good guys standing up for the underdog, the weak and the oppressed. Those heroes went through a lot but always prevailed.

Actually, I'd gotten into those novels earlier during the school year. They prompted me to spontaneously shout out a solution to the continuing battles between us guys living in the trailer park and the kids living in the surrounding subdivision. They all lived in real houses. The houses were usually built with expensive brick. They were really big houses. Well, at least they were pretty big when compared to the trailers we all lived in. The Cincinnati City Schools' bus would effectively mix the trailer kids with the real house kids. On the bus and in the school, we were all friends. After school it was different. It was usually us against them.

We would play war against the house kids. We always played it in the woods that separated the trailer park from the main road and the house-filled subdivision. The woods consisted of a deep ravine going down from the back of a long row of trailers that reached its lowest point at the always running creek and then climbed up to the top of the hill. At the top there was some level ground that extended for about half the length of a football field before it met the road. The back of the ten trailers or so was marked by a long cement patio construction that served as a community patio. It was about ten feet wide. We had a thick rope tied to one of the big trees next to the cement patio. The rope swing took advantage of a four-foot drop from the back of the patio to the ground that quickly fell away towards the creek.

Once, when I was taking the maximum swing off the patio from one side of the tree to the other, the rope broke. It broke at the apex of the swing. You had to get a good running start to launch your swing in order to land on the patio on the other side or you risked crashing into the supports keeping the patio from collapsing into the deep slant of the ground to the creek. As I reached the apex, my body was almost horizontal to the patio surface. The ground was a long way down as it dropped quickly at that spot. It was at that moment that the rope broke. I was frozen in place. I could not look down, sideways or up. I knew I would crash into a tree. My legs were spread wide apart. I hoped I wouldn't end up straddling a tree as I crashed into it. The few seconds of free fall seemed to last about five minutes as I waited for the pain that would come.

My stomach hit first. It wasn't a hard hit. I hit the slope of the hill at about the same angle it was sloping. Then I slid to a relatively gentle stop. Outside of a few scraps on my stomach, I was unhurt. My playmates on top of the hill rushed to my rescue. We all marveled at the good fortune that had landed on me. Once again, my luck had stood strong for me.

The far side of the ravine, the house side with the somewhat level boundary top, was where the house kids and we had our wars. Each side would take up defensive positions behind old piles of dirt left by long-forgotten construction crews. Then the battles would begin. We would pull up tall weeds that had large clumps of dirt attached to their roots and throw them at the other side. They were our hand grenades. If you got hit in the head with one, it would fill your hair with dirt. Usually, getting hit didn't hurt; it just got you uncomfortably dirty. It was important to pick a defensive position that had enough weeds to serve as ammunition. Eventually, one side prevailed over the other and that side would rush the other side with their hands full of ammunition, tossing it in rapid-fire mode.

Our side, the trailer park kids side, was being overrun. We ran down the hill to the creek with our pursuers close behind. Up the trailer park side of the bank and onto the patio we went. The house kids stopped two-thirds up the trailer park hill and shouted insults, which were returned in kind.

The whole process just seemed stupid to me at that moment. I liked some of the house kids in the gang who were taunting us. The others, I really didn't know although I had seen almost all of them on the school bus or at school.

Without inner reflection, I shouted out, "This is stupid. It's really dumb. We have to stop the fighting." Everyone stopped shouting. They all looked at me.

One of the house guys shouted at me, "How do we do that?"

My words surprised me as they shot from my mouth, "Let's match up someone from each of our sides and have them fight. We'll make sure that they are about the same size and age. Whoever wins, that side is the winner. The war is over."

"Ok," came the reply as both clusters of boys went into conference.

"Who shall we pick?" I asked our group. We had some pretty good fighters. We had a good shot of winning.

My question was met with silent stares. I was dumbfounded. Any one of them gave us a pretty good shot. I had expected several volunteers.

The silence was broken by one of the older kids, "It was your idea. You should be the one to fight."

Ahhh, no. Someone else was supposed to do this. Not me. I only fight when an injustice is being done and I'm trying to correct it or someone has jumped me out of the blue, raced my inner thoughts. *I don't want to fight anyone. I have to be mad or outraged to fight spontaneously. I can't just fight to be fighting. This is wrong.*

As they stared at me, I realized the spot I had put myself in. "You're right. It was my idea." There seemed to be a group gestalt acknowledging the truth of my words.

Reluctantly, I said, "OK, I'll do it." From my perspective, it was the only noble thing to do. If I ask it of others, then I have to be willing to step up in turn.

The kids shouted down to the house guys that I had been selected. The house kids argued among themselves. Ending their discussion, they announced their champion. He was a year older than I was and a little bigger. I liked him. He always seemed to play fair on the school playground and in the tackle football games we played in the subdivision in an open lot behind some houses. While none of us wore football gear, he was never afraid to hit a runner going through the lines. That runner was usually me.

We gathered near the creek bottom on a small spot of level ground. As the kid and I began circling each other looking for an opening to launch an attack, both groups of boys shouted encouragement into the center of their encirclement.

The attack was simultaneous. We sprang at each other with our arms widespread. Upon contact we embraced in the struggle with each other. Quickly we fell to the ground in a writhing snake-like frenzy. We rolled over and on top of each other time and again, each of us struggling to obtain an advantage over the other. Suddenly, I was on top. I had his shoulders pinned to the ground as I straddled his midsection. He was mine. I had him under complete control.

"Hit him. Hit him in the face. Punch his lights out. Go on, hit him," came the taunts from my guys.

This was incomprehensible to me. What? Why would I want to do that? I don't want to hurt him. He's a good guy. I was astounded at these calls to hit him.

"No, I won. It's over. We're friends." I stated as I slowly got up and extended a hand to the vanquished foe.

Pulling him up by the hand, I said, "It was a fair fight. We won."

Then I held out my hand to the guy. We shook hands.

Not much was said by anyone as we went back to the trailers and they went back to their houses.

Our two sides never played war again. We continued to play footfall together. They were nice guys.

That happened in the spring. This was summer. This was going to the Mt. Healthy swimming pool. A friend from the trailer park was going with me. We had about three quarters of an hour of riding our bicycles to the pool. It seemed like a long way, but it was worth it.

The afternoon passed quickly. It was fun. We regretted getting out of the pool. I needed to be home for supper. We turned in our basket number attached to the overly large-sized safety pin at the checkout both, retrieved our basket of clothes and dressed. The bikes were parked on the other side of the little park that surrounded the swimming pool.

As we were walking to the bike stands, there's this guy, about my size, build (wiry, stringy thin) and apparent age, trying to pull a girl's bicycle out of her hands.

"No, no, I've got it. Let go, let go."

"I'm taking it! Give it to me! Let go," he screamed in her face as he vigorously pulled the bike towards him, dragging the seven or eight-year-old girl with it.

"Hey, why don't you let the little girl alone," I shouted.

He stopped pulling on the bike and stepped towards me.

"Why don't you mind your own business!" he demanded, continuing his approach.

"Why don't you just let the little girl have her bike?" I shouted back.

As he got to within arm's reach, he spit out, "You should mind your own business," and tried to land a left hook.

Instinctively, I blocked the punch with my right forearm while landing a quick jab to the center of his forehead, one to his nose and one to his mouth in rapid succession. He took a half a step back, momentarily stunned by this unexpected turn of events. They were solid jabs but not given with my full strength as I was unprepared for his sudden attack.

Quickly he followed with a flurry of punches, none of which landed. It was easy to block them. Clearly, he didn't know how to fight with his fists. Again, I hit him with three quick jabs that had more force behind them but not ones that I would throw if I were really mad.

It was obvious to both of us that we were mismatched. I could beat him badly if I wanted to start pounding. He knew it.

He held back from throwing any more punches. His expression told me that he didn't know what to do next. He was in trouble.

"Hey, why you picking on him?" cried one of the five guys approaching the two of us as we circled each other with our fists up.

"Yeah," called out another, "you're older and bigger than him. How old are you? When's your birthday?"

This is trouble, I thought, as the five guys surrounded my friend and me. I lied as I reduced my age by a year.

"Well, they're about the same age," someone from the hostile group stated as they closed around me, "and about the same size."

My partner had slipped out of the ring. Keeping my eye on the two guys in front of me and slowly stepping backwards, I stated, "He tried to take a little girl's bike from her."

"That's none of your business," came the reply as they pressed towards me and I continued to back-peddle towards the bikes.

The lead aggressor moved his hand up to shove me. I started

to step back while bringing up a forearm to knock his hand aside as I felt something brush against my back leg. In my peripheral vision I saw one of their guys on his hands and knees ready to trip me as the frontal assailant moved forward.

Instantly, I moved my right leg back slightly in preparation to pivot my left leg over his crouching form. The heel of my shoe accidentally slammed onto the back of his hand pinning it to the ground. Knowingly, I immediately shifted my full weight onto the back of that hand. Instantly, I swung my other leg over his crouching form in such a manner that my pivoting heel ground deeply and painfully into the hand trapped between it and the hard surface. The tripper cried out in deep pain. The pivoting maneuver successfully allowed me to jump over my would-be assailant in such a manner as to allow me to once again face the two aggressors moving towards me.

As I continued to slowly walk backwards towards the bike rack, the aggressors stayed at the imaginary boundary created by their injured companion, who was standing at the spot where his injury occurred, holding the damaged appendage while whimpering in pain.

My friend rejoined me from the sidelines and we began walking quickly towards our bikes. The collection of hostiles stayed where they were, shouting that they would get the two of us if we ever came back. They began talking among themselves.

One of them was heard asking, "Why wouldn't his sister let him have the bike?"

INTO THE ADULT YEARS

CHAPTER THIRTEEN

Pittsburgh by Thumb

It seemed like a good idea at the time. For spring break, I'd hitchhike to Pittsburgh, Pennsylvania.

There wasn't enough time for me to go down to Port Lavaca, Texas. My father had been transferred from Pittsburgh to Port Lavaca last fall. I spent Christmas with the family there. My grandparents drove me all the way from Danville, Kentucky to Port Lavaca and back. It was a really long trip. It was too long and too expensive for me to get down there during that spring break of my sophomore year at Centre College, 1962.

During my freshman year, I had returned to Pittsburgh several times. It was a long, hard one-day trip, but it was a one-day trip. I'd do it. I'd make an adventure out of hitchhiking up there.

Arrangements had been made for me to stay at a high school classmate's home. He'd be back from Rice University to spend the break at his home. All my old Pittsburgh friends and I would get together for spring break. They were attending colleges in quite a few different states. We'd have fun telling stories about our adventures. Then I would catch a Greyhound bus back to Danville. It was all so simple.

The best ride I could catch out of the college going north would take me just south of Cincinnati. Erlanger, Kentucky, wasn't far from the Ohio River. Cincinnati was just on the other side of it. Everyone assured me that it would be easy to catch a ride from there going through Cincinnati and on up to Columbus. From Columbus it would be an easy hop up to Wheeling, West Virginia. Then it's a pretty straight shot from Wheeling to Pittsburgh. All of the guys at college thought that I wouldn't have any problems getting rides. With a little luck, I might make it in a single day. Just to be on the safe side, I had planned on the trip taking two days.

Of course, I'd travel light. I had one small suitcase packed with underwear and two changes of clothes. My spending money and my returning bus fare were rolled up and stuck in my sock.

In order for possible rides to know that I was not a desperado, I wore my sport jacket, a white shirt and a tie. I was a college guy going back home for spring break. That was the clear message I wanted to signal to possible rides. The sign I intended to hold up had clear, bold letters that said, "Pittsburgh." Anyone driving by would know that this was a college kid going to Pittsburgh. Who wouldn't want to give him a ride to help him on his way?

The ride to Erlanger was fast. We arrived at the outskirts around midmorning. My friend let me out at the main road to Cincinnati. In less than a half hour a car pulled over. I ran up to it.

"Going to Pittsburgh?" the driver asked.

"Yes sir."

"What route do you plan to take after you get through Cincinnati?"

"I plan to go to Columbus and then to Wheeling and across to Pittsburgh."

"Well, I can get you through Cincinnati, but I'm not going to

Columbus. I'm going to Chillicothe. You might consider riding with me to Chillicothe. From there you could go on up to Athens. It's a college town. The University of Ohio is there. It should be pretty easy to get a ride from there on north towards Pittsburgh. While you're thinking on that, hop in and I'll get you through Cinci."

I knew the Chillicothe, Ohio, area fairly well. All of my mother's relatives were from around that part of Ohio. For brief periods of time while visiting my aunt Virginia, I had attended Buckskin Elementary School in South Salem, Ohio, where she was a fifth-grade teacher. I also attended Greenfield, Ohio's elementary school with my cousin, Timmy. Both towns weren't all that far from Chillicothe. Sometimes Aunt Virginia's daughter and her husband would take my younger brother and me to a Chillicothe drive-in movie. We loved to watch the Ma and Pa Kettle movies. They were funny. I liked Chillicothe. During the four years we lived in Cincinnati, we would frequently drive to Greenfield and South Salem.

I got in the car. The guy seemed to know the roads up to Pittsburgh more thoroughly than I did. He thought it would be my best bet to go with him to Chillicothe. In actual miles, it would be shorter to go through Chillicothe to Pittsburgh than going through Columbus, my ride stated. That was good enough for me. I was off to Chillicothe.

In the course of our conversation during the three-hour or so ride to Chillicothe, he asked me if I knew the area around there. That led me to relate a story from each of those school experiences.

When we got to Chillicothe he let me out at an intersection that he speculated would provide me with the best chance of catching a ride that would take me some distance towards

Pittsburgh. I thanked him.

The mid-afternoon sun was hot. After about an hour of standing there, my armpits had begun to sweat. No one had stopped to offer a ride. I held up my Pittsburgh sign to no avail. The cars just whizzed on by. It was at this point that I began to have real doubts about the wisdom of my plan to hitchhike. I could be stuck at this intersection for days. What a depressing thought that was.

At last a car stopped. Walking up towards the rear of it, I could see that it was full of girls. When I approached the open window on the driver's side, the girl said, "We've driven by this spot several times and had seen that you were still here. This is the wrong side of town to get a ride going north. You need to get on the Athens City side. That's the best place to get a ride going north. Hop in the back."

The young lady in the front passenger seat had opened her door, gotten out of the car and pulled up the back of her seat for me to begin the struggle of getting into the rear seat area. The problem was that there were already three young women in the rear seat. When I looked into it, I stated that I didn't think there was room for me. They all laughed and said they'd make room. They did that by having one girl sit on another's lap. I sat in the middle crunched between the girl on the driver's side of the seat and the double girls on the passenger side.

All five girls were seniors at their high school. That night was their prom night. They were bubbling over with excitement. They wanted to know where I went to college and what it was like there and shared their hopes for college the next year. It didn't take long to reach our destination.

I thanked them. They drove off amidst a lot of laughter, waves and multiple honks of their horn.

No luck at this intersection either. I had been standing there for several hours. It was now dusk and nothing. Before long it would be totally dark. I didn't know how much longer I could continue to stand here with my thumb out and my Pittsburgh sign held chest high before I would have to find a place to sleep. I could pay for a motel room, but there weren't any motels in sight. I was worried. I had not planned for this at all. Everyone had told me it would be a simple task to get to Pittsburgh. Maybe I was a little naïve.

The Volkswagen bug slowed to a stop in front of me. A guy about my age or a little older leaned over from the driver side of the car and spoke to me through the passenger side's window, "You've been standing here a real long time. We drove in from Athens to get groceries this afternoon and you were here then."

The young lady in the passenger's seat nodded in affirmation, as he went on, "We're going back to Athens; we can give you a ride there if you want. You'll have a better chance of catching a ride to Pittsburgh from there than from here. We'll have to move some of the groceries around to make room for you in the back seat, but I think you'll fit. You might have to hold a bag of groceries in your lap, but we can get you in if you want."

I enthusiastically agreed. Anything to get out of here was better than great.

He was a graduate student in physics at the University of Ohio there in Athens. She had a job on campus that didn't pay much but it got them the money they needed.

They were both from the Cincinnati area and knew about where I had lived. The even knew where my elementary school, Kirby Road Elementary School, was. We shared old elementary school stories.

After stopping for gas and a restroom break just outside of

Athens, they invited me to supper.

"It's not much. Just spaghetti, but if you like that, we'd enjoy having you eat with us."

"Well, sure, but I don't want to impose."

"It's not an imposition, but it's pretty simple, just spaghetti."

"Thank you. That would just hit the spot."

By this time, I knew they were counting pennies. They had a really tight budget. I thought of offering to take them out to an inexpensive restaurant for a meal. I could afford that, but then I thought better of it. They would refuse. It would just be an awkward situation. I liked spaghetti even if it didn't have meatballs. I'd just put some grated cheese over the tomato sauce and eat away.

We unloaded the car together. It was fun. They were such a wonderfully joyous couple. She went to work in the kitchen preparing the meal as they directed me to the bathroom to freshen up. It didn't take long for her to call the two of us, the two men, to the supper table.

When I walked into the kitchen, I was surprised at the sight. She had lit a tall candle that stood in the center of the table. There was a big plate filled with spaghetti. That was it. There were three plates with the accompanying silverware, three glasses of water and the plate of spaghetti. There was no sauce. There was no cheese nor butter nor salt or pepper. There was just the spaghetti. They had repeatedly told me that it was just spaghetti for supper. They were right. I was touched. They had so little but were sharing what they had with me. As I stated, I could have paid for a cheap meal for all of us. It was clearly out of the question now. Continuing the pleasant sharing of stories we had begun during our trip from Chillicothe, we emptied the spaghetti plate.

As we were cleaning the dishes, they invited me to spend the night with them. They could put some sheets on the couch for me. I could sleep there. Then in the morning, they would drive me to a good intersection for catching rides. It was on the north side of Athens. After they dropped me off, he'd go to his classes and she would go to her job on campus. I accepted this gracious offer. Late into the evening we talked about a lot of things related to what we were learning, what we hoped to be doing in the future, our personal philosophies of life and how we had acquired them. They were such wonderful people.

The morning went just as they said it would. After dropping me off at the intersection, they gave me a hug. We said our goodbyes and off they drove.

It took about five hours of holding up the Pittsburgh sign before I got a ride. I had to take a break and get a hamburger for lunch. It took an hour or so after that before the car stopped. The driver was in a business suit.

"You're in luck, son. I'm driving all the way to Pittsburgh. Hop in. Your job will be to keep me awake as the night wears on."

Once we had joined the flow of traffic, he said with a big grin on his face, "That was a nice touch, the coat and tie. I don't normally pick up hitchhikers. That coat and tie did it. Congratulations!"

As it turned out, he meant just what he said about keeping him awake on the trip. We had a lot of hours to go before we got there. He was really great at asking me questions that got me talking. On the other hand, he was brief and non-informative in responding to my inquiries concerning the specifics of his work. He expected me to do the talking. Fortunately, I had accumulated a lot of interesting stories from the many places I had lived.

He said that he was based out of Cincinnati with his firm but had business in southeastern Ohio that caused him to go up to the firm's Pittsburgh office. He knew a lot about Cincinnati. He knew where my elementary school was located, where the trailer park we lived in was located and where my Boy Scout Troop had met in Finneytown. He even knew about the football game that made my college famous around 1920 or 1921. Little Centre College had beaten Harvard, the consensus number one college team of the country that year, by a score of six to zero.

Around ten that night, somewhere between Wheeling, West Virginia, and Pittsburgh, he started to get really sleepy. He wanted me to try singing some songs. Now, most people who've heard me sing will tell you it's best if you turn up the background music. He got into it though, and started to sing along. Then he would lead with some song he knew, and I would join in. We laughed at the fact that neither of us knew all of the lyrics to a single song.

"I haven't told you much about what I do for a living, have I?"

"No, sir."

"I'm a FBI agent."

Well, what do you say to someone who has just told you he was a FBI agent? I didn't know either.

"That's good."

"You don't believe me. Here, I'll show you," he said, pulling back the right side of his suit jacket. There was a shoulder holster with a gun in it.

"Yes, I believe you."

"I'm on a case. That's why I'm going to Pittsburgh."

Well, if he were an FBI agent, it would explain why he was so good at asking me questions and getting me to talk without his providing much information about himself. Of course, he could be a gangster. Wouldn't that just be my luck? It took a while before our conversation resumed its entertaining tempo, but it did.

He said he would drive me to my friend's house in Bellevue. Bellevue is a borough of Pittsburgh. It's northwest of the city near Sewickley and Avalon. When he asked for the street address, I couldn't give it to him. I knew where the house was because I had walked to it a lot the two and a half years I lived there. I never needed to know the address because I always knew where it was.

That didn't faze my chauffeur; he drove around the general area until I could identify the house. We shook hands vigorously before he let me out. I waved to him as he pulled away.

CHAPTER FOURTEEN

Justice

"Hey Kid, the captain wants you to turn that steel shaft," the big Mexican shouted at me from the deck of the dredge boat fifteen feet above.

"It's too big, I can't turn that," I shouted back, squinting as the early afternoon sun glared into my eyes at the bottom of the open hold. The stainless-steel shaft extended from the center of the dredge boat. This was my first day of being a deckhand on an ocean-going dredge boat in the summer of 1962. I had already deduced that the entire dredge, all 500 plus feet or so of it, was just one big diesel engine assigned the job of turning that shaft and operating the suction-pumps. It had to be at least ten feet across. I couldn't even get a good grip on it, let alone turn it.

"Sure you can. It's precision balanced with ball bearings and all. He just wants you to turn it a fraction of an inch. Hurry up! The whole dredge is waiting on you to do it."

"All right," I shouted back, thinking that this was really stupid. I stretched my arms around the protruding four or five inches as wide as my reach could possibly allow.

Damn, this is a waste of effort. This guy is stupid or he knows a whole hell of a lot more about dredges than I do, I thought to myself with a chuckle.

Straining as hard as I could with my arms slipping and my feet shifting for better leverage, I turned my head as a loud roar of laughter came from above. Twenty or thirty guys were looking down at me, laughing their heads off. I had to be ridiculous. I was hilariously ridiculous. I had to laugh as well. This was funny, no two ways about it.

"What's going on here," a voice shouted out from beyond the edge of the hold. "You men get back to work," it demanded authoritatively. As they quickly disappeared, the face of the deck captain loomed above me. Looking down at me, a smile crossed his face and then he disappeared.

The entire day had been strange. This event simply fit into the continuum. When my mom drove me to the isolated boat landing at sunrise, I was overwhelmed with doubt. This was my first real man's job. Last summer I had worked as a lifeguard at the local public swimming pool in my Pittsburgh, Pennsylvania, borough. That had been the second summer in a row I'd held the job. Now, one year of college was under my belt. I'd still be working at the pool if my dad hadn't had a transfer to Port Lavaca, Texas, during the fall. The main offices of the dredge boat company were located in Port Lavaca. Dad had talked to the director of personnel for the company and gotten me the job. It paid well. I'd work five days a week at $1.50 an hour with the possibility of getting in some overtime at time and a half pay. That was a lot of money in 1962. The company also provided room and board on the dredge. I'd really make enough to cover my living expenses during my junior year. A half tuition grant-in-aid helped my parent's budget out a lot. In addition to paying half of my tuition, my parents also paid for my dorm room. It was all they could do to pay those bills. All of the other expenses were my responsibility. The work I did in the dining hall provided free board and paid ten dollars a month. I could barely make it on that. The slivers of soap left in the showers at the college gym worked well enough in cleaning my clothes along with the free assistance of the dorm showers. That and other money-saving measures enabled me to maintain an acceptable level of decency. I needed to make and save money at some kind of a job during the summer in order to ease my burden of existence in school. This paid so much more than lifeguarding. I was really fortunate.

First of all, having your mother drive you to your first day of real man's work was embarrassing. The family had one car. Well, in those days most families had just one car unless they were living on the affluent side of the tracks. Anyway, there was no question that she had to drive me.

I had envisioned the crew-boat landing being in the middle of a shipyard type setting. It would be in the midst of boats coming and going with a lot of freight-related traffic driving here and there. That's how it was in Kenosha, Wisconsin's harbor when we lived there. We lived on the lake side of the harbor in the Coast Guard's CO's quarters. The dredge boat company was the second largest one in the world. Their landing would reflect that status, went my reasoning.

It had taken more than an hour to get to the landing from Port Lavaca. Once outside of the town, there was nothing. The road was surrounded by saltwater marshland with dozens and dozens of little streams whose flow was controlled by the tides. It was flat, and it was unending. At last, my mother turned off onto a gravel road that headed to an open space of water expanding into the ocean. At the end of the road was a lone telephone pole. A faded light at the top of it competed with the dawn. Several cars were parked near the pole. Finally, the boat landing appeared slightly mounded above the saltwater grass. It was a simple wooden platform suspended a few feet above the sea by the standard pilings. The seaward side of it was just long enough for a tugboat-sized craft to tie up to it.

Fifteen or so men were standing around huddled in small groups or in isolation on the planks of the landing. Women and little children stood on the landing and in the gravel parking lot to the rear of the platform. Some of the people in the small groups were engaged in conversation. Except for the children, movement was subdued.

Mom parked the car at the furthest spot from the landing that she could. I think she sensed my embarrassment and was trying to help out. As I was saying goodbye, she said she'd wait until the crew boat arrived to be sure I got aboard all right. I grabbed my gym bag full of clothes to take with me as I'd sleep on the dredge for the five-day shift.

Walking towards the lighted landing, I could see that everyone was a Latino. I assumed that they were all of Mexican descent. They were speaking Spanish. Spanish was the language I studied in college to meet the graduation requirements. I was a poor student of it. We studied Castilian Spanish. Except for a few words that sounded somewhat like the meager vocabulary I could remember, I had no clue as to what these guys were saying. I stood there in isolation. What was I getting into?

The energy level of the assembled group picked up as the crew boat came into view. The tug's big diesel engine sound began to drown out the suppressed conversations. It tied up to the landing in an efficient style. The deckhand worked the ropes with grace.

Once the tug was stable with the dock, some guy looking like an authority figure exited the pilot house, walked down the ladder to the main deck and assumed a guard-like pose as he motioned to a small group of the men to board. They jumped on with cat-like agility. As I approached to board, he held up his hand for me to stop. I leaned toward him so that he could hear me over the idling engine and said, "The central office told me to get on the boat here. This is my first day."

"OK." He sighed with a resigned note while motioning me aboard. Once on, I didn't know what to do. Several of the other men had gone inside the tug while some stood around the outside housing or climbed on top of it to sit. They were all putting on life jackets and hard hats. I went to the cabinet where they were stored and obtained a set.

"Hey, how about a job?" shouted one man from the dock. "I'm a hard worker." A woman and several small children stood beside him.

"You'll have to talk to the central office," shouted my gatekeeper. "I can't help you."

"Aw, come on, give me a job," he shouted back as the deckhand began releasing the lines that held the tug to the dock. As the engine revived up, the screw churned the water into a boiling muddy soup. We began to pull away from the dock.

"I've got a wife and five kids. Give me a job. I'll be your hardest worker. Come on man, my kids gotta eat."

I wanted to shout back, "Take my job. I'm just a college kid making summer money. You have a family to support. You need this more than I do." Then I thought, I could end up like him if I don't keep this job. I won't be able to stay in college without it. My guilt was heavy. I held my tongue.

The gatekeeper held up his hands and shrugged. Turning away, he went into the cabin. They had started a poker game there. Five or six guys were already betting. Some of the men on the main deck or on the roof of the tug's cabin huddled in groups of two or three, but mostly the men sat by themselves silently looking out to sea. No one approached me. I looked out to sea wondering what would happen to me.

I knew nothing about ocean-going dredge boats. I had seen dredges on the Ohio River, but they were small. I doubted that I was about to work on one of those. They had a crane-like construction on top of a flat barge that was pushed by a tugboat. The crane would lower a bucket-like scoop into the river and then pull it up full of dripping bottom sludge. The crane would swing to the side over a cargo barge and drop its load, then monotonously repeat the process. The crew boat had more men on it than would be necessary to operate one of those dredges.

Now, I did have some experience working lines and tying up craft to docks and the like. My dad had seen to that. The lines of the tug were far bigger than any lines I'd ever handled. They looked to be two inches thick. I'd have to learn to handle them. I could do it. That wasn't the question. The question in my mind was what was the IT?

How far out was the dredge? We had left sight of land more than forty-five minutes ago and were still headed out to sea. Another twenty minutes or so passed before I saw it. The thing was big. Three tugs larger than this one were moving around it like busy bees. The bulk of it was at least 500 feet long with a big ladder-like contraption on the front that, with its connecting cables, lowered another crane-like arm into the sea. It seemed to be like a big, long anteater's nose probing into the water. The dredge swayed in rhythm to the slow, methodical swings of the nose from one side to the other. The rear of the dredge had a long pipe floating on pontoons extending for fifteen or more lengths of the dredge leading to a series of low islands. The end section of the pipe was elevated so that it spouted a continuous flow of muddy water onto the last island. It was clear that this outpouring had made the narrow stretch of islands, just as it was in the process of creating another one. Tiny, ant-like men were at the spouting edge busily scurrying about.

The crew boat headed bow first into the rear third of the dredge as it continued its rocking rhythm. At the last possible second, the captain of the tug reversed the engine, causing the tug to gently nudge the side of the dredge with its massive bow fender. Instantly, the tug's engine roared forward, forcing the bow to be firmly attached to the dredge by the powerful thrust of the tug's propeller. Men deftly jumped from the tugs' point of contact onto the dredge's deck. I joined the mass and entered the world of dredge boatmen.

To my eyes, the deck was a mass confusion of men who knew where they were going. I was the lone exception. I did not fit. First off, I was clearly the youngest person on deck. Next, as a Caucasian, I was a member of a small minority group. Finally, my use of the English language did not fit the norm.

I explained to an older Mexican man who had been walking by me that I was new. This was my first day. I didn't know what to do or who to report to. He pointed out a white guy talking to a group of Mexicans and said that was Jerry, the deck captain. He would tell me what to do. Thanking the man, I walked over to the group.

It was clear that the deck captain had no idea I was coming. He was a little perplexed as to what to do with me. One could deduce that he didn't like to be perplexed. After explaining that the central office had told me to report, he finally seemed to allow that I was to be a part of the workforce. He resented the fact.

He directed me to a weathered man standing with a small group of men by one of the spuds that was in the process of being raised. He said he was my section's mate.

Approaching the mate, I introduced myself. He said something to me that was pretty much incomprehensible. His Cajun accent was thick and my ear for understanding was thin. The noise of the spuds shifting positions seemed to dominate all other sounds as I shouted, 'What?"

He told me to go into the galley and eat breakfast with the rest of our watch. Well, the galley was total confusion. You stood in line, got a plate and then when you got up to the cook, he would say something in Spanish to you. You told him what you wanted. The cook fixed it on the stove top just behind the counter. When it was done, you held out your plate and he put your food on it. Then you moved on to the double line of tables in the open eating space, grabbed a chair and ate. Following the lead of the man in front of me, I responded to the cook's unintelligible Spanish with, "Scrambled eggs and pancakes." In short order, they were on my plate, and I sat at the only open seat for a table of six. The Mexicans were all speaking Spanish. They nodded to me and I returned the nod. They continued to talk. I ate in silence.

When the guys at my table got up, I followed. Outside, the mate met me. He said I would be with the guys chipping rust as he led me to four middle-aged Mexican men. After introducing me as the new kid, he told us to get the chipping hammers and get started.

We chipped all day on the lower deck's walkway. I had chipped rust on the deck of the coast guard buoy tender my dad was on during the summers when I was around eight or nine years old in Cincinnati. Back then it had been a great adventure. I could prove to the crew and my dad that I could do important work. Now, I understood that it was just hot, hard work. However, I also knew that I needed to prove myself to these men, the mate and the deck captain. Following the example of the seasoned men, I got on my hands and knees to begin the tedious tapping of the tapered end of the hammer on the deck.

Fortunately, my dad had advised me to wear a long-sleeved, heavy cotton shirt; and he had purchased some work shoes for me. The shirt would keep me cool; and the shoes would help to absorb the constant deck vibrations from the diesel engines, he said. The first fifteen minutes of chipping was horrible. The heat just pressed down on you. The life jacket and the hard hat just make the misery factor all the worse. Sweat simply poured out of every possible pore that existed on my body. Suddenly, I didn't notice the heat. It just wasn't bothering me. My shirt was soaking wet from the sweat. Once it was soaked, it served as a natural cooling system. Fortunately, the work kept us sweating all day. We stayed cool. As long as you worked hard enough to sweat, which was almost all of the time, the heat was not an issue on deck.

There seemed to be no set time when you took a break. You just took a few minutes off when you needed to. The mate, Boone, seemed to be a little agitated when I took a break. It wasn't that he said anything. It was just the way he looked at me that told me he thought something was wrong. By mid-afternoon, I had picked up on the source of his problem. He could understand a man needing to take a cigarette break. He just didn't feel comfortable with someone standing around doing nothing just because he needed a rest. When I got into town, I'd buy a couple of packs. I'd never learned to inhale the smoke but could hold it in my mouth and blow it out my nose convincingly enough. Time proved the accuracy of my observations.

Anyway, the day passed. During the breaks I got to know my section mates better. They were all middle-aged. One man, Luis, who spoke English, was particularly kind to me. After I made a fool out of myself in the hold that afternoon, we both laughed as I explained how I had gotten myself into that embarrassing predicament.

Luis explained that the guy who had pulled the joke on me was Felipe. He was crew chief of the pipeline crew. That was the most dangerous work on the dredge. The pipeline crew got paid the least of any crew on the dredge. This wasn't fair in Luis's view. Felipe had a couple of children around my age and was a powerful force among the Mexicans on the dredge. It was good that I had laughed at myself when everyone broke out laughing at the stupid gringo, Luis said. He thought I would learn and do all right. I could come to him any time I had questions. I was appreciative.

Luis helped me understand the basics of the dredge boat operation a little more during our breaks and over lunch. The dredge boat had no engine to propel the boat. It moved by walking itself up the swing-anchor cables. The leverman controlled all this. The leverman sat up in the housing on the top deck of the dredge and controlled the cutter head and the suctioning up of the loosened sea floor. If the leverman made a mistake and got the water/mud mixtures too heavy with mud, the pipeline would get plugged. When the pipeline got plugged up, one or more of the pipes on the pontoons behind the dredge could explode. Another problem could be that the last pipe at the end of the long line could buckle, jump wildly or explode. When that happened, someone almost always got injured on the pipeline crew. A few had been killed over the years. Of course, if you happened to be walking the pipeline checking it at the time a pipe buckled or exploded, you'd get buried, pinned to the sea floor by the flood of mud. Your life jacket wasn't enough to bring you to the surface. You'd just drown. Maybe they'd never find your body. It had happened a few times since he'd been working on the dredges, he solemnly noted.

The three tugs were critical to the dredge's operation. The civil engineer would tell the tugboat captains where to place the swing cable anchors out in front of the dredge so that the cutter head would stay on course in cutting the underwater channel. The leverman would keep the left rear spud down in the mud with the right rear spud raised as he pulled in the cable of the left swing anchor while releasing the cable of the right one. As the dredge was swinging to the left, the leverman controlled the depth of the cutter head and the mud/water mixture going through the pipeline making sure that the cutter head didn't cut the swing anchor cable. Everyone else on the dredge supported whatever task the leverman needed. The company was paid for the amount of mud cleared from the channel being created. The less time it took to dig the channel, the higher the profits for the company. If the dredge had to be shut down, all three crew shifts were called out to work non-stop until the dredge was operating again. The dredge only made money for the company when it moved the mud. It was as simple as that. The dredge boat had a captain, a deck captain and an engineer in charge of the three crews operating the dredge's diesel engine. Each work crew had a mate. There were three working crews for operations on the deck and three for the engine room. Each crew worked an eight-hour shift. The crews for deck operations had seven or eight men plus a mate. In addition, every crew had one leverman and his runner. There were also the three pipeline crews and their chiefs, the cooks, the welders and the tugboat captains. The tugboat captains would take one or two men from the deck crew to function as their deckhands when they needed them. Oh, yes, the employees also included the civil engineer and his assistant. There may have been others, but it got to be more than I could absorb at the time.

My forearms really hurt as four o'clock arrived. I told Luis that I guessed that they would have me sleep on the dredge boat that evening. Jerry, the deck captain, had not told me otherwise; and Boone was about as uncommunicative as a living human being could be thus far in my interaction with him. Luis took me to Milo.

Milo assigned me a bunk and wall locker in a two-bunk room. Milo said that I was lucky to be on this dredge boat. I had the whole room to myself. No one would be using it from the other two shifts. If I wanted, I never needed to go ashore even on my two days a week off. Four meals a day were served in the galley. There was the one breakfast meal. It was the only one served cafeteria style. The others were served family style. They were full dinner meals. Milo said I didn't have to stay overnight on the dredge, but I'd have to catch the crew-boat early tomorrow morning. I told him I'd just stay on the dredge. He said he'd tell the deck captain what I had decided.

Back on deck, guys were crowding around the rear area of the dredge, the open workspace between the spuds and the entrance to the galley, watching the crew boat approach. I watched as well with nothing else to do and no one telling me what to do.

"Hey kid, do you want to work an extra shift? The leverman on this shift needs a runner," the short redhead said in his thick Cajun accent.

"Sure, that's fine." What a lucky break. Sure, I was tired but I'd be making $2.25 an hour for the next eight hours. This was great.

The fiftyish Cajun motioned for me to follow him up the ladders. I hadn't been on the roof of the top deck, let alone in the control center of the dredge, that day. I hadn't been anywhere but the main deck chipping rust or in the hold making a fool of myself except for eating in the galley. This was high country.

On a ship, this area would have been considered the captain's bridge. Here it was the leverman's room. Entering the leverman's room, I could feel the sway of the dredge boat as the height accentuated the swinging and dipping of the dredge tugging on the swing anchors and pivoting on the spuds. In the center of the hissing and pressure-releasing sounds of hidden cables, pulleys and compressors sat a diminutive man with his hands extended on two of the many levers and knobs before him on the control panel. A cigarette dangled from his lips. He stared directly out the wide windows in deep concentration. After a few accentuated swings of the dredge with accompanying compressor hisses, he looked over at the two of us.

"This the kid?" his Cajun drawl asked of the redheaded mate.

"Yep."

"Ok," he said while quickly taking his hand off a lever and holding it out to me.

"Long," he said shaking my hand.

Red left without a word.

"I need you to do what I ask when I ask and as quickly as you can. Can you do that?"

"Yes, sir."

"Good. Now go down to the galley and get me a cup of coffee and get one for yourself. It's going to be a long night for you."

"Yes, sir," came my sharp reply as I turned to leave for the galley.

Through that first night, Long became a friend and mentor. In between his giving me orders to do something or delivering his orders to someone else, he asked me a lot of questions about myself. In turn, he told me more about the detailed operations of the dredge and details of the Cajun community he had grown up in. He had two children who were about my age. He didn't know them well as they lived with his ex-wife and he was off at sea a lot. He had been on dredges out of Germany, Spain and South America, among other exotic places. Over the course of the summer, we became close. But that's another story.

The one thing of note that happened that first night occurred when I asked Long if I could take my work shoes off and massage my feet. It was late in the shift. I had been working straight through for about twelve hours or so. With this being my first day and all, Long understandingly approved. As I was sitting on the floor massaging my bare feet, Jerry, the deck captain, walked in. He looked over at me as he approached Long about something. I could tell from his expression that my behavior had just confirmed some disparagingly negative thoughts he had about this "kid" forced upon him by the central office.

Late into the summer after some of my exploits had earned me a place of respect, Jerry asked me a question relating to that first night with Long. As I was leaving the regular Friday night poker game, Jerry called out to me, "Why didn't you tell me that first night you were pulling a double shift?"

Speaking over my shoulder as I reached for the door handle, I replied, "Because I thought you knew."

As time passed over that summer, I got to know my first day's prankster, Felipe, much better. He seemed to gravitate to me on the crew-boat rides when we were coming or going at the same time. Other times, on the dredge, when all the crews were working to solve a problem to make the dredge operational again, our paths would cross. When they did, Felipe would tease me a little in a most friendly manner. He had a son just about my age and seemed to identify me with the lad. I also think he felt a little guilty about pulling that stunt on me. Anyway, we grew to like each other and naturally seemed to find ourselves together. I enjoyed his company and admired him for the respect his pipeline crew showed him. He was a real leader and a man of integrity.

One thing that I truly marveled at was Felipe's restraint at responding to the crew boat captain's constant taunting and derogatory comments concerning Mexicans. They took place almost constantly but were the worst and most blatant when he was obviously drunk. It astounded me that he could pilot the crew boat at predawn hours so skillfully when drunk. As a drunken captain, he was most cruel and foul in his shouted hate talk directed at any Mexican within sight.

Felipe never responded to the captain even when his worst racist comments were directed specifically at him. It was Felipe's example that kept his crew and others from confronting the crew boat racist. Often were the times when I would observe him counseling a young pipeline crew member not to respond to the taunts. To respond was to feed into the guy's craziness, he would say. Felipe's opinion seemed to be that with his power status as captain of the crew boat, he would always win any confrontation. The poor Mexican who lost his cool with the racist would lose his job. The captain would always win, which would simply feed into his racist superiority concepts and feed the monster. How Felipe became so wise and self-controlled in the face of so many years of discrimination was a puzzle to me but reinforced my admiration of him. Everyone on the dredge knew that he and I had a special relationship. His approval of me seemed to give me a special status among his crew. I felt he almost treated me like his son.

Late in the summer this one morning, the crew boat captain was particularly drunk. Being particularly drunk meant that he was shouting the whole trip that morning to his passengers about how rotten Mexicans were. Felipe would signal to his young crew members to ignore him when it was becoming obvious that the captain's comments were directed at a specific individual and it was getting to that person. I just admired him for his patience and marveled at his calm in the midst of this verbal storm.

The captain was so drunk that he drove the bow of the crew boat into the side of the dredge without backing the engine off at the last second. There was a large thud as we crashed into the side of the dredge. We all lurched forward at the impact. After regaining their balance, several of the crew began jumping off of the bow to the deck of the dredge. I was in my usual place immediately following Felipe as he went forward to the bow in preparation to jump onto the dredge when the captain came out of the crew boat pilothouse to hurl a vile insult specifically at Felipe. It was just a nasty comment shouted loud enough for everyone on the crew boat and on the rear deck of the dredge to hear. Everyone stopped. It was just filth directed at Felipe.

It was too much for Felipe. I knew that he would lose status with his crew if he let this one go.

Standing on the bow fender poised to jump onto the dredge, Felipe paused, slowly turned his head to the captain and calmly stated, "The day will come when your hate will cause you trouble."

"You son of a bitch. You….." screamed the captain as he jumped from the bridge to the deck, charging Felipe. Felipe's momentum at the bow fender had carried him onto the deck of the dredge. I had moved to the bow fender for my jump but was stopped by the rush of the captain as he pushed past me and lunged for Felipe. No one was in the pilothouse. No one was in control of the crew boat. In the corner of my eye, I saw the deckhand running to the wheelhouse.

Grabbing for Felipe's shirt collar, the captain's hands seemed to fumble as he suddenly jerked a hand up to slap Felipe's face. He continued screaming insults as fast as his slurred speech would allow as he latched on to Felipe's shirt collar. I jumped to the deck, landing beside the two men. Felipe slapped the captain's hands from his collar in amazement. Felipe probably weighed fifty pounds more than the raving drunk and had him by four inches in height. Despite the captain's physical fitness, he was clearly no match for Felipe in a fight.

Reaching into his pants' pocket in one swift movement, the captain pulled out a pocketknife. He fumbled with the blade as he struggled to open it. The process seemed to happen in slow motion, but the reality was much quicker despite the fact that both Felipe and I were stunned by the clumsiness and sheer stupidity of this move. Where was this going?

As the open blade of the knife was brought up to Felipe's throat, Felipe slapped the knife hand causing the knife to fly loose and skid across the deck into the open space of the rear section by the galley doors. Just as quickly, Felipe grabbed the captain's arms. The two of them went into an embrace of rage as they followed the knife onto the deck. They rolled over each other in their struggle. The rolling stopped with Felipe straddling the captain. The knife was lying beside the captain's head. As soon as he saw it, Felipe picked it up. There was a split second of hesitation as to what to do with the knife. Felipe moved the point of it to within an inch of the captain's neck.

Time stood still. My God, I thought, he will have to kill the captain or maim him at the very least. He will lose face with his crew if he does nothing. I looked at the crowd of men standing around the two on the deck. Breakfast always brought the largest number of men into the open area behind the galley. Senior tugboat captains, deckhands, mates, pipeline crews and others were frozen in movement. They could not intervene. To move in at this moment could get them stabbed or start a racial fight with Felipe's crew coming to his defense.

It was clear. I was the one to stop it. I was the only one Felipe would not attack. He would not attack me. His crew would understand why he would not attack. Instantly, I body-slammed Felipe. My shoulder and side slammed into his. He rolled and sprang to his feet with the knife in the attack position. He started to take a step towards me and then stopped before his trailing foot left the deck. Moving from his crouching attack position, he straightened up. Never taking his eyes off of mine, he slowly relaxed into a tall, proud stance. With a slightly backward glance, he tossed the knife over the railing into the sea. Then he turned and started towards the pipeline to walk to it like any other workday. His crew followed him in silence.

To my amazement, everyone else turned away to walk to wherever they needed to go. No one said anything. No one spoke to me. We went and ate breakfast. There was little conversation in the galley that morning. No one spoke to me about the event.

As a week or two came and went, Felipe avoided me. He never got close enough to me for us to speak even on those few occasions when we were in line of sight of each other.

About three weeks after the event, someone told me that the director of personnel for the company was aboard and wanted to talk with me. I went to the cabin he was in.

"I want you to tell me what happened between Felipe and the captain."

"Ah, I was just there. There were others there. Why don't you just ask them?"

"Damn it, I'm tired of this shit! That's what everyone on this boat says. They say ask the kid. He's the one who broke it up. Now stop this shit and tell me what happened!"

I was stunned at the outburst and at the fact that others acknowledged what I had done.

"Ok. The captain was drunk. He's almost always drunk when he's operating the crew boat. He hates Mexicans. He is constantly calling out to them and making racist statements to them or about them. Felipe has been the model of restraint. He's kept the others from responding. He has treated me like a son. Everyone knows it. Felipe likes me. As Felipe and I were preparing to jump on the dredge, the captain came out of the bridge and shouted a really bad insult at Felipe. Just as he was ready to jump off the bow to the dredge, Felipe stopped and told the captain that his hate comments would get him into trouble one day. The captain rushed off of the bridge screaming racist things, pushed past me and jumped on the deck, slapping Felipe in the face and grabbing him by the shirt. I landed right beside the two of them as Felipe knocked his hands away. The captain pulled out a pocketknife and fumbled to open it because he was so drunk. It was quick but seemed long. He started to put the point of the blade to Felipe's neck. Felipe slapped it away and the two of them wrestled to the deck. Felipe ended up straddling him. The knife was right beside the captain's head. Felipe picked it up and held it near the captain's neck. Things kind of froze for a second or two. I looked at the crew watching it. No one could move. Felipe might think they were attacking. Something had to be done. If Felipe backed down now he would lose all the respect of his crew. Something had to make it stop. Something had to let Felipe stop with honor.

It would only end badly for him if something weren't done. I thought that he would understand if I did something. He wouldn't hurt me. He likes me too much. I body slammed him. He rolled off the captain, stood up and looked at me. He threw the knife overboard and walked away. His crew went with him. That's all."

The personnel director looked at me in silence for the longest time. Then, calmly, quietly, he said, "Felipe won't lose his job. We will fire the captain. It will take us a couple of weeks to fire him. Don't tell anyone about this. That's all."

I left. I never told anyone what the personnel director had told me. No one ever spoke to me about the incident or the interview. Felipe never spoke to me again. The crew boat captain never appeared on that crew boat again. No one ever mentioned him to me after that incident. A couple of weeks after the interview, I asked one of my Mexican deckhand friends if he knew what had happened to the old crew-boat captain. He told me that he had heard that the captain was no longer with the dredge boat company. I returned to college not long after that.

CHAPTER FIFTEEN

Getting Through Houston

My Saturday night hitchhiking adventure in downtown Houston needs some background so that you can appreciate the full impact of it.

The summer of 1963 was coming to an end. Friday was my last day of working as a deckhand on a state-of-the-art ocean-going dredge boat. This was my second summer of working on one. It was dredging out a deep-water channel for the intercoastal waterway of the Texas coast. Saturday morning I was to catch a bus to Houston. I'd arrive in Houston about 10:30 in the evening, go to the train station and sleep there overnight. At 6:00 a.m., Sunday, my train would pull out.

My wonderful Anna would meet me at the train stop in Danville, Kentucky. She'd already gotten settled into the women's dorm. We'd walk up to the men's college dorm. I'd drop off my luggage. We'd eat supper at a downtown restaurant. I had my summer's wages and modest poker winnings on me. The $800 plus was wrapped around my foot covered by my sock. We could afford the meal thanks to the money in my sock. I had so many stories to tell her about my summer job.

This was the start of a great year. Almost a month earlier, I had turned twenty-one. Being isolated from land delayed any celebrations. When I wasn't working overtime, I'd just go to my folks' home in Port Lavaca and sleep until it was time to catch the crew-boat back to the dredge. Being twenty-one was nice. I was a real man now. Anna and I would get married at the end of the academic year, then go on to find jobs, go to graduate school or whatever to begin our lives for real.

The Saturday morning that I was to leave Port Lavaca for Houston, my parents went with me to the bus station. There were few parked cars in front of the station that early morning, but then there were probably not many cars there at any time. The bus station in Port Lavaca was small. It was the right size for the town. When my parents and I walked into it, I immediately saw a fellow dredge boatman. He wasn't a member of my section, but we had worked some together when all the shifts were working. That happened whenever the dredge boat had to shut down. We had to correct the problem as fast as possible. The company didn't make money when the dredge boat was out of action. I had pulled a couple of twenty-four hour shifts during the summer. After the first eight hours, you got time and a half. That was an extra seventy-five cents an hour. That was big money. The college student kitchen staff I worked with during the year made sixty-five cents an hour. Making $2.25 an hour built up my savings to make it through the school year. It was important money.

My shipmate looked bad. He looked about the way he did on the dredge-boat, but that was a different context. His gray beard was just unshaven stubble that seemed as unruly as his short-cropped gray hair. His thin body had a slight forward lean to it that continuously suggested he was about to fall over. The blood-shot eyes with their deep shadows hinted that he was hung over.

Briskly walking up to him, I held out my hand. We shook hands and exchanged greetings as my folks walked up to us. After I introduced him to my parents and determined that we would not be traveling on the same bus, he stated to my father, "He's a good man. He's really a good man."

Poor dad was a little taken aback by this but responded graciously enough. Being a career Coast Guard man, I was fairly certain he was reading rather well the signs this guy wore. The fellow was a nice man. He'd been very quiet on the dredge boat, but you could count on him to do his job. I wondered what caused him to be a lowly deckhand at this stage in his life. Gratefully, the call to board my bus came quickly. I said goodbye one more time to my shipmate, hugged my Mom, shook my Dad's hand and boarded the bus.

It was an all-day-and-into-the-night long trip from Port Lavaca to Houston. Last summer's trip back on the bus had been an adventure. The last half of the trip was the most uncomfortable, I remembered. The bus got really crowded. Someone would end up sitting beside you. This kept you from lying on the two seats and sleeping. I had worked seven days straight before catching the bus. I was tired and planned to sleep as much as I could. Once I got from the bus station in Houston to the train station, I planned to see the nightlife. I mean, I was twenty-one. I was a man. Maybe I'd even go into a bar and have a drink. I'd never done that before and wasn't sure how not to feel awkward while pretending to behave naturally. Well, I wasn't sure how the night was going to work out. Maybe I'd just stay in the train station all night. Anyway, the whole trip was going to be an adventure. I wanted to have slept as much as I could before reaching Houston.

My overall strategy was to pretend to be asleep at all of the little towns where we stopped. The entering passengers would see me stretched out on the seat as they walked down the first third of the bus and go to the back for an open seat. They would not want to wake me. That was the unspoken rule I had learned from last summer's trip.

Texas is a big place. It seemed the bus traveled forever without passing a house, let alone a little town. It was just open rangeland. Last summer the bus had stopped in the middle of nothing to pick up a frail, elderly man carrying only a violin case. When he entered the bus, he and the driver conversed. There was no exchange of a ticket or money. Once the bus resumed traveling, he opened the case and took out the violin. He began playing it. The little Hispanic children would peek at him from behind their seats with big grins on their faces while their mothers tugged at them to keep them from going to him. He played terribly but with great vigor, smiling and dipping the violin at the kids. They loved it.

After ten or twenty minutes of playing, the elderly man simply stopped playing, replaced his violin in its case, walked to the front of the bus and said something to the bus driver. The bus stopped. He got off. It was the middle of nowhere. There were no houses, no cars, and no hint of civilization anywhere except for the road, the bus and the telephone poles. As the bus pulled away, the man waved to the children. A few waved back.

Unusual characters rode the bus. I didn't want to interact with anyone on this trip. My pretend sleep at the bus stops was working even as the bus slowly filled with the approach of sunset.

I could tell the bus was about full, which served as a greater incentive to pretend to be asleep at each small-town stop. Awaking to the commotion outside my bus window, I was pleased to realize that I had been asleep. The bus had stopped in some unknown town. A lot of voices were right outside my window. Stretching my neck up to the window's edge, I was shocked to see what was going on. In the center of the crowd stood a huge black man holding out his hands for a uniformed officer to unlock his handcuffs. The crowd was definitely agitated. They were pressing the bald black man and officer as his shackles were removed. Then the whole mob moved toward the front of the bus.

That is one man I don't want sitting beside me, I thought as a hunkered down into my fetal position with a determination to do the best job of pretending sleep an awake person could do. Sure enough, through the tiniest peek between my shut eyes I could see him approach my seat. He stood there for a few seconds just looking down at me. Thank God, he finally moved towards the back. I relaxed and snuggled into the comfort of the seat.

As the bus pulled out, I heard a sound in the aisle by my feet. Cracking my eyes open just the tiniest bit, I saw him sitting in the aisle facing the front of the bus. The bus must be full.

Pretending to be just waking up, I began to stretch and sit up. Our eyes met.

"Oh, excuse me sir. Please sit here," I said in pretend surprise and humility.

He rose from the aisle and towered over me. "Can I sit by the window?"

"You sure can," I said, starting to move behind him to the aisle. "I actually prefer to sit in the aisle seat," I exclaimed as we squeezed past each other.

Once we settled in, I began a little small talk with him. He responded quite pleasantly.

Suddenly getting serious, he stated, "They didn't treat me right back there. I didn't do anything wrong and me a World War II vet."

Well, my dad was a WW II vet and had told me lots of stories about that time. For most of my childhood it was assumed that I would be a career military officer. I knew a lot of stories from that time and was always interested in hearing more of them.

"They shot me in the head," he almost shouted as he twisted his heavily muscled body from the window to show me the indentation in the upper part of his bald skull. "There's no bone there. Go ahead, you can touch it. It's just skin."

I really didn't have a need to touch it. There was a clear bullet hole there and it certainly looked as if there was no bone under its depression into his head.

"Did you have to stay in the hospital a long time?"

"I've been in and out of the VA hospitals ever since. My brain doesn't work right. For the last few years, I've lived in that VA hospital up from the town. Those people didn't treat me right, those cops and the others. I can leave the hospital whenever I want. They arrested me and put me in jail. The hospital told them it was OK. I'm going to Houston to see my friends. They haven't been to see me for a while."

He went on and on talking about himself. I asked questions and sympathized with him. Then he started asking me questions. I told him about college and working on the dredge boat. He asked some good questions and seemed to be genuinely interested. I even told him about turning twenty-one.

As we were pulling into Houston, he enthusiastically exclaimed, "Let's go out and party with my friends. They'll be at the bus station. I'll fix you up with a good woman who knows how to take care of a man."

Right off, I knew this was going to be delicate. "It's like I said, I have to get to the train station because the train to Kentucky leaves so early in the morning, but thank you. I appreciate the offer."

"Naw, you come on with me and my friends. There's a Houston most white folks know nothin' about. Come on now."

It took considerable persuading, but I got it across as to how important it was to me not to miss my train. Anna would be waiting for me at the Danville stop. She would be really stressed if I weren't on the train. I had no way of calling her to let her know I'd be late if I missed it.

Most reluctantly, he accepted the fact that I had best not go with him. However, when we got off the bus and met the two rather attractive women waiting for him, he tried to enlist them in convincing me to allow them to show me a good time. Once again, I had a diplomatic challenge not to offend anyone. In the end, the guy shook my hand with great relish and the women waved goodbye. We left the bus depot in opposite directions.

I caught a taxi to the train station. It was on the far side of town. There weren't many people in the huge station. The ones who were there were mainly trying to sleep on the benches or read. There were a few military guys scattered about obviously moving to a new assignment of some kind. I felt sorry for them. They all looked tired and sad. Their big duffle bags sat in the seat beside them or at their feet.

Placing my satchel in one of the storage lockers, inserting the coins and locking the door, I was ready for Houston. Well, I wasn't sure what I wanted to do. It was about 11:30 p.m. I was tired. Maybe I'd just catch some z's. Fortunately, I had the knack of being able to sleep just about anywhere. On the early morning crew boat's hour and a half run from the company dock to the dredge, I'd curl around the warm smokestack and sleep. You'd think that the summer heat on the gulf would make it uncomfortable to experience the heat of the stack. The truth was that the early morning coolness was enhanced by the wind generated by the speed of the tug's movement through the water. The ocean-going tug's diesel engine was powerful. Even with my hardhat and life jacket on, I was really comfortable hugging the stack. With the warmth of the stack and the rocking movement of the tug through the sea, I napped most comfortably.

Lying down on the bench in the train station didn't work. I was too excited about getting back to Kentucky and kept thinking I was missing out on having fun in Houston this first real night I had to celebrate being twenty-one.

I'd just walk towards downtown and see what was going on. Maybe I'd get a drink in a bar.

At first, it was just dark streets with nothing open. After ten blocks or so I was in the bright lights. There were bars on both sides of the street. Several of the bars had guys in top hats calling to people to go inside. They said that there were beautiful girls inside who would take care of you. The pictures of the almost fully nude women on the windows of the bars suggested that they were right.

"Come on in. This is what you're looking for," the top hat shouted with a smile and a hand on my arm.

"No, I've got an appointment."

He smiled with a knowing look and tipped his hat to me. I briskly walked down the street, ignoring the other calls for my attention. This was not what I wanted. What would I do? Go into a bar and order a drink. They would probably want to see my ID because I looked so young. I'd sit by the bar, alone and afraid to talk to anyone. No telling what kind of character would be a bar stool or two from me, certainly not anyone I'd want to talk to. Let's face it, I'm a babe-in-the-woods in this setting. I could get robbed of my entire summer's earnings. They'd easily find the money in my sock. I would be unable to look at the nude girls because of my embarrassment at being in the place to begin with. What a bad fantasy this whole thing had been.

What I really wanted to do was to talk to some college-age kids like myself and share stories with them. I'd ask them about living in Houston, where they went to college or work. You know, stuff like that. Well, I reasoned, if that's what I wanted then I'd better go where the high school and college kids hang out. That would be at a drive-in restaurant. There ought to be some around here in a big city like this. That's where we all hung out in Pittsburgh during my high school years. Yeah, that was a good plan. I set out to find my drive-in.

After walking what seemed like several miles into the downtown area of the city (I was careful to note various landmarks to find my way back to the train station) I could see the drive-in restaurant. It was huge. The parking spaces were all full and cars were slowly cruising around it and through the parking area. Walking up the street corner just opposite it, I looked into the maze. Music was blaring from dozens of parked cars. They all seemed full of boys and girls. Everyone seemed happy and engaged in talking.

Now, just what was I going to do? Was I simply going to walk up to a full car and say, "Hi, I'm just passing through. I've just been working on the dredge boats. It was a great adventure. It's a totally different way of living. I'm going back to Kentucky to go to college and be with Anna and I just want to talk with people tonight before my train leaves in the morning."

This was stupid. If someone had come up to my car window in Pittsburgh, I'd have thought they were strange and rolled up the window and driven off. Well, maybe I wouldn't do that, but I know a lot of people in Pittsburgh who would. This was simply dumb.

With this discussion going on in my mind, I just stood there on the street corner looking in. Just as I decided to walk back to the train station and sleep the rest of the night, a car stopped in front of me.

The driver leaned over to the passenger side window and said, "Where are you going?"

"I'm going back to the train station," came my spontaneous reply, noting that the guy looked to be a clean-cut-college type fellow.

"I'll take you there."

"No. Thank you, but I'll just walk."

"It's a long way. Not a problem for me. I'm just killing time."

"Ok. Thank you."

Opening the door, I got in. He was very personable. When I explained how I came to be in Houston that night, he said he'd drive me around the downtown area and give me a tour. He had gone to college for a couple of years but was working a good job somewhere. I really liked talking with him. As we came to a stop at a red light, he suddenly reached across my upper thigh and began rubbing the inside of my leg.

"Never happen," I hissed. I was ready to fight.

He jerked his hand back. With a shocked expression on his face, he blurted out, "But why...why did you get in the car? I thought you knew."

"It's like I told you. What I told you about me was true."

"I'm so sorry. I didn't know. I just thought you knew."

"Just let me out here. I can make it to the train station."

"No. No, you'd get lost. I'll take you back to where I picked you up."

"OK."

There was a long silence as we drove across the streets. At last,

I recognized the drive-in restaurant coming up ahead. As he slowed to a stop at the very intersection where I had gotten in his car, he said, "I'm really very sorry. I just thought you knew why I stopped for you at this corner. That's understood here. I'm sorry."

As I opened the door to leave, I said, "It's OK. I'm sorry, too."

So there I was on the street corner again. Without hesitation, I turned and began walking back to the station. I was pretty certain that I knew the way back even though it would be a long walk. Maybe I'd have that drink now. That experience was a first for me. It was upsetting. Damn, all of the bars were closed. It was just straight back to the station. I decided to take a short cut off the main streets to save time.

There were hardly any cars on the back streets. Just a lone one would drive quickly down the deserted corridors every now and then. The traffic lights commanded empty space to stop and go with a relentless vigor. Of course it was late. I didn't have a watch but guessed it to be about 1:00 or 1:30 in the morning. The tall buildings hemmed me into the four-lane canyon of a road I was walking down. The backs of the buildings faced me with their windowless walls. A few people came out of a steel door at street level from what looked like the back of a movie theatre on the opposite side of the street. They quickly turned a corner and began to disappear up the two-lane side street as I started to step off the curb.

When I started to step off the curb, the intersection light was green. It said I could go. Just as my lead foot touched the road, a small, red convertible sports car came roaring down the side street towards me. I hesitated. In that second my signal light turned red. I stepped back as the two-seater was gearing down to stop.

The whole scene brought laughter to my lips. Here I am on Houston's deserted streets with no one in sight, trying to be a good citizen crossing the street on a green light when it suddenly changes. A fancy convertible sports car roars down the street and stops, first to keep from hitting me and then to motion me across the street while the driver waits for me to pass.

Both the driver and I burst into laughter at the ridiculousness of the situation.

"Go on across," he said, waving me to move.

"No, it's OK. You go ahead."

"No, you go on."

We both laughed out loud.

"Where are you going? I can give you a ride," he shouted at me over the purr of his engine.

"Oh, no. Thank you anyway. I'm just going to the train station."

"That's alright. I can drive you there. It's no problem really. I just got off work and was going home."

"No, you don't understand," I stated a little more seriously, "I just had a bad situation happen. I was walking down the street and someone else offered to give me a ride. When I got in, he put his hand in my lap. I don't want to risk that happening again."

"Oh, no! What a situation! I'm not like that. I really can give you a ride. It's not any trouble. You're safe with me," he stated with an understanding smile. "Come on. It will save you a lot of walking."

Well, I was tired. He seemed really nice. It was a funny situation. He seemed to be about my age or a little older with a good sense of humor.

"Ok," and with that I walked over to the passenger side of the car as he pushed the door open.

We got talking as he drove down the road, making a turn here, a turn there and then a couple more turns. I was working hard to keep oriented just in case this guy had another agenda. He was truly personable and asked good questions. Quickly, he got my story; going back to college, the dredge boat summer, the bus ride and the loneliness of being in Houston.

He told me that he was working the night shift just to make money for his next adventure. It was good pay for what it was. After a year or so of college he left before he declared a major. He just wanted to experience life away from studying for a while. That was when he had gotten the sports car. A buddy of his joined him for a multi-month adventure driving the entire distance on Route 66.

His whole story resonated with me. There had been several times in college when I felt stifled by all of the studying and questioned the whole purpose of it all. Life was roaring by me, and I had another test coming up. If it hadn't been for Anna, I'd probably have flunked out by now. She kept me studying. I wanted to be with her. I loved her. There had been a TV series about a couple of guys traveling on Route 66. They kept having adventure after adventure. In a way, this guy was living part of my fantasy life.

"I can tell you why the bars were closed. Houston has a law that says they have to close at midnight on Saturdays. They can't be open on Sundays," he explained. "Hey, I have a friend who has this great bachelor's pad right in the center of the city. We could go and have a drink there. He's got a great liquor cabinet. He's out of town right now, but he lets me have a key for anytime I want to use it."

"Naw, that'd be too much. I don't want to impose."

"No, no, really, he wouldn't mind. He's got all kinds of money. It's a great place. He's got it air-conditioned and a fireplace that you just press a button and it starts up. It's really neat. Besides, we got a good thing going. I want to hear more of your stories."

That place sounded impressive. On a hot night like tonight to have air conditioning counteracting a burning fireplace took a lot of expensive electricity. It sounded like something from a James Bond movie.

"OK, but just one drink, then it's on to the train station."

The apartment was all he said it was. Wall-to-wall thick white carpeting for the first floor living room greeted me as walked in the door. The large room's ceiling was two stories up. The back of the first level opened up to a beautiful kitchen. It was the most modern kitchen I had ever seen. Everything appeared to be shiny-new. It was stocked with good food and all kinds of beverages. The shiny pots were hung up on a rack the way you see them in the TV cooking shows. I was impressed. The stairwell to the upstairs was just to the front of the kitchen and supported by a sidewall. It went to a balcony that overlooked the living room area.

With the press of a button, he started the gas-log fireplace. Then he gave me a tour of the downstairs. The liquor cabinet matched everything else. I decided to have a scotch and water. He poured.

After putting on some soft background music that played gently from hidden speakers, we continued our conversation. My host had considered studying to be a minister. He speculated that he still might do that. I was amazed. I had considered going into the ministry late in my high school years. My family had always tried to be active in the Presbyterian Church. My last two and a half years of high school in Pittsburgh had church and a Sunday School session on the schedule almost every Sunday. Among the things that discouraged me from seriously pursuing that vocation was the idea that everything that could be said about Jesus, God and the Presbyterian Church had no doubt been said. All that was left was for people to believe it. The position appeared to be pretty boring to me. I wanted to help people. I particularly wanted to help juveniles who lived hard lives. Some of the communities my family kept relocating to were pretty rough. The kids there had been or were going to end up in jail a lot. It wasn't necessary. They were smart and capable even though they were flunking out of school. They just needed help. I wanted to help them.

Amazingly, my host seemed to be the same way. We just clicked. I loved talking with him. We thought the same way. I really liked him. One drink became two and then three. I was feeling it.

"Gee, its late," the guy noted, looking at his wrist. "Why don't you just sleep over here for a couple of hours? Then I'll fix breakfast and take you to the station."

Wait just a minute here. Was this guy really trying to set me up? Maybe he was going to have someone come in and the two of them rob me, beat me up and throw me out on the street. I could take him. I was a pretty good street fighter and in great shape. If there were two of them, I'd probably get beat. I had made that mistake once. I'd taken on two guys at the same time that I had beaten individually before. Those things don't work the way you see them in the movies or on television. I lost.

"No thanks. I think it would be best if we went to the train station now."

"Aw, come on. That doesn't make sense. You won't be able to sleep on those benches. My friend won't mind. It's no trouble. You're safe here and I don't mind. We can share a little more time together that way."

Well, I was being foolish if this guy was as nice as I thought he was. I mean, I'd do the same thing if our roles had been reversed. He really was a nice guy, and I was ruining a great new friendship with my doubts. Besides, I could take care of myself.

"Well, if you're sure it's no trouble, OK."

That was it. I was staying.

We went to the kitchen to rinse out the glasses. We continued to talk. We just seemed to think the same things. It was remarkable.

Walking back into the living room, I asked, "Where should I sleep?"

"Upstairs. I'll show you the bed."

We walked up the stairwell. The view of the living room was just great. There was one large bedroom and a large bathroom with a tub and a shower. The bed was huge.

"This is a great bed. Thank you, but where will you sleep?" I inquired. I hadn't seen another bedroom downstairs.

"Oh," he said with surprise, "There's just one bed. We'll both sleep in it."

Damn, this was it. The guy was gay. I was in trouble.

"Well, I could sleep on the couch downstairs."

"No, that won't work. Besides, I just wouldn't feel comfortable with you downstairs and me upstairs. Anyway, the bed is plenty big enough."

Damn, double damn, what was going on here? raced through my mind. This guy is so nice. If he is straight and on the up and up, I am being a fool. I don't like this. It would be so easy to jump me in the night. I'd hear someone come in. I can take this guy if I have to. He is so nice. I just don't know.

"Are you sure about the two of us in the same bed?" I asked.

"Yeah, it will be alright," he stated looking so honestly and innocently at me.

All right, I thought, I can take care of myself. I'll stay on the very edge of the bed. If he touches me in the slightest way, I'll spring out of it and that's it. I'm gone. I'm ready to fight. He'll not fight me. He's too nice a person for that. There's no question that I could take him. I could do him some real harm. Damn, double damn, was I ruining a chance for a life-long friendship? It was like talking to a mirror image of myself. I wanted this to be right so badly.

"Ok," I said with a sigh.

He began undressing.

"I'm going to take a shower. Do you want to take one?"

"No, I'm OK," I lied. I wasn't about to get nude with this guy in the building. Actually, I would have loved to take a shower. The air conditioning in the bus had not been up to the task of keeping the passengers comfortably cool. It barely met the minimum needs. Houston was hot. The night air was hot and muggy. Then all the walking I had done had caused me to sweat some. Overall, I was clammy. I needed a shower and would not feel comfortable until I had one.

He walked to the bathroom and closed the door. He still had his pants on but had taken everything else off. Taking my shirt and shoes off. I sat on the edge of the bed pondering what I was going to do. Well, I'd keep my Fruit-of-the-Loom underpants on. I'd have to take my sock off. The sock with the cash in it would be stuffed in the right shoe. I always put the right shoe on first. If I had to run, I'd need my pants on and my shoes on. I'd lay them out so that I could immediately jump into them at the sign of trouble. There'd be no time to put the socks on. I'd better stuff the money in my pants pockets before I took my pants off. I'd lie there in the bed pretending to be asleep. There was no way I was going to sleep this night. Just the slightest touch from him and I was out of here.

God, what would I do if he slept nude in the bed? Well that was it. I'd insist on leaving. Now, wait a minute, was my next thought. I sleep nude most of the time. Yes, but not when there were other people sleeping in the room with me as at Boy Scout camp and the like. That would be the line to draw. If he got in the bed nude, I was gone.

As I was thinking all of this I moved to the top of the stairwell and sat on the top step. This was such a nice place. Everything the guy had told me seemed so authentic. There was nothing he had said or done to suggest that he was anything but what he appeared to be, a very nice person that was kind and thoughtful who was going out of his way to be helpful to another nice person. I was the crazy one here, thinking of all the bad things that could happen but never would. They would never happen because this guy was just what he appeared to be and my mistrust was ruining the possibility of a great friendship.

He came out of the bathroom drying his hair with a towel. He was wearing his Fruit-of-the-Looms. Stopping in surprise at seeing me sitting at the top of the stairs, he smiled and asked, "Are you sure you don't want to take a shower?"

"Thanks, actually, I would. If it's OK."

"Sure, the towels are in the closet in there," he said motioning into the bathroom.

We both entered the bedroom. I went into the bathroom and took a shower.

When I came out in my Fruit-of-the-Looms, I could hear him talking to someone. My guard was up. He was downstairs talking to someone. I crept to the edge of the wall separating the bedroom from the balcony. The back of his head was to me. He was talking to someone on the phone. I couldn't hear all of what he was saying, just a few words and phrases.

"Yes...well... I'm staying overnight... He's a nice... Yes, mom. ...But...well...call...in the morning...first thing...love you..."

As he hung up the phone, I quietly moved back to the bedroom.

When he entered, we exchanged a few words, and then he climbed into bed staying on the far wall edge. I hugged the opposite edge of the bed, which was closest to the door. I lay on my side facing the doorway. That was so that if he touched me, I could spring from the bed, grab my clothes and dash out down the stairwell to the door.

We said goodnight. He turned out his bedside light. The hall light stayed on, lighting the bedroom up well enough.

He remained motionless, as did I. There was no way I was going to sleep. I just had to endure. Every once in a while, he would slightly stir on his side of the bed. There were no movements towards me. Time seemed to pass so slowly.

His foot touched mine. My God, I'd fallen asleep. The slight touch of his foot triggered my automatic reaction. I sprang from the bed, grabbed my pants and shoes and shot into the hallway.

He hadn't moved. He must still be asleep. He must have just rolled over in his sleep and accidentally touched my foot with his. I was just ruining this whole night. This whole adventure could have been simply great except for my distrust, but then again... *Damn*, I thought. Well there was no going back to bed. I'd just sit here on the stairwell until dawn.

"What's going on? It's four a.m.?" he sleepily asked, looking at me from the bedroom doorway.

"This last week on the dredge boat I was working the first shift. This is the time I usually wake up," I lied. "I'll just sit here until it's time for you to get up."

"No, that won't work. I can't sleep with you up in the apartment."

I understood that.

He went on, "How about I fix us breakfast now and take you to the station early?"

I agreed. We were both subdued. He fixed bacon and eggs. We were both polite but cautious with each other.

He drove me to the station. We shook hands, said goodbye and that was it.

The train ride back to Danville, Kentucky was long, boring and uncomfortable. There rarely seemed to be more than five or six passengers in each car. As usual, the passenger cars had trash on the floors. The seats were hard. I had to go through three cars before I found one with a bathroom that worked or a working water fountain. You'd think having the bathrooms work would be a simple thing. When you flushed the commode, you could see the bottom trapdoor open to a clear view of the railroad tracks below. A sign was always over the commodes advising you not to flush while the train was in a station area.

The ride through north Texas always seemed to take forever. There is nothing to see but the same continuous open country with no sign of human habitation, period.

Hours into this ride through sameness, the train inexplicably began slowing. It finally came to a complete stop. It had stopped in the middle of nothing. There was no station, no house, no road, no nothing except open land with patches of scrub grass and brush. Maybe there was a little station by the engine that I couldn't see. I doubted it.

Out of the silence I heard a sound at the back of the car. Someone was moving and bumping around. I heard the creak of the gate to enter the car from the ground in the open passage between the cars. Suddenly the gate slammed against the outside of the train. The door to the compartment slammed open. A real cowboy entered the compartment carrying a saddle with lasso rope attached to it. He was a young man, thin and wiry. Throwing his saddle onto the window side of the seat nearest the entrance, he plopped down and propped his feet on the seat in front of him. Someone on an early trip had reversed that seat so that four people could sit facing each other and talk, play cards or whatever. Pulling the brim of his cowboy hat down to cover his eyes, he promptly went to sleep.

About an hour later, the train stopped in the middle of sameness. The land looked the same to me as it had when he first got on. The cowboy pushed his hat back, picked up his saddle and put it on his shoulder. Getting off the train, he just stood there with the saddle at his feet. There was no station, no road, no one there. It was just him and the land. He didn't seem worried so I decided not to worry for him.

Somewhere in Arkansas, a guy about my age got on the train and we talked all the way to Danville. He was in the Army and was going home to a small town near Lexington, Kentucky. His big stories were about the high school he graduated from and the wild things he and his classmates had done. They sounded a lot like things you see in coming-of-age movies. They were hard to believe. He swore that they were true. Listening to him helped the time pass.

I arrived in Danville in the late afternoon. The train just stopped at a railroad crossing, and you got off. There was a small railroad station. Anna was standing on the sidewalk beside the station. It was wonderful to kiss her and hug her. We walked up to my dorm where I dropped off my satchel. Then we went hand and hand towards the small business district in downtown

Danville. We were so happy to be together. We talked and laughed as we walked.

As we were passing the open driveway of a gas station, someone shouted out my name. Looking into the housed section of the station, I saw him running up to me with a big grin.

It was the guy. It was the guy from Houston. I was stunned. I couldn't believe it. It was him but it wasn't him. There was no way he could be here. He would not be wearing the uniform of the gasoline company. This was crazy. Giving me a big hug, he said it was so great to see me. He had gotten admitted to the college. I could not think of his name or what he was talking about. He looked like the identical twin of my bed companion from Houston.

Turning to Anna, he said, "He hasn't told you about me, has he?"

This was where I was to introduce him to her. I didn't know his name. Things were beginning to come back to me. I was still reeling from the shock of seeing him as the Houston guy. The awkward silence told him I didn't remember his name and maybe not even him.

He was embarrassed and clearly disappointed. I felt terrible as my memory started working. It was prompted by his calmly telling her his name and saying that in the spring he had come to the fraternity house asking for guidance about getting into the college. I had helped him a lot, he said.

It all came rushing back to me. Yes, he was a good guy. I had spent a lot of time talking to him about college and what he wanted for himself. It was clear that his friendship with me was important. I had just disappointed him greatly. We shook hands, and I praised his efforts.

Anna and I went to the little restaurant we always went to.

The elderly black man waited on us as he always did. He was so kind. You could tell that he thought it was wonderful the way Anna and I loved each other.

CHAPTER SIXTEEN

"How Dare You!"

"Don't let Tom Butler go through the cafeteria line. He has never signed up for the college's food service. He's been freeloading all this time," stated the manager of the food service operation.

What a bombshell! This was going to go down badly. I sure didn't want to do this. From all I could tell, Tom was OK. He lived in the small college town with his family. His father had a national reputation in his professional work. Tom clearly came from a wealthy family. Why would he want to do this?

Well, I had my orders from my immediate supervisor. As the coordinator of student workers in the dining hall, I had responsibilities to fulfill. It was the highest position a student at the college could have with the food service company. I got free board and ten dollars a month. It was better than the sixty-five cents an hour I got as a dishwasher when I started three years ago as a freshman in 1960.

I told the servers on the cafeteria lunch line that Tom was not to be served if he ever showed up. Of course, they asked me what was going on. I didn't want to unduly embarrass Tom with the story, so I just said there was a management issue and left it at that.

Very soon after the order had been given, Tom appeared at the beginning of the cafeteria line. The salad server told him that I had said they were not to serve him. He demanded to talk to me.

Tom was in a rage. He was shouting and cursing. His arms were moving in unison to the ebb and flow of his voice as I approached.

"Just what the hell is going on here? You have no right to keep me off the line."

I motioned for him to move out of the mainstream flow of the cafeteria line. He rushed towards me screaming, "How dare you! How dare you?"

"You have not paid for meals here. Until you do, you can't go through the line."

"That's a lie. You are lying!"

I wanted to tell him that the decision wasn't mine. I was just carrying out orders. Then, I thought, that's a cop-out. I have to take responsibility for my actions. I was the one who had told the staff not to serve him. I had to bear the brunt of his anger.

"You need to prove that you've paid. Until then, you can't get the food here."

"I'm going to get you! I'm going to beat the shit out of you! Step outside right now!"

"I can't. I've got a class to go to."

"All right then, you son-of-a-bitch, name a time and place. I'm going to kick your ass."

"How about tomorrow at three, behind the football stadium. Just the two of us, no audience."

"I'll be there. You'd better show, you dickhead."

I nodded in agreement. The encounter was over. Damn, I

didn't want to get into a fight. The guy had to be embarrassed. Maybe he did pay for the meals. All that I had to go on was what Mike told me. I trusted Mike. Over the two years I had worked under him in this position, he had always been honest with me. I could count on Mike. He was a good man. I looked up to him. He had suggested that I turn professional in his food service company after I graduated. Mike was pretty certain that he would rapidly rise up in the company hierarchy. He wanted to take me with him. I was tempted to accept the offer. At this point, I didn't know what I would be doing after graduation. My broad goal was to get a job helping children, maybe becoming a teacher, or going to graduate school to be a guidance counselor or something. At this point, I didn't know what my options would be. Working with Mike was an attractive one and always a fallback position if nothing else came through.

That evening, I began to dread the next day. When it came, it was like this dark cloud hanging over me. I did not want to fight Tom. It wasn't that I thought I would get hurt that was the most depressing. It was that I understood why Tom thought he had to fight me. He was fighting for his honor.

I didn't know if he would be able to beat me up or not. He was smaller in size than I was. However, he appeared to be more muscular. Several of the guys attending the college had black belts in karate. Maybe Tom was trained in the martial arts. All I had going for me was a little training in boxing plus many rounds of being called out by bullies in the different schools I had attended growing up. I never felt comfortable in any of those fights. They happened by surprise. I would be assaulted and spontaneously fight back in self-defense. At least that's how I was interpreting those past fights. There was no doubt I had experience in fighting. Whether or not that would carry me through the pending encounter was yet to be determined.

It wasn't a long walk from my dorm to the back of the football field. I got there a little early. How I wished this wasn't going to happen. Tom drove up in his late model car, got out and briskly walked right to me.

I raised my fists, ready to fend off his first punches and prepared to throw mine. He did the same. We circled each other like two roosters preparing for the immediate cockfight. His eyes kept darting back and forth. He continued to circle me and I turned to front him as he moved, our fists maintained at a constant ready. The circling started to frustrate me.

"You'll have to throw the first punch," I told him with our eyes locked into the other's.

"No, you have to hit me first."

It is always best for me to have been hit first or to be really angry in order for me to fight with aggression. I can't just hit someone to be hitting him.

"No, you asked for this fight. You have to throw the first punch."

"You did this to me. You have to hit me first," he stated with those eyes continuing to dart back and forth.

Then it dawned on me. He was afraid. He was afraid of what I was about to do to him. I knew in that moment that I could beat him badly. I could make him a bloody mess. With his fear, it must have taken a great deal of courage for him to have even shown up to face me.

"I quit," I stated dropping my fists. "I won't fight you. There's nothing you can do to me to make me fight you. I quit. If you want, you can tell people that we fought, and you won. If anyone asks me about it, I'll tell them you won. That's all there is to it."

He dropped his fists and stared at me. I turned around and

walked back to the dorm.

No one ever asked about the outcome of the fight. Tom never again appeared in the cafeteria.

CHAPTER SEVENTEEN

Water Tower

Another late-night studying was underway. That night was just before the DKEs were to have their Saturday night celebration of St. Patrick's Day. The year was 1963, my junior year at Centre College. I remember it well.

I had applied to be a dorm counselor during my senior year. If I got it, the college's cost for living in the dorm would be waived; plus, I got a phone in my room. All the expenses of my senior year would be lifted from my parents. My meals were free in payment for my work as the coordinator of the student dining hall workers, I had a grant in-aid for half of my tuition, and the other half of the tuition was covered by my student loan. If I got appointed to be a dorm counselor, my parents wouldn't have a bill from the college for my senior year. The pay from my summer jobs and pickup work on campus provided me with the funds I needed to cover my living expenses during the school year. Sometime that March, I would learn if I had been selected to be a dorm counselor. I remember the date of the water tower adventure well.

A little background information will help you understand the stress the water tower adventure produced at the time of its occurrence. Back in the early 1960s, the principal social activities on campus revolved around the six fraternities. The campus had no sororities at that time. During the middle of my sophomore year, the college relocated all six fraternities from their frat houses off campus to three large duplexes recently built on campus for that purpose. My fraternity, Sigma Alpha Epsilon, shared the duplex with the DKEs. Many of the DKEs upper classmen worked in the dining hall when I started as a dishwasher my freshman year. We quickly became friends. I found them to be smart, funny, adventuresome, honest, and kind.

Drinking was allowed on campus, but an inebriated student could be cited and brought before a judicial council. The council would decide on what punishments would be imposed on the violator of the drinking policy. The assigned punishment could be as stern as expulsion from the college.

The DKEs had a reputation for being a little on the wild side. That reputation was earned. Their parties were reported to be the most rambunctious on campus. When there was a boundary-challenging incident, it was usually the DKEs who did it. So it was not surprising to me to hear that, once again, DKE fraternity brothers from several other universities were staying at the DKE house in preparation for a major blowout of a St. Patrick's Day party the next night. Saturday night. From the sounds coming from next door, the wild celebrations had already started.

I just got tired of studying that night. I decided to quit, go down to the Cup to have a coke and then come back and go to bed. The Cup, a coffee shop type place, was just a few blocks from the dorm down by the railroad tracks. Few college guys went there as townies and day laborers preferred the setting more than most of the college men. As I passed the open living room of our fraternity house, I saw my friend, Nate, there.

"Nate, I'm going to the Cup. You want to go?"

"Yeah, that's just what I need right now."

With that, we set off on our adventure. As we passed the DKE portion of our duplex, we heard music, laughter, and other joyous sounds. We were passing the town's nearby water tower as we progressed towards the Cup when I commented.

"You know, the DKEs and most of the other fraternities have always done something to make themselves stand out from the others at one time or another. Our fraternity has never done a thing. 'Just plug along,' seems to be our motto. We ought to do something."

"You're right! Let's do something. Let's be daring just once. Let's do it."

"Ok, but what will 'IT' be?"

Passing the water tower stimulated us to agree spontaneously that we needed to paint our fraternity letters on the side of the water tower tank. It seemed as if every other fraternity except ours had at one time or another painted their Greek letters on it over the years we had been at the college. We turned back to the dorm to look for some paint and paintbrushes in the storage closet. As if divine intervention was working in partnership with us, we found an almost full gallon can of cream-colored paint and two large paintbrushes. Once we climbed all the way to the top of the water tower, I would use a screwdriver to open the can.

Never having climbed a water tower before, I had little experience to draw upon as we threw ourselves over the eight-foot chain link fence designed to keep folks like us from getting to the ladder and climbing up to the water tower tank. I had slipped my pants belt through the handle of the paint can and re-buckled it to free my hands for getting over the fence and making the long climb up the water tower ladder. Once inside the enclosed area, looking up to the top of the water tower caused me to realize that it would be a strenuous climb getting to the actual water-containing globe at the top. Nate and I were up to it.

When we reached the top of the town's water source and maneuvered under the guardrail to get to the tower's surrounding walkway, we were surprised. We were surprised to see that the city's public workers had already painted over most of the old fraternity Greek lettering and other graffiti in black paint. The black-painted area was huge. It had to be at least six feet high and ten feet wide, maybe larger. To me it was clear that the city's paint crew had tired of the painting project and intended to return another day to complete the entire water tank paint job. Once they had laid down this black undercoating, they would repaint the tower white and then paint the town's name in large, bold letters.

Anyway, it was clear to Nate and me that the blacked-out space was perfect for painting SAE on the water tank's side. The large letters would be clearly seen all over campus and around town tomorrow morning. We would have done something of note!

Setting the can of paint between us, Nate and I got busy. Gosh, the first two letters stood out against the black background. The cream-colored paint was just the perfect color. The full moon and cloudless sky seemed to make our Greek letters glow as if they had a light of their own.

As we were working to complete painting the last letter, a commotion seemed to be coming from the back entrance of the DKE house, the entrance facing the water tower. Guys were spilling out the back door shouting and pointing at the water tower. They were screaming. Most of them had cups of beer in their hands. It was clear that many of them were well into their suds.

They were an angry mob as they rushed to the chain-link fence protecting the water tower. Some climbed the fence, while others were falling off of it either inside or outside its boundaries. They were screaming, cursing, shaking their fists at us and shouting something. Nate and I looked down at the chaos below, not knowing why they were so hostile. They were clearly angry.

Finally, I pieced some words together through all the noise. They were upset that we had painted our fraternity letters on the water tower. Well, that was an understatement, as curses and threats as to what was going to happen to us when we came down were worrisome.

Since we couldn't make out much more than what we had deciphered up to this point, I suggested to Nate that we go down some rungs on the ladder. We wouldn't go all the way down to the ground until we understood why everyone was so upset and we could explain what we had done. Since I was friends with several of the DKEs, it was decided that I would go down the ladder first with Nate close behind me. Once again, I looped my belt through the handle of the paint bucket. We didn't take the time to put the lid back on. Since the paint bucket was a little less than half full, I figured that it wouldn't spill.

I stopped descending the ladder about ten feet off the ground. People were jumping in the air trying to grab my foot and pull me down into the mob. That would have been a disaster.

Some of the guys I knew began asking me if we purposefully decided to paint SAE on the water tower to ruin their St. Patty's Day's party.

"No, why would we do that?" came my surprised reply. More shouts and curses and guys jumping to grab a leg followed my statement, making it hard to hear the follow- up questions. I kept having to pull up one or the other leg as some of these hostiles could really jump.

"You saw that we had blocked out a space to paint DKE on the water tower. You know. That black painted clear spot. That was for us. We did it! We were going to climb up at midnight and paint DKE on the water tower to announce the beginning of our all-day/all-night party. You knew that and tried to finesse us."

"No, No, we had no idea this was going on."

"Sure you did! You saw that black painted area from the ground. You tried to pull one over on us. Now you're going to pay."

Just then some guy sprang high up into the air grabbing for my waist. He missed it but caught the edge of the paint bucket. The paint followed him back down to the ground covering his head and shoulders with creamy white paint along with several heads and shoulders of those standing near him. They were packed tightly together at the foot of the ladder allowing several to become baptized in this manner. The paint shower did not calm the maddened mob. It added a creamy color to several mugs of beer.

Out of nowhere, four or five of my good dining hall DKE friends appeared at the foot of ladder. They miraculously formed a protective circle around the foot of the ladder and called for me and Nate to come down.

As soon as our feet touched the ground, Nate and I pressed our backs together as the crowd lunged for us with their clawing hands stretching to possess us. Our circle of protection pushed them back as several other DKEs I knew and respected joined our friends in shielding us from those who would do us harm.

Amidst the shouts and curses, the senior DKE leadership grilled me about the possibility of our intentionally trying to ruin their celebration. As I was explaining how Nate and I were just being spontaneous in our behavior, an occasional drunk would break through the circle of protection. One by one they would come with a fist and its extended arm trying to do damage to my face. They would miss by several feet as the inner circle of protectors and I just leaned out of the way and the poor fellow followed his feeble weapon to the other side of the crowd. Through this circle of protection/explanation period I was unsure of what was happening to Nate. Our backs were pressed tightly together in the hope that we formed a shield of protection for ourselves. There was no time to discuss any other strategy. We were simply trying to survive.

Just as my protectors were agreeing on the truth of our story, the dean of men for the college showed up with his dog on a leash. He was clearly the immediate authority figure of the college. He didn't seem to shout when he spoke to the mob but everyone heard him. "Get out of the fenced-in area! NOW!"

Immediately, the shouting stopped. All of the guys suddenly appeared meek and subdued as they climbed over the fence and walked back to their fraternity houses. I was surprised to realize that a large audience of college students had accumulated on the open side of the fence to witness the chaos. As my turn came to climb over chain-link barrier, all my fears about not getting the dorm counselor position for next year became written on my face. Dr. Cavnes, the dean of men, looked me directly in the eye as I cleared the top of the fence with my feet landing on the neutral ground.

Well, I thought, *he knows I was in the mob. He'll learn that I was the cause of the whole thing. I guess this is it. I'll not get the position.*

Two weeks later, I got a letter from Dr. Cavnes. I was appointed to be next year's dorm counselor in an upper classmen's dorm.

CHAPTER EIGHTEEN

Calls in the Night

It was a big deal to have a telephone in your dorm room. That privilege was provided as part of my responsibility as a dorm counselor in an upper-classman dorm during my senior year at Centre College. Centre College is located near the center of Kentucky in Danville.

Remember, this was the 1963-1964 school year. At that time small towns like Danville used manually operated switchboards. It was just as you saw it in the old movies with big switchboards being controlled by telephone operators. They wore earphones and an extended voice microphone over their chests. The operator would ask the party on the other line what telephone number they were calling and then pull a cable from one outlet on the switchboard to plug it into another outlet. The more sophisticated switchboards allowed the operator to hear the dialed number and move the switchboard cable to another plug-in without speaking to the caller. At least that's how I understood it back then. In truth, I wasn't sure how Danville's operators handled phone calls, but they did have some degree of "hands on" as this story will explain.

Making a telephone call was expensive in those years. Payphones were plentiful but consumed dimes and quarters at a rapid rate. When I worked on the dredge boats off the Gulf of Mexico during the summer months of 1962 and 1963, I'd call my wonderful Anna in Kentucky on the Saturdays I was free. I'd get a ten dollar roll of quarters for the payphone. Every three minutes the pay phone would automatically interrupt our conversation to coldly state that if I wished to continue to be connected, I needed to deposit one more quarter. When I was out of quarters, we would be forced to say goodbye. My guess is that in today's economy, that roll of quarters represented around one hundred dollars. That was money well spent.

It was hard calling Anna at her college dormitory. The one phone on her dorm floor was always busy. All of the co-eds would naturally want to use it or have it not in use to receive calls. The calls could be from their favorite guy asking for a date and other such important issues to those in their college years. The phone hung in the dorm's open hallway. There was little privacy for anyone talking into it. However, late at night that phone was dormant. That's when I'd call. It was usually around 11:30 or a little later, one, two or three nights a week. During the week, it was hard to get face-time to talk. We weren't in many classes together. My role as the coordinator of the student workers for the dining-hall took up my time during the meals and late into the evening completing the cleaning chores of the day as well as setting up for the next morning. Those evening calls were about the only time we had to share our day with each other.

Towards the middle of the second semester, our late evening calls became more intense as we prepared for our graduation, wedding plans and finding a path in life after graduation. This included arranging for interviews to graduate schools and/or finding teaching positions. Both of us would graduate with high school teaching certificates in our areas of specialization.

One night in the spring, round two in the morning, my dorm room phone rang. As I awoke, all I could think was, there has to be a major emergency. The phone never rings this late at night.

"Hello, this is Jerry."

"Hi, Jerry. Are you OK tonight?" the female voice inquired.

"Ahhha, yes. Who is this please?"

"Oh, I was just wondering if Alice was going to continue dating Jim?" the friendly voice responded.

Now this must be someone from the college to be knowing about the tension between Alice and Jim. Anna seemed to be concerned for Alice in our last phone conversation.

"I really don't know, but who is this?"

"Oh, you know who I am. I don't want Alice to know about my asking you. We'll just let it go for tonight. I'm sorry to have called you so late. Good night." With that she just hung up.

As the weeks progressed, this mysterious female voice would call more than once during the week. She would never tell me who she was. Some nights it sounded like a different female voice. The person or persons would never identify themselves. I'd ask if they were one of the women in the college. It became somewhat of a game with the mystery caller having detailed information about college issues that an outsider would never have known. Sometimes, I would just tell the caller that I was too tired to talk that night. The caller would apologize and hang up. Overall, it became a game to try and figure out who the callers were. Sometimes it was fun asking for clues. Other times, I just couldn't afford to miss much sleep particularly during that last month of school. I told the callers that. They said they understood and would stop calling. They did until late one night two weeks or so before graduation.

"Sorry to call you so late when you are so busy," the female voice gently stated.

"It's OK."

"Have you figured out who we are?"

"No. I've tried, but I just can't put it all together."

"Well, I'll tell you, but you have to promise not to tell anyone except your Anna."

"OK."

"If you tell someone and our bosses learn of the calls, we'll be fired. We'll lose our jobs."

"OK. I won't tell anyone."

"We are the Danville telephone operators. We work the night shift. It gets so boring most nights. No one makes calls late at night. We listen in to your calls to Anna. The two of you are so sweet and in love. We can't help it. Your calls are just…well, it just makes us so happy. We couldn't help ourselves. Then when we called you, you were just as kind as we thought you would be. Your voice is soft and calming. We all want to wish you and Anna a happy life. We know it will be full of your love. I just thought one of us ought to tell you. That's all."

"Well, thank you. I would never have figured that out. Maybe we could all get together one time. Ah, no that wouldn't work out. Not with our getting married in a couple of weeks. There just isn't any time. Thank you for letting us know. Goodbye."

"Goodbye."

Two days after we graduated, we were married. We'll never do that again! We were really pressed for time. There were so many things to do as we started our lives together. I had obtained a summer job in Cincinnati working with the food service firm serving Centre College. We had to get a car and find an apartment near my work in the city. We needed to find a place to live in Oxford, Ohio, in the fall for the two years I would be at Miami University of Ohio while allowing Anna time to prepare to be a high school teacher in a Cincinnati suburb that fall. Since we were together, it was all a wonderful adventure.

CHAPTER NINETEEN

A Reading

Since childhood, I have been interested in psychic phenomena, which, as a child, I equated with magic. I knew magic was not real, but I could not help wishing it were.

A spontaneous incident related to psychic phenomena took place at my infantry officer's Officer Candidate School celebration of our class's passage to senior candidate status. As a review of events leading up to this occurrence will show, this incident seemed entirely out of context. Yet the memory of it has stayed with me over the years.

That evening of celebration could have been a disaster. The training officer (TAC) of another platoon in the company had boxed in our platoon's lieutenant, our TAC. The other TAC's trainees had presented him with a pink rabbit for some reason. The rabbit's fur had been dyed pink. During the evening meal, the recipient of the pink rabbit had gone on and on about how his platoon valued him. They had surprised him with the miracle rabbit. What he was really pleased about was that his trainees had found a way to break the training program's rules without getting caught. They had smuggled a rabbit into the barracks, kept it hidden for some time and then truly surprised the tactical officer at the time of the presentation.

All of the company's tactical officers were seated at their usual places behind their dining table, eating dinner on the raised platform that made it easier to watch the OCS candidates eat. The 200 or so trainees were seated four to a table eating on the square. We had to eat all of our meals on the square, and that was with no "eyeballing." Eating on the square meant that while looking straight ahead you raised your fork to eye level, then moved it in a straight line out until it was directly over your plate, then dropped your hand and fork straight down to the plate. While continuing to look straight ahead, you allowed your fork to obtain food. Once it had, you reversed the maneuver. In one smooth, straight line, you raised your fork straight up to eye level. Then, in a sharp 90-degree angle, you pulled the fork straight back and into your mouth. This process was repeated until you were full, you were caught eyeballing or the TACs determined that no more time would be wasted on eating. Getting caught eyeballing was very bad. Eyeballing was looking anywhere but straight ahead while you sat at your table eating. If you were caught eyeballing, you would be ordered from your seat and assigned various unpleasant tasks. These tasks included but were not limited to such things as doing fifty pushups, running out of the dining hall and around the barracks several times, or climbing into the large garbage dumpster and standing at attention while garbage was poured into it. After four months of eating on the square and learning to avoid being caught eyeballing, I found the process of eating not all that bad.

To increase their ability at catching someone eyeballing, TACs would leave their dining table to walk among the candidates as they ate. In the middle of one of these walking tours, the owner of the pink rabbit began shouting out his love for the pink rabbit, declaring that it was a natural pink, not a dyed pink as some had speculated. He went on and on about how his men, his candidates, were the best at all kinds of things.

I instinctively knew it was time for me to leave the dining hall during this boastful tirade. No good was going to come of it. As I was taking my tray to the collection point for the kitchen, the TAC laid down a challenge to our lieutenant. He charged our platoon with not valuing our TAC and lacking the "balls" to do anything out of the norm.

Our TAC rose to the challenge. Addressing me specifically, he ordered our platoon to present him with a chipmunk at the senior candidates' "coming out" party. The senior candidates' party was the celebration party for our reaching the senior candidate level of the six-month training program. From this point on, the harassment of the OCS candidates was basically over. During the remaining month or so of training, we were treated as if we were decent human beings. Our lieutenant stated that he wanted a live chipmunk, not a stuffed one that had wood chips glued to its shoulder or some other stupid substitute for a live chipmunk. If we failed to give him a live chipmunk at that Friday night dance, our platoon would not get a weekend pass for Saturday or Sunday. My gut feelings about our TAC were that he was a decent considerate man. His decree was out of sync with that assessment. Hidden issues were at work between our lieutenant and the pink rabbit TAC.

This was serious. A lot of the guys were inviting their wives and sweethearts to the party, and they anticipated a weekend pass. These women lived all across the country. They would have gone to all of the expense and travel to be here for the celebration but would not be able to spend time with their loved one Friday evening after the celebration or all-day Saturday and into Sunday if we failed in this mission. For example, my wife was in Danville, Kentucky.

It would have been a huge financial and emotional blow to us if she had left her high school teaching position to come to Ft. Benning to learn that Friday night we couldn't spend the weekend together. As it was, we had decided that she wouldn't come for the event. That was the last week of school for her. She had to close out the school year, but then she was going to come to Columbus, Georgia, and live with me until I graduated.

We didn't know where they would send me. I was probably going directly to Viet Nam as a combat platoon leader. That was what all of my colleagues and I expected. It was the way it was at that time. It wouldn't be easy living off-post as a senior candidate but it would be harder not being with my wife for the remainder of my time in the states. I'd still have to make the 6:00 a.m. muster and participate in all of the training activities of the day. The nighttime barrack's chores would need to be completed in order for us to pass the morning inspections before I could be with her.

The main plan to get the chipmunk revolved around one of our platoon mates' sweetheart. She worked in a large pet store in Atlanta. She would get one for us. If her store didn't have a chipmunk, she would call stores across the country and get it. This was an easy task to accomplish, we thought. We were wrong. About two weeks before the party, my platoon mate reported that his girlfriend could not find a chipmunk. She had called pet stores all across the country with no luck. She could get us a gerbil, if that would do. I didn't know what a gerbil was. A gerbil looks just like a chipmunk except it doesn't have the two light brown stripes running down its back, was the explanation. It is the same size, color and shape as a chipmunk.

Well, it would have to do if we couldn't find one or get someone to trap one in the wild. It was suggested that we just paint two stripes on its back. I was sure that wouldn't work. The hostile TAC would point out the paint when we presented it to our TAC and box our lieutenant into rejecting it.

The burden was on me to solve this dilemma. I had to figure out a way the gerbil could be presented to our TAC so that he would accept it as a real chipmunk. Just days before the party, it came to me. I would tell this outrageous story about the chipmunk that everyone would buy into. I could not reveal the story to anyone. I needed it to be a surprise when I told it to the lieutenant so that the audience's spontaneous reaction to the story would be so forcibly positive that our lieutenant would willingly accept the gerbil as a chipmunk. The crowd's positive support had to be so strong that the pink rabbit TAC's anticipated objections would be shallow and, within the military context, un-American.

The strategy worked. Shortly after the party had started, our TAC shouted out for his chipmunk. We all gathered around him and the other officers seated at the tables near the band. Everyone knew that the stakes were high for our platoon. All 200 plus men and their dates crowded around the seated officers. As prearranged, I called for the chipmunk to be presented. A couple of our guys pushed through the crowd holding up a stuffed monkey with woodchips glued to its shoulders.

This brought an angry response for our lieutenant. He stated that he had told us not to give him this object. I agreed, pointing out that this stuffed monkey was just what unworthy candidates would present to their TAC. The crowd muttered its agreement. I went on to say that we had a true hero of a chipmunk to present to him; one worthy of the honor of our lieutenant and his OCS candidates. A chipmunk with no other peer.

As our guys brought forth the caged gerbil, I went on to tell a story about how, as a sergeant with sergeant stripes proudly displayed on his back, he had routed a herd of elephants in Viet Nam that were rushing needed supplies to the Viet Cong. The battle was won because of this chipmunk's single-minded bravery. As a reward for his heroism, he was allowed to give up his stripes and become an infantry officer candidate right here at Ft. Benning. The story brought a roar of laughter and applause.

Our lieutenant happily declared the gerbil a chipmunk with a roar of approval from the audience and the muted protests of the pink rabbit TAC. We were all in a joyous state of celebration for the rest of the party. Our guys would be able to spend the weekend with their loved ones.

Towards the end of the party, one of the guys from another platoon introduced his date to me. We laughed about the chipmunk stunt. I really liked this guy, as did so many of the OCS candidates. He went on to tell me that his girlfriend was psychic.

That grabbed my attention. I told her how much I regretted not being able to talk with her about her experiences. I stated that I was very interested in the subject. My classmate said that he knew that I would be interested, which was why he wanted to introduce her to me.

How did he know I was interested in psychic questions? I had never openly spoken about my interest. Throughout my childhood and into graduate school I had always had an interest in psychic phenomena. It was just that you never spoke openly about psychic things. You would be ridiculed if you did. That's not to deny that once in a while, in hushed tones, you would talk to someone about psychic stuff, but just as a topic of mystery, not something that was so real that it happened to people you knew.

So, I had a real interest in psychic phenomena that I would

never openly discuss with anyone. Somehow, some people knew about that interest but seldom let me know that they knew.

As an escape from the tensions of my first job after leaving the Army in June of 1969, I read a book I had run across about Edgar Cayce, the sleeping prophet. It was the first time I had ever encountered some documented, unexplained psychic type of phenomena that I considered to be credible. Now, there were things in that material that were just beyond any level of credibility, like reincarnation and life after death. However, there were reports of documented psychic predictions from Edgar Cayce that impressed me. Cayce's trance-like readings on someone's health and the recommended treatments that were documented to have worked were convincing. The material strongly suggested that something beyond our understanding was real.

I didn't pretend to know what real was. Whatever it was, it gave me hope that there was something more than what we saw in front of us. A guiding force knew what was happening and directed us when we allowed ourselves to listen. Now, I understood this was not the scientific view of the world, nor the mainstream view of the world. You couldn't just openly discuss these things. You would quickly be ostracized from any well-educated group of people. The risk of believing such things was being labeled a religious fanatic or worse.

After two years of functioning as the only school psychologist serving seven inner city schools being integrated for the first time in St. Petersburg, Florida, I got admitted to the University of Tennessee's Psychology Department's doctoral program in school psychology. Even though I had a master's degree in school psychology, I was told that it would take me five years or longer to complete the program. The length of time it would take me to graduate was dependent upon my passage through well-defined evaluation levels the doctoral program had established for all of its Ph.D. psychology students. There were five basic levels to get past. Each one would take an estimated year of preparation to accomplish. Somewhere along the line, at least one of the levels would take you more than a year.

Leaving my Florida position with a wife and two toddlers to enter a five-year plus doctoral program was stressful. My wife had a high school teaching job at a school near the house that we had to buy in order for me to get in-state tuition. Thank heaven for the GI bill and its funds supporting education. The psychology department didn't trust my masters level training in psychological testing, so I had to do extra things in that area along with the eighteen hours of course work I was taking. It was a stressful time.

Adding to my stress was the fact that I had not passed the department's first hurdle. The entering class in the psychology doctoral program had to take a test on the mastery of current facts established in the nine domains of psychology. The test was created by the department's faculty. A passing score was not established until the test had been administered. The faculty would review the test results and determine the passing score in such a manner that at least forty percent of those taking it would fail.

Those who failed would be allowed to retake the test in the spring. Those graduate students who failed the test the second time would be dropped from the program. The word among the senior graduate students was that you could appeal to take the test a third time in the fall with the newly entered class of graduate students. Failing the test the third time was it. You were gone.

I was stressed. Here I was with a wife and two toddlers

competing against these brilliant graduate students straight out of undergraduate school knowing all of the current research in the nine areas of psychology. I had been out of graduate school for five years and didn't even know there were nine areas of psychology. I repeat, I was stressed.

I could manage the course work. My experiences at the Army's special warfare center working on psychological issues for two years had prepared me extremely well for the graduate work. The Army provided me the opportunity to work with some highly regarded psychology professors. In turn, my work as a practicing masters level school psychologist for the last two years had made student evaluations comparatively easy for me when contrasted to the other graduate students. I had administered the standard psychoeducational tests at least three hundred times compared to the ten or so times expected of the normal graduate school student. The course work wasn't my problem.

My fellow graduate students were at a disadvantage when compared to the hard intellectual work demanded of me by the Army. I knew that no one had worked harder or longer hours than I did on issues related to psychology during my two years at the special warfare center. My problem was getting through the department's big testing events and doing the research for a dissertation. Test results never reflected my true knowledge of a subject. With the exception of the few times I got lucky on a test. Then I did extraordinarily well. I couldn't count on getting lucky in this graduate school.

Well, there were two other problems. One was having enough time to do all that had to be done. The other problem was money. My wife worked all day in a highly demanding job. We had two toddlers to raise. I needed to study in the evenings. She needed to grade papers and develop lesson plans. Daycare, diaper services and normal living issues consumed our income and a lot of time.

I found reading the Edgar Cayce material sent from the Cayce center at Virginia Beach, Virginia, helpful in reducing my stress level. It gave me hope of something bigger than the constant struggle to get ahead. There were just a few very close graduate school friends to whom I even dared to mention a little of the Cayce material. They were surprisingly receptive. Being rigorously trained in the scientific method, we naturally challenged every concept of reported explanations for verified events.

One of the graduate student's wives told me about a psychic who lived near the part of town where my family and I lived. She thought the psychic was able to hit on some things for her that she had no way of knowing about beforehand. She gave me the woman's name and phone number.

After thinking about it for several weeks, I mentioned the psychic to my wife. Our first summer in Knoxville was under way. It provided a break for my wife from teaching school. She was able to spend more time with the children. I continued taking courses at the university. I was trying to get through the program as rapidly as possible. I also needed extra time to study in preparation for getting through the second of the five hurdles in the fall. I had passed the first testing phase in the spring. It was the one I had failed last fall.

It wasn't until the third or fourth year of graduate school that the senior graduate students attempted to pass the generals examination that I was targeting in the fall. It was two days of writing essay answers on very broad psychological issues that required you to cite specific research or literature on the topic in writing your answer to each question. Approximately 40% or more of those taking the test failed it. Those who failed it could appeal to take it the following year. Reportedly, it was rare for a graduate student to be allowed to try to pass generals a third time.

My wife suggested that I call the psychic, Vivian, and see how much she would charge and when she could see me. We could consider a reading from Vivian a birthday present since my birthday was fast approaching.

Vivian could see me two weeks from the day I called her. She would charge me $5.00 for a reading. We set the date. Her house was on Chapman Highway near John Sevier Highway. It was about three miles from our house.

The day to get a reading arrived. I felt like such a fool. This was a waste of money. These fortunetellers were fakes. This was so un-scientific. Why was I doing this to myself? On top of all of those feelings of self-doubt I was afraid. What if she was accurate on some things? What would I do then? How would my worldview be forced to change? Why was I putting myself under this pressure?

It was with mixed emotions that I drove to the address Vivian had given me over the phone. I'm not sure what I expected to see, but what I saw was definitely not what I expected. This house was a poor excuse of a house. It was tiny. It was more of a run-down shack than a house. I knocked on the screen door. The screen was torn in one corner. Because of the heat of the day, the windows and the front door were open. I knocked again. A parrot in the house screeched from the left side of the screen door. A weak voice coming from the right side said, "Come in, Sweetie."

The squeaky screen door opened and bumped on the flooring as I walked into the dimly lit room. The elderly, overweight woman was propped up in the bed, pressed between the back wall and the opening for the door. Her hands were obviously crippled as she raised a glass to her dry lips. The glass was clasped between her thumb and forefinger as her other fingers were pressed deeply into her palm in such a manner that it was apparent that they had not moved from that position in years.

"Sit down, sweetie. Bring that chair over there, here. Sit right here beside me now," she wheezed between little gasps for air.

Vivian was an old woman with not long to live. She appeared to live in pain and poverty.

"SCRRREEECH, CHAWW, EAT IT, EAT IT, SCRREEECHHH," screamed the parrot.

"Shut up, you damned old bird," screamed Vivian.

Yes, I thought, *I've been had.*

"Don't mind that old bird. Now you're the one who called for the reading, right?"

"Yes, ma'am."

"Good. You're right on time. Now give me those playing cards," she mumbled pointing to an old deck of regular playing cards sitting on the little end table beside her bed.

As I handed her the cards, she said with a pleasant smile, "Now reach that bottle of Southern Comfort and pour a little into my glass, please."

I did. She took a little sip of it and set the glass down.

"Now take the cards and shuffle them nice and long for me. That's right. Do a good job. Pull that board over here. Put it on my lap. That's good. I can lay some of the cards down on it."

She proceeded to lay the first few cards on the make-do table and studied them.

Looking up at me, she said, "I see you're a graduate student in medicine about to become a doctor."

"No, ma'am. I'm in psychology."

"Well that's a healing profession. That's what I meant. You're about to graduate aren't you?"

"No, ma'am. I just started. It will take at least four or five more years if I ever do graduate."

"No, you are wrong. This time next year you will be through with school. You will have a job as a psychologist. It will be here in Tennessee. You will not have to move from the house you live in now. Honey, would you pour me a little more of that Southern Comfort?" she asked, after finishing a long drag on her glass of the same.

"That's all for now. Don't pay me. You will be back. You will be back next year. You will be back after you start that new job," she stated, taking another sip of the Southern Comfort.

I tried to pay her, but she vigorously refused to accept the five-dollar bill. As I was leaving, a brand-new Mercedes-Benz sedan pulled up in front of her house. It was driven by an extremely well-dressed older lady. As I got into my car, the woman got out of hers, made a friendly wave to me and entered Vivian's house as she was greeted by the screams of the parrot.

My wife and I laughed at the telling of my visit with Vivian. She was an obvious total failure as a psychic but what a wonderful character as a human being. You just couldn't help but like Vivian a whole lot.

I did go back to see her a year and a half after that reading. Her predictions of the future were so far-fetched that I had just forgotten about her. It wasn't until the year and a half had passed that I paused to reflect on what Vivian had told me.

I had finished the doctoral program the following July. I had gotten through the department's fact-check test, the two days of writing the generals exams, my specialty project in psychology and my dissertation, an analysis of variance research project that tracked twenty-six factors across an experimental group of subjects, a control group of subjects and a placebo group of subjects.

I didn't receive the doctoral degree officially from the university until that December because my major professor had missed the filing date for receiving the degree in August by two days. I had a job that started on the first of July, as predicted by Vivian.

I was to develop the first comprehensive school psychological services for seven small school systems through an educational cooperative and to provide training to the area school systems' staffs on the implementation of the newly passed special education laws being enforced by the state for the first time. The cooperative's offices were less than ten miles from home.

CHAPTER TWENTY

Which One?

As I have stated before, the last year of graduate school was stressful. While it was highly successful, there was never time to enjoy any of the success, as the next challenge was right before me. For inspiration and relaxation, I continued to read the Edgar Cayce material. This instilled a desire to explore the world of psychic phenomena.

Since I had determined that the psychic I saw the summer before launching into my second and final year of graduate school had not made a single successful prediction at the time, she had been dropped from my conscious awareness. That year it never occurred to me to visit her again.

Every Friday afternoon I drove by a house where a large sign in the yard announced that Madam Sophia gave psychic readings. The house was on the four-lane highway I drove to do the week's grocery shopping for our family. I was tempted to pull into her driveway on numerous occasions but would change my mind for a multitude of reasons.

However, the chief reason was that I was embarrassed to go there. I had always assumed that such people with their signs and pictures of a crystal ball with a gypsy woman looking into it were just a carnival show. This was a business for taking people's money for simply making up some tall story about them. Since her home/place of business was right on the edge of a major four-lane highway, all the passing traffic saw any car parked in front of her house. If I pulled into her lot, my classmates, my professors, my neighbors and everyone else would know that I was there seeing Madam Sophia. They would know I was a fool throwing away my family's money.

Time and again I would drive by Madam Sophia's big sign and wonder what if she were real. Maybe it wouldn't be as I suspected. Maybe she wasn't a fraud. A lot of people treated Edgar Cayce as a fraud. I had read in some of the Cayce foundation material that way back when, the American Medical Association brought legal charges against him for practicing medicine without a license. After investigating some of his trance-state readings in which medical remedies were recommended and finding out what happened to the person given those remedies, the AMA dropped its charges. Instead of pursuing the charges, the AMA listed Cayce as a medical consultant, the material stated.

Maybe Madam Sophia was like that. Maybe it was just my long-established prejudices that kept me from investigating Madam Sophia. Wasn't I supposed to be a supporter of the scientific approach? You have to be open to whatever the data presents to you. You can't pre-determine the outcome of something without observing, collecting the observed data and objectively analyzing that data to determine the truth of something. How would we ever learn anything new if we just relied on our personal prejudices to make a determination of what is true or not true? My inner dialogue continued for some months along those lines as I routinely passed Madam Sophia's place.

While out in the car on a Saturday morning with a little time to spare, I approached Madam Sophia's sign. Gritting my teeth, I turned the steering wheel and drove into the graveled parking area in front of her house. I backed the car up to the house. That way, I thought, no one would see my license plate. Someone who knew me might not recognize the car if they didn't see the license plate.

I really felt awkward walking up to her door. This was a fool's errand, I thought as I knocked. When the door opened, I was standing face-to-face with a very young-looking woman.

"Madam Sophia?" I hesitantly asked.

"Yes," she said, with a pleasant smile on her face.

"I'd like a reading or a palm reading or whatever it is that you do."

"Please come in."

I entered the little hallway that led to a large living room. Behind the living room was the kitchen area. Off to the right was a hallway that I assumed led to bedrooms.

As Madam Sophia led me to the living room, I reflected that I had expected Madam Sophia to be in her forties or fifties. This Madam Sophia looked like a college student or younger.

"Well," I thought to myself, "you learn about your in-grained prejudices every day."

"Please sit down," she said motioning to the couch.

As I sat, she sat down beside me. With the two of us sitting side-by-side she turned her head and part of her body towards me.

"One palm reading is five dollars; reading both palms is ten dollars and an in-depth analysis is twenty-five dollars. Which of these would you like?"

I had forgotten that there would be a fee for this. Of course there would be a fee. Why hadn't I planned for a fee? Well, it was an unplanned stop. I hadn't planned anything. I was operating on impulse.

"This is embarrassing. I don't think I have $5.00 on me."

"How much do you have?"

Standing up to pull out my wallet from my pants pocket, I pulled out three dollars. She could see that it was all the money I had in it. Then reaching into my front pockets, I pulled out the change I had in them. Sitting back down on the couch, I counted out one dollar and thirty-seven cents.

Self-consciously laughing, I held out the money and stated, "four dollars and thirty-seven cents."

"That will be all right. I'll give you a palm reading."

She held out her two hands, and I placed my right-hand, palm up, in them.

She proceeded to tell me what the lines in the palm meant. She went into considerable detail about the meaning of several lines in my hand.

"You are experiencing a lot of resistance to what you want to accomplish."

I studiously resisted saying yes or displaying any facial or body clues to her that she was right. I was aware of the massive amount of non-verbal communication we all display and read from others. Reading non-verbal messages sent by someone was how so-called psychics could determine if their statements about you were accurate or not. I wasn't knowingly going to provide her with non-verbal or verbal clues as to the accuracy of her comments to me.

"You will overcome this resistance, but it will take a long time without help"

Suddenly, the front door burst open. Both Madam Sophia and

I involuntarily flinched with the abrupt opening. In walked this fortyish plus woman carrying two bags of groceries. She walked into the open passageway beside the living room leading into the kitchen. As she walked past the two of us, me with my hand, palm up, being held in the young woman's two hands, her look of surprise at seeing us quickly transformed into a smile as she looked directly into the girl's eyes. Without a word, the obviously "real" Madam Sophia walked into the kitchen and began putting the groceries away.

I knew I had been had. What a fool I was.

Pulling my hand from Madam Sophia's daughter's two hands, I asked, "What kind of help are you talking about?"

"We can light candles for you and pray once a week for half an hour. It will cost you ten dollars for each half-hour of prayer. You will need us to do this for several months."

Getting up from the couch and backing towards the door, I commented, "I'll have to talk it over with my wife. That's a little costly for us right now."

She kept pace with my backing to the door, "I'm sure we can work something out."

At that moment my back hit the sidewall of the little hallway. Immediately, a framed picture fell off the wall, wedging itself between the wall and the back of my leg. Bending over to pick it up, I apologized profusely. The glass in the frame had a big crack in it.

"That's all right. Don't worry about it," she said as she took the picture from my hand.

My back hit the door. I turned to open it, still expressing my regret at breaking the glass with the girl reassuring me that it was all right.

Outside the door, I said my final goodbye; and she responded with the same.

Driving back home. I had to laugh at myself. I had suspected that it would be foolish for me to stop to check out Madam Sophia. As I pulled into the gravel driveway of Madam Sophia, I had thought that I was being very foolish. Having the young Madam Sophia hold my hand reading my palm made me feel even more foolish. Then when the real Madam Sophia so dramatically entered the house, I knew I had been and was being foolish. Knocking the picture off the wall as I was leaving the house proved how foolish I was.

Driving down the highway gave me such a sense of relief. It's good to be foolish every once in a while. You don't have to pretend you're not being foolish while in the process of being foolish. It's such a relief.

CHAPTER TWENTY

Doc Hanson

That second and last year of graduate school at UT was intense. It was moving fast. The lack of a break from the intensity, even when a major hurdle had just been accomplished, produced a great deal of stress for me. Where was it all going? If I graduated at the end of the year, where would I find a job? No doubt we would have to move.

In 1973, the big cities in Tennessee were the only ones employing doctoral level school psychologists. All of their positions were filled with competent young adults. They were not about to leave their jobs, and the systems weren't about to hire new ones. They were strapped for money. It wasn't reasonable to expect them to be adding new positions for doctoral level school psychologists.

There didn't seem to be any relief from the stress with one exception. Reading the Edgar Cayce material gave me hope that there was more to life than jumping through hoops. I really didn't know what to make of Cayce's many readings about people's past lives. I was unaware of any way to validate that aspect of his readings. The same was true for his readings about Atlantis and the spiritual side of his trance-induced pronouncements.

Still, the medical readings could be validated according to material I had read. Maybe the reincarnation stuff was real too. I just didn't know what to make of that. Overall, the readings gave me hope. They helped me manage my stress levels. Of course, there was no one I could converse with in great detail about the Cayce material or other similar material I was reading. They would consider me to be having a breakdown, or so I thought. I did share some of my interest in psychic phenomena with a few close friends in graduate school. To my surprise, they seemed to have a strong interest in the subject as well. We agreed that it would be interesting to investigate the phenomena if we ever had the time to do it.

It was a big surprise to learn that a fourth-year graduate student in the education department had written a book about a psychic in Chattanooga, Doc Hanson. I made a point of introducing myself to the guy. I wanted to know about his research on Doc Hanson and how to get a copy of the graduate student's book. The guy was quite open about the information he had collected on the psychic. He said many people for whom Doc Hanson had given readings had reported on the accuracy of what he told them. Doc Hanson had been written up in several major newspapers and interviewed on numerous of radio shows, the graduate student reported.

I obtained a copy of the book. My acquaintance, the author, went into great detail about his interviews of individuals who had reported on the accuracy of Doc Hanson's readings and predictions for them. His research confirmed the claims of several of Doc Hanson's supporters. It was true that he had difficulty finding some of the people referred to in newspaper stories who spoke in support of Doc Hanson's psychic talents, but that was to be expected.

It was exciting to know that there was a "real psychic" just one hundred miles south of Knoxville and that he was giving readings to the general public. I wanted to try to get a reading from him. Maybe he could tell me what was about to happen. Would I be able to graduate at the end of the year? Reportedly, no one knew of another graduate student who had completed the doctoral program in psychology in two years. I was told that many students who entered the program with a master's degree, as I did, had taken five or more years to complete the program. That was why I had been advised that it would take me at least five years to graduate from the program. If I were lucky enough to get through the program, where would I find a job? Doc Hanson might provide me with the guidance I needed to allow me to correctly steer myself into the future.

After I discussed the information I had about Doc Hanson with my wife, we decided I would just drive down to Chattanooga one Saturday to his office and see if he would do a reading for me. In the book about Doc Hanson, it was stated that you didn't have to have an appointment to see him on Saturdays. He saw people on a first-come, first-serve basis. Often more people would want a reading on Saturdays than he could give. It was important to get there as early as you could so that you would have a chance of being seen. He charged a fee for his readings, but the book didn't say how much it was.

My wife and I agreed that I would take twenty dollars to pay for the reading. If he were a true psychic, he would know that we couldn't afford any more than that. Actually, twenty dollars was a big dent in our budget. I took an additional five dollars to cover the cost of lunch and sodas while I waited. Twenty-five dollars on non-essential expenses was a lot of money to spend in 1973. With inflation added into the calculation, I would estimate that twenty-five dollars then would be one hundred-seventy-five dollars today. That's a lot of money to take out of most people's monthly budget and certainly a lot to take out of a graduate student's budget.

I could hardly sleep that Friday night. The plan was to get up at 5:00 a.m., dress, eat breakfast and be on the road by 6:00 a.m. That way I should arrive at Doc. Hanson's office right at 8:00 a.m. and be one of the first to be put on his waiting list for the day. I was excited and nervous. What if he told me some things that were really negative? Would I be able to deal with it? Even worse, what if he were like Vivian, the Southern Comfort drinker who had been so far out with her predictions that I knew she was a fake?

Deciding what to wear seemed like a task that would never end. It wouldn't be appropriate to wear my sport coat and a tie. I wanted to look nice but not overly casual. After all, this guy might actually be able to see who I was. If he were a true psychic, he'd know me when I walked into his office. That seemed to be the way it was with Edgar Cayce. As soon as he went into his trance to give a reading for someone, he just began talking and seemed to know all the relevant information about the person.

Doc Hanson just might be as good as Cayce was. After all, Doc Hanson had been studied by many people. People he had given readings to said that he knew things about them that he could not have known beforehand. His predictions for them came true as well. I anticipated that I would have the same report to make. He would know the real person I was, and he would guide me into the future. It was exciting, but in the words of an old song, "a little bit frightening."

I got into the car just a few minutes after 6:00 a.m. The fact that

I was starting out a little later than I had planned added to my anxiety about see Doc Hanson. Once in the car, my wife handed me the ritual cup of coffee I liked to take at the start of a long trip. She kissed me, and I was off.

Not more than three miles down the road, I needed to make a sharp left hand turn onto a major highway. It was a dangerous intersection even at the crack of dawn. Coming to a complete stop, I looked both ways. It was clear. I gave the car some gas and turned quickly to the left. The quick turn caused my arm on the steering wheel to collide with my coffee cup. The entire cup of coffee dumped into my lap. It was hot. I squirmed around some but completed the turn. Once traveling in a straight direction, I checked my pants. The khaki pants were soaked all around the crotch. It was a big soaking. The cup had been full. Well, it should all dry by the time I got to Chattanooga, I thought.

Yes, but there would be a big ring of coffee stain around my crotch. I would be sitting in Doc Hanson's waiting room for untold hours with everyone staring at my coffee-stained crotch. There was no other choice: I had to go back home and change my pants. This would mean that I wouldn't get to Doc Hanson's waiting room until around 10:00 a.m. If a lot of people showed up before I got there, I might have to wait all day and still not get a reading. There was nothing to be done about it. I had to change my pants.

As predicted, I got to Doc Hanson's complex around 10:00 or 10:30 in the morning. The place was huge. When you entered the door, you were confronted with a large open room. The room was surrounded with windows. Benches were placed against the four walls. Nine or ten people were seated on the benches. The room was so large that it seemed empty. In one corner of the room sat a large black lady. She sat behind a desk.

189

"Come on in, sir," she cried out to me with a big smile on her face. "You're here for a reading from Doc?"

"Yes, ma'am."

"Well, sit you down on one of those benches. It won't be til mid-or late afternoon that he'll be able to see ya. Is that going to be OK?"

"Yes, ma'am."

"Maybe he won't have time to see ya, with all these people here and all. But I think you've got a chance. Sit down now. I got your number. I'll tell you when you can go on back to see him," she instructed as she nodded her head to a doorway behind her that I had not noticed until then.

I wished I had brought something to read. After the first hour, the time dragged on. It took an hour before someone exited from the door behind the lady guarding it, and she pointed at one of my fellow bench-sitters to go on back to see Doc Hanson.

To pass the time, I began reading the many newspaper stories stuck to the walls between the windows. They all told of remarkable things that Doc Hanson had done. Testimonial stories after stories affirmed Doc Hanson's psychic abilities. This guy appeared to be the real thing. I was staying until they closed at 5:00 p.m. that evening in the hopes of getting a reading.

After twenty minutes or so, the person called to go into Doc Hanson's room came out. He thanked the informal receptionist as he walked by. She called the next person on the list to go in.

It was close to noon. I was getting hungry. Rather than risk losing my place in line to get something to eat, I was determined to stay right there in the large room. Fifteen minutes or so passed, and the second person to be called into the room during my presence exited it. I heard a deep male voice from within the psychic reading room call to the receptionist.

She went into the room and quickly returned to announce that Doc Hanson was taking a break for lunch. He would take his next reading a 1:00 p.m. I decided to walk over to a nearby convenience store and get a package of nuts and maybe some cheese crackers. There was a soda machine in Doc Hanson's big waiting room. When I got back with my lunch in hand, I'd buy a soda.

To my surprise, when I returned there were three new people who arrived hoping to get a reading from Doc Hanson. I checked with the receptionist to ensure that my place on the waiting list had not been disturbed by the new arrivals. She assured me that she wouldn't do that to me. I thanked her.

By 2:30 p.m., I had conversed with most of those waiting to see Doc Hanson. They were all confident that Doc would give them important advice. I questioned them about how they had heard of Doc Hanson. Their explanations were tied into what they had read about him or what friends of theirs had told them. The things they wanted to ask Doc Hanson about ranged from getting a divorce to wanting to become rich. I kept thinking how sad it all was. These people wanted the Doc to tell them what life decisions they should make on some very important issues. If Doc Hanson really wasn't psychic, if he was just making his answers up, these people were in serious trouble. This psychic business was risky for those willing to pay for answers. The Doc could be like Madam Sophia. That would be a disaster.

Some of the waiting souls that were here when I arrived began expressing disappointment about how long they had been waiting. They had other things they had to do that day. Gradually, several decided to leave and try to come back on another Saturday when there wouldn't be as many people wanting to see him.

If the few remaining people ahead of me spent a half hour or less with Doc Hanson, I would get to see him around four or four thirty. That was cutting it close, but it looked as if I would be able to get a reading from him. It was worth the wait.

Around 3:15 that afternoon, a speeding taxi drove up to the waiting room door. A middle-aged woman rushed from the cab and into the waiting room. She ran to the receptionist and stated that she had to see Doc Hanson. She had flown in from Chicago. As soon as her plane landed, she explained, she caught the cab and rushed over here.

The receptionist explained that she would have to wait her turn. She could go in after me. Everyone waiting to see Doc Hanson that had arrived after my arrival had done the math. They had all left. I would be the last person Doc Hanson would see.

The lady asked the two people ahead of me if she could take their place. She had a family emergency that she had to get Doc Hanson's advice about. It was critical that she see him that day. They told her that they, too, had important questions to ask Doc Hanson. They were sorry, but they could not let her have their spot.

She came to me. With tears in her eyes, she said I was her only hope. She had to catch her plane back to Chicago at 5:45 p.m. She was afraid that she would miss it, but it was so important that she talk to Doc Hanson about the crisis that she had to risk it.

What did I know? I wasn't about to follow anything he told me if it didn't fit into my life. I wasn't about to turn my life decisions over to some psychic whether it was Edgar Cayce or Doc Hanson or Madam Sophia. Nothing in my life was about to pivot around what Doc Hanson said.

"Sure," I said. "You can go ahead of me."

She was so pleased. She clasped my hands in hers and asked

God to bless me. Sitting beside each other while we waited for the last two to conclude their sessions with Doc Hanson, the lady and I talked. It was clear that she was very, very wealthy. You would think that someone with all the money she had wouldn't have such dramatic problems that she would fly down from Chicago to ask a psychic about them and then fly immediately back to Chicago. It caused me to reflect on the things we pursue to gain our happiness and how little happiness many have when they had obtained the objects of their pursuit.

I guess it was about 4:15 p.m. when the Chicago lady was called into Doc Hanson's chamber. All of the other hopefuls had left. I was the only one waiting, hoping to get the last reading. Around 4:45 p.m. she came rushing out of that room, waved goodbye to me and ran into the taxi that had been waiting for her all this time.

I heard Doc Hanson call to the receptionist, "That's it. That's the end of the day. Tell the rest they'll just have to come back another Saturday."

"Oh, Doc, let me talk to you," she said entering into his chamber. I could make out voices talking but had no clue as to what was being said.

Returning to the reception room beaming a big smile my way, she said, "Doc will see you now."

The room was dark. It took a minute for my eyes to adjust. Doc Hanson sat behind a big desk. He was a large man. He was quite tall, clearly several inches over six feet. His shoulders were wide. This guy had been an athlete of some kind in his youth. I'd guess he was in his seventies at this point. However, he was still lean and fit.

"Sit down," he said, motioning to a chair slightly off center from his desk. "You've been waiting a long time."

"Yes, sir. Since about 10 or 10:30 this morning."

"Yet you gave that lady your slot to see me. You are a kind man," he said with a fatherly smile.

"Thank you, sir. She seemed to be very stressed and to need your guidance."

"Well, yes. Now tell me your birth date, the time you were born and where you were born. The longitude and latitude of your birthplace is important."

I gave him the information.

With a big grin and leaning towards me, he said, "I was born in Duluth as well. It's good to be with a Minnesotan again. This is very good. Oh, this is very good, your birth date, the time of birth and Duluth. My goodness, this is so good. Before we go on, the reading is fifty dollars."

I was stunned. In my wildest imagination, I never dreamed the reading would cost such a huge amount of money.

I sputtered, "I don't have fifty dollars with me. I've got a twenty-dollar bill and maybe three dollars and some change."

"I'm sorry, but I have to have the money up front."

My mind rushed through so many thoughts. He was for real. He was famous. I needed to have his insights. People from Chicago flew down here just to get a reading from him. I wanted this reading.

"I have a check in my wallet. I could write you a check for the fifty dollars."

Even as I spoke these words, I knew how hard it would be for us to be out fifty dollars. It just couldn't be helped. This was the chance of a lifetime. My wife would understand. We would make it.

"No, I can't take a check. I used to do that, but so many people wrote me bad checks. I just can't take checks anymore."

"Well, that's it. I can't pay. Thank you for talking with me."

"I'm sorry too. Your chart is most unusual."

I turned and left his counseling room. The receptionist had left. By the time I got home, I was chuckling to myself about the encounter with Doc Hanson. It would be a great story to tell.

My desire for a reading from Doc Hanson never returned.

CHAPTER TWENTY-ONE

Searching

As it turned out, a handful of friends, fellow graduate students, had an interest in exploring psychic phenomena. We formed an informal investigation group the year after I graduated. Some in the group had graduated the year I did, and a few of the others were in their last year or two of school. We decided to meet the third Monday evening of each month. At the meeting we would report on any so-called psychic phenomena that a member of the group had followed up on the previous month. We would also inform each other of coming issues that someone might want to look into. It was a good way for friends to get together. Our expectation was that we would be debunking those who reported to be psychic or to have experienced a psychic event.

After several months of meetings, our expectations were being met. One member of our group attended an advertised tent revival/healing in a nearby rural county. He reported that it was a total fake. There was a lot of shouting, praying and hallelujahing going on, but there were no healings. When the lead preacher told those who wanted to be healed to come to the front of the tent to be healed, about ten to fifteen people came forward. A few of them were limping, but there were no obvious catastrophic conditions observed. Most of the participants looked healthy. The preacher approached each of the petitioners, placed the palm of his hand on the person's forehead and then seemed to babble. His assistants cried out that it was a miracle because the preacher was speaking in tongues. Our group member said it was clearly babble with no sign of rational communication. No one, not even the assistants, pretended to have a clue as to what the babble meant.

At the end of the utterances, the preacher would push the petitioners hard on the forehead with the heel of his hand, which knocked the faithful one off-balance and often down to the floor. The assistants anticipating this action had strategically placed themselves behind the off-balance seeker to keep the person from being hurt in the fall.

Another faith healing/tent revival was revealed it to be a front for the purpose of presenting a girly show. I guess the men found it easier to get out of the house by telling their wives they were going to a tent revival than out to observe scantily clad young ladies dancing. Who knows, the young women may have danced to gospel music.

Two situations I went to visit on behalf of the group dealt with a reported poltergeist event and a visiting psychic's presentation. I discovered the announcement of the events in the local newspaper.

The story in the paper concerning the poltergeist experience involved a teenage boy and his family. The family reported that when the boy was in the living room, objects would fly off the fireplace mantel. The objects would hit the floor or the far wall with such force that they broke. The names of the interviewed family members were part of the newspaper story. I obtained the family's phone number from the phone book and called them.

They agreed for me to interview them in their home. I had explained that I was just an interested person who wanted to know more about the phenomena. It surprised me that they were so open about having a visitor and willing to be interviewed.

After talking to the parents and their son, I was convinced that they truly believed that what they reported had happened. They were sure that the objects flying off the mantle had not simply fallen. They reported seeing the picture frame moving through the air as if an invisible hand had thrown it. The glass in the frame had shattered, and the frame was badly bent. They showed me its remains, which had been stored in a cardboard box. Nothing out of the ordinary happened while I was there. It was clear to me that these people were frightened by the events they described. They had no explanation for what had happened and hoped I would have one. I did not. The last event had occurred a little more than two weeks prior to my visit. They hoped that it had stopped.

While I could not verify any of their reports, I could verify to the group that this family believed that the events had actually happened. Their verbal and non-verbal communications to me were congruent.

The Reverend Peter event was strange. It was held in the large conference room of the Holiday Inn across from the West Town Mall of Knoxville. There was a large ad in the newspaper announcing Reverend Peter's free presentation on his psychic powers. It was scheduled on a weekday in the early evening. I decided to attend it. Even though I had arrived a little early, a large crowd had already assembled. I guess there were seventy-five to one hundred people in the room with several more arriving as I sat down on a folding chair near the rear. Many of those in attendance were clearly well-dressed, middle-aged professionals with their spouses. This was a surprise to me as I had expected to see primarily hippie-looking young people and poor rural folks seeking a meaningful religious experience.

As the time neared for Reverend Peter to appear and make his presentation, I noticed several people in the back of the room increasing their activities. One man was adjusting some small spotlights to focus on the stage while another began dimming the room lights. As the lights dimmed, the conversations between audience members began to decrease significantly. From a door in the rear of the room, Reverend Peter appeared. With a brisk pace he walked up to the raised stage-like platform in the front of the room. As he walked by me in his flowing white robe, I could clearly see that he wore heavy makeup. He wore black eye shadow, and powdered makeup covered his face down to the full, flowing black beard that had been meticulously trimmed. Once on the stage with the spotlights focused on him, he looked just like a classic picture of Jesus.

After thanking the audience for attending the presentation, particularly the physicians that he understood were in the audience, he explained that he would share some of his wisdom with us before he channeled TOBY. TOBY wanted to speak to the group. After TOBY had spoken, Reverend Peter would perform a healing for anyone who wanted to come forward to receive it.

The good reverend began walking up and down the center aisle as he explained that he was simply a channel for God's work. God wanted all of us to do his will and share in his bounty, Reverend Peter explained. As he stopped beside an elderly-looking man wearing a coat and tie, Reverend Peter stated that there were some in this room who knew of God's work through the reverend who were not fully sharing of their bounty to assist the reverend and his good works. Reverend Peter said he would not identify those individuals, but they knew who they were.

These words seemed to depress the elderly coat-and-tie gentleman as he nodded in agreement. He held his head down as if he were ashamed of something. My guess was that Reverend Peter was in the process of shaking this guy down.

Then Reverend Peter stated that someone in the room was worried about his or her spouse. He wanted to know who that person was. Where was that person in this room? A timid female voice spoke up. She said that she might be the one. Reverend said that she was in fact the person he was getting information about. He then advised the woman to pray with all her heart for God to listen to her pleas for help, and God would give her a clear sign within the week as to how to deal with the situation. Reverend Peter asked the woman if she understood the message. She quietly nodded her head yes.

Returning to the platform, Reverend Peter began a singsong kind of chanting while he swayed to his own music in such a way that his robe picked up the movement of his body in a most beautiful manner.

TOBY came through speaking in a much deeper voice than that just used by Reverend Peter. TOBY spoke about Jesus' love for all of us and the true meaning of his Sermon on the Mount. The true meaning of the Sermon on the Mount as expressed by TOBY fit the meaning I had learned in my Pittsburgh Sunday school class. When TOBY finished, he asked if there were any questions from the audience. A man sitting in the well-dressed middle-aged group asked what TOBY thought about spiritual healing. TOBY's answer was long and involved but seemed to be saying that all healing ultimately had a spiritual base. Then he asked if there were any more questions. After a long pause he started to say he was pleased that so many seekers were present when I stood up with my hand raised.

"TOBY, TOBY, I have a question."

Reverend Peter began coughing violently. He could not speak. He bent over with the force of the violent coughs rushing through his windpipes and out of his mouth. His face became beet red as if he were choking to death. Staff members rushed to him, but he held his hands out for them to not touch him.

Finally, he regained his composure. He seemed different. It was as if an iron force held his body perfectly rigid except for his head. He turned his head towards me and calmly said, "Please ask your question." The tonal quality of his voice had dramatically changed.

A little in shock over the dramatic coughing and equally dramatic recovery and this change in body control, I hesitatingly asked, "How does one acquire and then teach wisdom?"

"Wisdom can only be gained from life's experiences over time. Once acquired, it can be taught only by living it."

"Thank you."

With that TOBY seemed to leave Reverend Peter's body, as the Reverend began speaking in a normal voice. His aides rushed up to him and gave him a glass of water. He drank all of it. I thought that the answer TOBY provided in response to my question was a good one, particularly good given the fact that there was no time given to prepare an answer to the question.

Next came the healing part. Several people came forward to be healed. Reverend Peter started to pray for them. His prayer was spoken in an ever-increasing rapid speech pattern until you could not understand what he was saying. He was making sounds, but none of the sounds sounded like words to me.

Suddenly one of Reverend Peter's aides shouted out, "He's speaking in tongues. He's speaking in tongues. This is a special healing. He's speaking in tongues."

Well, the tongue-speaking went on for several more seconds, which seemed like a needlessly long time to me. Abruptly, he stopped speaking in tongues and spoke plain English to those hoping to be healed. Reverend Peter calmly told the gathered that they had been healed although some of them would not realize the full extent of the healing until several weeks had passed.

Abruptly, several of Reverend Peter's aides rushed up to him with a blood pressure cuff and pump.

"Everyone, come up close to Reverend Peter. Come on. Come up close so you can witness his stopping his heart. He will stop his heart from beating. It will come to a complete stop."

A crowd formed around Reverend Peter and his aides as the blood pressure cuff was placed around his upper arm. The crowd became packed close to Reverend Peter as this was happening. I stood on the periphery of it but close enough to see the blood pressure gauge as someone began pumping the air into the cuff and it momentarily squeezed Reverend Peter's arm. It was chaotic around Reverend Peter. A lot of people were talking and shouting above the confusion and voices of others so that they could be heard.

"There! Look, look! His heart has stopped! You can see it on the gauge," shouted one of the aides holding up the gauge by the hose connecting it to the inflated cuff. I strained to see it. From what I could see, there was nothing strange about it. It seemed to be reflecting a systolic and diastolic reading. I leaned into the crowd just a little bit to see if there was something I was missing. Abruptly, the aide began to quickly remove the blood pressure cuff as he dramatically stated, "That proves it. That proves Reverend Peter stopped his heart. What more do you need to believe?"

Well, I thought, *I need more than that.* I didn't think that chaotic mess demonstrated that Reverend Peter's heart had ever stopped. If it had stopped, it couldn't have been for more than a microsecond. This was a good stage show, but that was all it was. The coughing spell that took place after I asked my question was not a planned event. I didn't know what to make of it. These were some of the thoughts floating through my head as I moved to the back of the room.

Moving to the back, I overheard one aide say to another, "His performance was a little off the mark tonight."

"Yes, but that cough scared me," replied the second aide as they walked to the lighting equipment. His partner nodded in agreement.

I sat down in a chair on the back row. All of the surrounding seats had now been emptied. I just wanted to think about what I had witnessed when down the aisle walked Reverend Peter. He was alone. Up front the last of the attendees were exiting by a recently opened door. As the Reverend walked to the end of the aisle, he stopped beside the row I was sitting in. I was the row's only occupant. Reverend Peter turned his head and stared at me. He just stared at me. I looked back at him. The two of us remained motionless, staring at each other. Finally, I broke the spell. I nodded to him. He nodded back and walked out of the room.

When I reported the Reverend Peter story to our Monday night group of observers, it was met with laughter, thoughtful analysis of group manipulation strategies and a collective puzzlement over the coughing spell.

CHAPTER TWENTY-TWO

What If?

Our monthly gathering of newly graduated or about-to-graduate Ph.D. psychology students continued to meet every third Monday of the month into the late spring of 1974. Thus far our investigation into psychic claims or miraculous healings had found fraud and manipulation but nothing of fact to verify the existence of actual psychic phenomena. It was what we expected to find, but it was disappointing. One thing we all did agree upon: our activities were entertaining. We enjoyed doing the investigations, reporting our personal observations and hearing the reports of the others about theirs. In this respect, our time was not wasted.

We were running out of things to check out. It looked as if we would have to end the gatherings, or at least the gatherings for the purpose of investigating psychic phenomena before long.

One member of our group reported that he had heard of a woman, a Black woman, who read palms. She was reported to be very good at it. Since he knew where she worked in one of the region's major institutions, he could get her phone number and invite her to meet with the group. That sounded like a good idea.

It was agreed that she would be invited to meet with us in two weeks. That would be on a Monday evening at 7:00 at my house. He would call her and get the date arranged. Once she agreed, he would let me know, and I would call the others.

A day or two later our contact man called to say that he had reached the woman, Melba. She had agreed to come and give us a demonstration of her palm reading skills. I called the others. It was all set. The Sunday afternoon before the meeting, our contact person called to report that Melba could not attend the meeting the next night. She had unexpected meetings she needed to attend that evening. She was most apologetic, he said. She suggested that she meet with us a week from Monday. That was fine with my wife and me. I called the others. We all agreed to meet with Melba a week from Monday at 7:00 at our house.

We were gathered in the basement family room waiting for Melba to arrive that Monday evening. The meeting time, 7:00, arrived without Melba. By 7:15 we began to think that this was a bust. Melba was not coming. Our contact member said he would call her tomorrow and see if another meeting date could be arranged.

The phone upstairs rang. My wife, who was walking up the stairs, said she would get it. As our group continued to share the news of the weeks since we had last met, I could hear my wife's voice as she talked on the phone.

"I can get him for you. No, it's no trouble. OK, I can take a message if you want me to."

I walked up the stairs to see who it was.

"Oh, here he is. You can tell him," she said into the phone and then handed it to me mouthing the words, "It's Melba."

"Hello, this is Melba. I am so sorry to call like this. I was in a meeting, and it has just ended. I will have to reschedule your meeting. Oh, my, oh, I can't believe it. I'm getting such strong psychic impressions. I am getting such strong impressions. It's so strong."

"Yes," I'm thinking, *"I've got me a crazy on the line."*

I can hear Anna telling the others that Melba was in a meeting and won't be coming. She tells them that I am talking to her now.

"You are very interested in the ancient Mayan civilization and the ancient Egyptian civilization, aren't you?"

Well, I guess I was. I mean, I read everything that comes out about the two civilizations. I had a book teaching you how to read Mayan hieroglyphs that I sometimes looked at. Then again, I thought to myself, isn't everyone interested in these two civilizations? Another thought that rapidly crossed my mind was to be careful not to give Melba too much verbal or non-verbal information that she could use later in the conversation to prove her so-called psychic abilities.

"Yes," came my cryptic reply. I couldn't help but be a little impressed that she would know this about me.

"Well," she went on, "the reason you are so interested in them is that you set those two civilizations up. You were the one that led the groups that created these civilizations."

I have a wacko on the line was my immediate thought. *What a piece of science fiction this is.*

"You need to wear something purple for the next three days."

Wow, this woman is long gone. Why am I listening to her? It will be fun to tell the group about this conversation, I told myself.

"You have been thinking about a girl you dated in high school, a petite red head. You were the one who broke off the relationship. She has been on your mind for the last two weeks. You have been puzzled as to why she has entered your mind and stayed there after all of this time. You can't stop thinking about her."

That's absolutely true. The girl has been on my mind. I had been constantly thinking about her these past few weeks. It has disturbed me that she has stayed in my mind like this. Melba has just read my mind. What is going on? I am completely shaken. I have not mentioned to anyone that I have been thinking so much about this girl. How could Melba know this? My wife didn't even know that she was petite or had red hair. Only a few friends in Pittsburgh knew about her because the girl went to a different high school than mine. Only one close friend in Pittsburgh knew that I was the one who broke off the relationship. Melba has stunned me. There is no possible way she could have acquired this information about me from another person.

"The reason you broke off the relationship is that you knew that the two of you were not to be together for this lifetime. You two had been together in ancient Egypt. You were co-rulers of the kingdom during that time together. The reason you have been thinking about her for the last two weeks is that she needs your prayers. You are to pray for her and send her your blessings."

This is crazy. This Melba person is speaking crazy talk. I don't pray for people. A past ruler of Egypt, a co-ruler of Egypt? Give me a break! Hey, the woman knew I was thinking about the girl for the last two weeks or more when no one else knew it. I had not told a soul about thinking about the girl. She knew the girl was a petite redhead. She knew I was the one who broke it off. There's no way Melba could know these things, but she did. My world is being turned upside down.

"You have been thinking about putting yourself in therapy. You are displeased with your behavior patterns while under extreme stress. Don't do it. You will master the behavior patterns within the month because of the new insights about yourself you are now receiving."

My God, how could she know this? I hadn't even mentioned this to my wife. After trying to use behavior modification strategies on myself without success, I had concluded that I just might need to seek out a therapist. I had reached that decision just a day or two ago. This woman is walking around inside my mind. How can this be possible?

"You and your wife have been noticing and commenting on the fact that young children seem to follow you with their eyes or try to leave their parents to come to you when they see you in places like the grocery store. The reason for this is that the veil has not yet fallen over their eyes. At that young age they can still see through the three-dimensional blocks to the spirit world. They recognize you as their former teacher. They recognize you and love you."

Oh, Lord, what is happening to me? She is absolutely correct. My wife and I have been commenting on this strange happening.

Young infants and toddlers sitting in strollers or grocery carts had been looking at me with big smiles on their faces and tracking me with their eyes as I walk the aisle where they are. Some of the children would raise themselves from their seated positions to be able to better view me as I moved past the edge of their aisle. Some toddlers would even try to walk away from their caregivers to follow me. Often, the mothers would look at their children, gain eye contact with me and just shrug their shoulders. I would smile and shrug back. Naturally, I always smiled back at the children and would sometimes wave goodbye. I thought the children looked at me just because of the skills I had acquired to work with young children with emotional issues. I had learned how to read many of their non-verbal communications and to communicate back to them without the use of words. The explanation Melba was giving for this happening was just too much, but how did she know this was even happening? Only my wife and I were aware of it. We had never spoken of this phenomenon to anyone. I was badly shaken. My concept of reality was being confronted by another way of interpreting the world. I was dismayed.

Then Melba launched into talking about my career, going far into the future. She went into how I would not fully understand the impact I would have on others until long after I had left the field, if then. My work in education and my writings would be valued in many countries and particularly in Canada. She went on like this for at least fifteen minutes. What can you say about predictions made far into your future? There's not a way you can know until the predicted future comes if the predictions are correct. Even if they are, would you be able remember anything but the basic generalities of the predictions?

Towards the conclusion of Melba's monologue to me, she stated, "A young child will be presented to you this Friday. The child is being brought to you for the specific purpose of having you bless it. The child is six months old; no that's not right. Anyway, six is in its age somehow. It is extremely important for you to bless this child. You are to place your hand on the top of the child's head, over the soft spot that hasn't closed on top of its skull, and ask God to bless this child. Do you understand?"

"Yes."

Oh, no, I don't bless children. I don't ask God to bless children. I'll make a fool out of myself. Friday is a horrible day. Some of the spouses of the graduate students working for the educational cooperative bring in their young children during the working day to say hello to everyone. Friday is the day this is most likely to happen. What am I going to do if one of them brings in a young child? How will I know which of the young children that come in is the right one if more than one comes in? Will I try to bless all of them just to be safe? Blessing any of them will make me out to be a wacko! What am I to do?

"Now, I am serious about your wearing something with

purple in it for the next three days. It is important that you do this! Do you understand?"

"Well, I've been thinking about that. I don't have any purple articles of clothing." Until this point, I had purposely refrained from saying anything. I did not want to give Melba any verbal or non-verbal cues as to the accuracy of her statements.

"See if this makes any sense to you. I am standing in a small space looking through a partially opened doorway. I see half of a dresser bureau. I see half a drawer. It is a small drawer that can be seen on the visible half of the dresser. I am thinking Fruit of the Loom. Does that make sense to you?"

"Yes, my wife puts my boxer shorts in that drawer. I have a pair of boxer shorts with purple designs, like purple flower petals."

"Ok, you know what to do. I have to go now. Remember to wear purple for the next three days and to bless that child on Friday. Tell the others that I apologize for having to miss the meeting with them again. I'll get back in touch with you later. Goodbye."

"Goodbye."

I was in shock. There was no way that this woman could have known about my interest in the Mayan culture or the ancient Egyptian culture, the girl in Pittsburgh, the children staring at me or my decision to consider going into therapy to better manage my internal behavior in dealing with stress.

Then there's the whole issue concerning my purple underwear.

The fact that she accurately described the view of that dresser was the final demonstration that something beyond the three-dimensional world was being proven to me. When Melba said that she was "standing in a small space looking through a partially open doorway," she was accurately describing our bathroom doorway to the master bedroom. At that time, our house had one bathroom. You could enter it from the hallway or from our bedroom. Entering from the hallway, you were actually entered the vanity area and then progressed into the second area of the bathroom, the commode and bathtub/shower space. A little in front of the commode and to the left of the bathtub/shower was a short hallway leading to the master bedroom. A door opened from the bedroom into the bathroom. The door could not be fully opened as the floor weight scales blocked it. Looking through the partially open door, you could see the left corner of our bedroom. Sitting catty-corner in the far-left corner of the room was our dresser. Standing at the half-opened door separating the bedroom from the bathroom, you could see the right half of the dresser. The drawer area of the dresser was approximately four feet high with two sections of drawers. The top section consisted of two small drawers, side by side. Beneath those drawers was a large drawer running the length of the two small drawers above it. The right side of the dresser was all that you could see of the whole dresser while you stood looking through the half-open bathroom door. That view included the right half-drawer. We stored my boxer shorts in that drawer.

Melba had described that dresser as if she were standing in the bathroom/bedroom doorway, as if she were physically there.

"I am standing in a small space looking through a partially opened doorway. I see half of a dresser. I see half a drawer. It is a small drawer that can be seen on the visible half of the dresser. It is a drawer that is just half of the dresser, and I am thinking Fruit of the Loom. Does that make sense to you?"

Well, yes, it made perfect sense to me; and it scared the hell out of me! She was completely accurate in describing my bathroom, bedroom and the dresser. She was even accurate in identifying the maker of the boxer shorts.

When I walked down the stairs to report to the rest of the group, they could tell that I was in some kind of state of shock. I described the phone conversation in great detail to the group. Somehow, they did not seem as excited as I felt.

One of the members asked, "Do you think it was real? Do you think you encountered a real psychic?"

"Yes, there is no doubt about it. I don't know what to make of her explanations for the factual information she somehow acquired. I still can't deny that she simply knew things about me that she could not have known. I can't explain that."

The next morning I did put on those boxer shorts, the ones with the purple flower petals. Well, I wasn't going to take any chances. Yes, I felt foolish doing it. Until I could figure out what was going on, I wasn't taking any chances. There was a whole world that I knew nothing about. This was no longer a parlor game. This was real.

For the rest of the week, I was in emotional turmoil. I had trouble sleeping at night. What would I do if a six-month-old child or a young child with six in its age were somehow presented to me? Would I actually ask God to bless the child? Would I embarrass myself in front of my peers to do some voodoo-like behavior based on debunked superstition? Would I risk hurting an innocent child by not asking God to bless it when that child had been specifically brought to me to bless? I did pray for the girl from Pittsburgh. She was a very kind person. I wanted only happiness for her.

A member of the group bought me three pairs of purple socks. He delivered them with many humorous comments. After all of the laughter had subsided, we both agreed that it was better to be cautious and follow Melba's instructions while we tried to make sense out of her psychic reading.

I tried every way I could think of to rationally explain how Melba knew all of those details about me that no one else knew.

Since she had my phone number and address, she could have sneaked into our house late one night while my wife and the two kids and I were sleeping, I thought. *Yes, she crept into the house, went into our bedroom, opened the dresser drawers to discover where I kept my clean underwear and then walked into the bathroom to get a good view from my bathroom door of my underwear drawer.*

Yes, that would explain her knowledge in a clear, three-dimensional worldview. That explanation was more science fiction than her explanations. I needed to do much more serious reading on psychic phenomena, including the Edgar Cayce materials. Of course, bookstores had all kinds of books on psychic phenomena. I would begin reading to find real answers. This was important.

Friday arrived, and I was worried. Noon came and went with no young children showing up. I was feeling better. I just might not have to embarrass myself by blessing a little child in a public setting. Then it was four o'clock. I was free. We locked up the offices. No one had brought a young child to the office. Melba had been wrong about at least one thing. Hope remained for a normal three-dimensional world, for at least some sense of order in what I had always known to be real.

As I left the office to continue the Friday evening routine my wife and I had established, I went to the nearby shopping mall to buy the week's groceries in the large chain supermarket there. I had the grocery list that my wife and I had prepared. The store was always packed with shoppers at that time of day on Fridays. It was a good day and a good time to shop for many families.

The exit doors of the store were the same doors used to enter the supermarket. With the numerous checkout counters feeding into those exit/entrance doors, during the peak shopping hours entering and leaving the store was hectic. Since I'd been shopping at that store every late Friday afternoon for almost three years, I knew how to manage it.

Just as I entered the store, an elementary school principal that I knew saw me. I (as well as some of the graduate students interning at the cooperative) had been having some major disagreements with him concerning changes his school had to make to accommodate the needs of several disabled students. In front of him he had two grocery carts full of food that he had just bought.

"Jerry," he called out, motioning me to come to him, "I didn't know you shopped here. How long have you been shopping here?"

"About three years now. Although, this is the first time I have seen you here."

"How great it is to see you. Now tell me about your family."

He kept me there talking to me as if we were long-lost brothers. The time just dragged on as people from his checkout line finished their purchases and pushed their full carts past us into the parking lot. The bag boys stared at us from time to time. I made several attempts to leave, but the principal would grab me by the shoulders and hold me as he continued to talk. I didn't want to be rude, but I had shopping to do. I needed to get on with it. Still, he kept me there. I don't know exactly how long we stood there talking, but it had to be at least a good thirty minutes when suddenly he moved his hand over my shoulder and grabbed a woman by the arm. I turned to see what was going on. A youngish-looking woman was pushing a grocery cart with a little girl in the child's seat, and an older woman was walking beside the cart.

"Oh, let me introduce these ladies to you,"

Pointing to the older woman, he said, "This is Mrs. ... .'

I lost the name as I realized that this little girl with the pretty blond curls might be the child that I was to bless.

"She was in the first elementary class I ever taught."

Placing his hand on the shoulder of the woman pushing the cart with the little girl in it, he said, "And this is her daughter, who was in the first school where I was a principal; and this little girl is her daughter."

Nodding to the women with a warm smile while bending over to the little girl with my hand moving to her forehead as if to brush some of the curls from her eyes, I asked, "How old is she?"

The mother proudly replied, "Sixteen months."

Lightly brushing the curls on her forehead, my hand moved to the top of the child's head as I spoke to myself, "God bless you, little child."

After a few more brief exchanges, the women moved on, and the principal and I said goodbye. When I got home that evening and related the encounter with the child to my wife, it surely seemed to us that I had been kept at the front of that grocery store for the specific purpose of meeting that child. It seemed that she had been presented to me for a blessing. I did ask God to bless her. I did it because I was afraid not to do it. Clearly, I had entered a new world, a world where things happened outside the commonly accepted beliefs about what constitutes reality. There was no going back. I would never be able to deny what Melba had so dramatically demonstrated to me. I did not understand what this new reality was, but I could not deny its existence.

CHAPTER TWENTY-THREE

Pat Sisson

My internal life was in complete chaos. To my astonishment, the Friday late afternoon confirmation of Melba's Monday prediction that a young child would be brought to me to bless on Friday had come true. Added to that was Melba's inexplicable accuracy about past and current events in my life and my inner thoughts about them. It was too much. My concept of reality did not account for Melba's explanation of my life's events, her statements about past lives or her suggestions to pray for and to prepare for future events.

Since I could not empirically explain how Melba knew the facts about my life, my house, and the future, I had to consider seriously her mysterious knowledge of these things. To do that meant risking being considered a wacko. The people I valued could consider me to have become dissociated from reality if I started to suggest I actually believed that she had acquired this knowledge psychically.

I could not, I would not, deny what had taken place. I had to be true to what I thought was the truth, no matter the consequences. There was more to the reality of our existence, my existence, than I had ever imagined. I did not know what else was out there, in what other dimensions we humans functioned; but they were there. I had to find the truth. Simply denying what Melba had so dramatically demonstrated to me would not bring me to the truth. There was no choice. I had to investigate the world of psychic phenomena with intensity.

Naturally, I re-contacted Melba. I knew that she worked at a major institution in the Knoxville area, but I didn't know what role she played in that organization. I learned she had a doctorate degree and was the assistant director of a multi-million-dollar project. Her employers did not know of her psychic endeavors. If they did, they would probably sever her relationship with them. I thought it was a big risk for Melba to reveal her psychic gifts.

In the several times I met with Melba after that first telephone conversation, I could not discern that she was ever as dramatically accurate again in her predictions as they related to me. In some cases, her answers to my questions about immediate concerns of mine simply did not make sense. Our informal study group met with Melba on several occasions for lunch. The other members had the same reaction to her during those discussions as I did. She seemed to speak in generalities concerning questions asked of her. It wasn't that she was not accurate; rather it was like talking to an old friend asking for advice. The friend would reassure you that you were doing okay and end up confirming what you had already decided to do about a specific situation. We all agreed that she was more accurate than wrong in her statements about situational outcomes. It was just the fact that she could have come up with the same information from studying the facts of the situations and reaching a logical "good guess."

Anna and I became members of the Association for Research and Enlightenment, the Edgar Cayce Foundation. I began sending off for copies of the original transcripts of the Edgar Cayce readings and devouring them. Trips to the local bookstores found me buying lots of paperback books on psychic encounters.

Then I remembered Vivian. She was the bedridden psychic who liked to sip Southern Comfort. Vivian had given me a reading about two years ago that had seemed so fantastically impossible that I had dismissed her from my mind. At the time of the reading, I had a number of academic hurdles to accomplish that would take several years to complete. Vivian had said that by a year from her reading I would have completed all of them and be employed in my specialty area without moving from our house. That set of predictions had no chance of ever happening. My conclusion was that Vivian was a sweet, elderly lady providing some fantastical feel-good stories to people, telling them things they liked to hear as a form of entertainment. Well, all of her predictions for that year had come true. My dismissal of that reading was so complete that it wasn't until the overwhelming impact of Melba's first reading for me had set in that I remembered Vivian's reading.

I revisited Vivian several times after my dramatic encounter with Melba. Those visits with Vivian were pleasant but not dramatically life changing. They were like my lunch meetings with Melba. I received reassuring advice concerning the stressing issues of the moment but nothing more dramatic than those a good friend would give in support of me as a person. It was true that neither Melba nor Vivian had the detailed information about my life situations that my close friends had. Both women had minimal background information about me. It was unusual that these two psychics could focus on my issues and provide supportive statements that fit the situations. I grew to consider both these unusual women to be friends.

Melba moved away from the region a year or two after her telephone reading for me. I lost contact with her, as did many others who valued her as a kind and caring person who happened to have a gift. Vivian died about ten years after my first meeting with her. She was a wonderful character in the community. It seemed that anyone who was seeking to know more about psychic phenomena knew of Vivian. To my surprise, a large number of well-educated people in the area were seriously exploring psychic issues. They did so discreetly as the mainstream culture of the region was quite hostile to the concept of psychic phenomena. City ordinances made it illegal to give psychic readings.

Gradually, I became a member of the area's underground community committed to exploring the reality of psychic phenomena. There were individuals among this group who clearly had psychological problems, family problems and interpersonal relationship issues they sought to solve through a psychic's advice. They would have been better off seeing a licensed professional than a psychic. However, a number of people whose lives seemed to have only ordinary difficulties, so-called "normal" people, appeared to be exploring psychic phenomena for their own development. I use the term "normal people" with a bit of humor as I have found it difficult to define what a normal person is, let alone find one who fits any definition of normal.

One of my fellow psychic searchers whom I had met at the Unitarian church, of all places, told me about a woman who would be giving a presentation about her psychic abilities at the local university's student center before long. I was surprised that the university would allow such an event. My informant said that it was part of an evening series of presentations on a wide range of topics sponsored through some extra-curricular lecture series. The students themselves coordinated it, she thought. I decided to go.

The lecture room was packed with people. Tables and chairs had been moved to the four sides of the large room. Young people filled the seats, sat on the tables and sat on the floor. Scattered among the college students were older adults and gray-haired ones. It was clear that I should have arrived earlier if I were to sit in a chair or on a table. As it was, I found a spot on the floor directly in front of a table full of college students seated on it. This suited me just fine, as I was a little self-conscious about being there. I just wanted to blend in, hoping to be unnoticed.

As we all awaited the appointed time for the psychic to make her presentation, the room was full of friendly conversations all going on at once among the attendees. In the crowd was an air of excited anticipation. I kept looking for the psychic. I thought she would probably be dressed as a gypsy or some other culturally different garb.

Finally, two middle-aged women walked into the center of the room. They could have been clerical staff at the center, or they could have played some role in the organizing of the event. Their dress and general appearance were in no way unusual. One of the ladies held up her hand for the crowd to quiet down. They responded. She said how happy she was to see such a large turnout for one of their program's non-credit lecture series. Then she gave the titles and dates of future lectures that would be presented in coming weeks.

"With no further ado, I'd like to introduce Pat Sisson, a psychic," she said raising her hand in acknowledgement to the woman standing beside her. "Pat has begun a path of psychic discovery which has resulted in the development of unusual abilities that some refer to as psychic abilities. Pat, please share with all of us your experiences."

Polite applause greeted Mrs. Sisson as she turned to the hostess, "Thank you for the opportunity to speak to this group tonight."

Then Mrs. Sisson began telling her story of discovery. She started by explaining that it all began when she picked up a Ouija board by chance that was lying around the house. To her surprise, it started to spell out answers to questions she had formulated in her mind. The answers made sense. Some of those answers were given to questions about events to happen in the future for her and her family. To her surprise, the answers proved to be correct. This captured her attention, and she continued to experiment with the Ouija board.

She had always been a practicing Christian, she explained. She was raised outside Paris, Kentucky, in the Christian Church. The Christian Church (also called the Disciples of Christ) was the church that Edgar Cayce belonged to, Mrs. Sisson noted. She stated she didn't want to be involved with anything that would conflict with the beliefs of the church but felt that the answers she was receiving through the Ouija board were compatible with those basic teachings. Since Edgar Cayce was a psychic who spent most of his life-giving psychic readings to people and was a member of the Christian Church, she felt even more comfortable about it. Pat related that she felt that as long as Christ was acknowledged as the source of all information, the way one got the information was not important. It was the information for those receiving it that was important. That was the way she thought Edgar Cayce dealt with the phenomena he had experienced and that was the way she was dealing with it.

Before long she started to hear a voice speaking to her when she approached the Ouija board. She was initially frightened by the experience, considering the possibility that she was becoming mentally ill. The voice assured her that such was not the case. She began asking the voice questions like those she would ask the Ouija board. The answers proved helpful and supportive of her Christian heritage, she noted. As this process rapidly progressed, the voice told her that he was Flemon of the Blue Green Ray. When her work in the hotel industry presented her with challenges, she began asking the voice, Flemon, for answers to her problems. The answers were helpful. Future predictions provided by Flemon about her issues of frustration proved to be remarkably accurate.

As this process progressed, she reported that she began to be able to read other people's thoughts. She didn't want to "walk in other people's spaces," so she would only allow herself to get inside other people's "mind talk" when they gave her permission to do so. Remarkably, she found people coming to her and asking for advice. The answers to their questions would suddenly come to her mind. She would provide the answers that came to her. Often those answers included other related information that demonstrated the relevancy of the answer or put the answer into a greater context of the individual's life. This information would astonish the questioner, as there was no possible way for Pat to have known that information.

Pat Sisson's presentation lasted about an hour. She provided the audience with many detailed examples of her giving someone information about themselves that no one could have known without an intimate knowledge of that person. She also gave examples of the amazing accuracy of the predictions she often made to individuals about their lives. She said that she was unsure where all of this was going but she had learned to trust her guide. She was still in the learning process as she tried to understand and live with her developing abilities. Then she said that she would demonstrate what she meant when she said that she could pick up information about people if they allowed her to do so. She seemed to be looking all around the room at people trying to decide from whom to pick up psychic vibrations when suddenly she pointed at me.

"You have been stressed out about your business accounting course. You have a major exam coming up later this week. It is critical to you that you do well. You are particularly concerned about (I didn't understand the terminology she used as it was not my field of study). You do not need to worry. You will do well on the exam. You will be very pleased with the results. Does that make sense to you?"

I was in total chaos. I did not want to be singled out before this group. I was not a student taking accounting courses. None of this made sense to me.

"No ma'am. It makes no sense to me at all. I am not even a student here."

"Oh," said the startled Pat.

There was a long moment of silence in the room.

A voice directly above me broke the silence. It was a guy sitting on the table directly behind and above me. "I can help here. It fits me to a tee. I am a business major here and I do have an accounting examination on Friday. I am concerned about doing well on it because I don't feel I fully understand the (he used the same term the psychic used)."

"As I said, you will do well on it."

Then she turned and addressed someone else in the same manner. I could not follow what was said because of my emotional turmoil. I did not want to be a focus of the group's attention. It was embarrassing to me. It deeply upset me that this woman made statements about me that were totally untrue but were true for the person directly behind and above me because she seemed to have derived the information psychically. I was simply too busy with my thoughts to follow any more of Pat Sisson's demonstrations.

As the session came to a close, Mrs. Sisson said that anyone who wanted to talk with her in greater detail about her psychic experiences could call her. She would be glad to meet with anyone interested in the topic. I wrote down her phone number. I wanted to talk with her. Something real was taking place with this woman and I wanted to know more about it. Perhaps she would be willing to meet with our informal psychic investigators group.

I did call Pat and made an appointment to meet her at the hotel where she worked one evening the following week. That week she was serving as the night manager. Her infant daughter and husband would be in a room adjacent to the room we would meet in if that wouldn't bother me, she said. The meeting was set.

Half expecting to get some kind of reading from Mrs. Sisson, I went into the meeting with some trepidation. What if she said that something bad was going to happen to me or at my work or for someone I valued? Would I believe it? Would I take unusual precautions? Would I start becoming a fanatic follower? I just didn't know what to expect.

The meeting with Pat ended up being nothing like what I had anticipated. Almost all of our meeting time was consumed with Pat's relating in great detail her fears and self-doubt concerning the development of her psychic abilities. Just about the time she started to feel comfortable with some ability, some other highly unusual psychic phenomena would start to happen to her which produced new challenges to her belief system.

I found myself reassuring her that her fears and doubts were totally understandable. I shared my encounters with Melba, the professional with a doctorate, and Vivian, the Southern Comfort sipper. I knew that there was something going on that none of us could explain and encouraged Pat to continue her development in this area.

It was important work. Just because we could not fully understand the phenomena was no reason to deny the truth of their reality. Our problem was not the phenomena, but how to explain them and our fear of the unknown. Once a phenomenon was independently verified, we knew it to be real. We just didn't know why it existed or was being manifested as it was. The meeting ended with Pat enthusiastically agreeing to meet with our investigative group. The time and date were set. We would meet at Pat's house, as she would have to be with her infant during the time we met.

As it turned out, most of the members of our investigative group who could meet with her for the scheduled meeting had completed their doctoral programs. Our group ended up sitting on the floor facing Pat as she explained how she read palms. Each one of us had our palms read. She did hit on some interesting facts that all of us knew about each other but there was nothing in her statements that was overly astonishing. It was curious that she could tell us things we knew about ourselves that she could not have known.

One member of our group had been practicing as a school psychologist and held a senior-level administrative position in a nearby school system. He kept asking Pat where she had gone to college. She was a little evasive in answering the question. My friend kept pressing her. I was puzzled as to why he was doing this. It was clear that she really didn't want to answer the question. He continued to press for an answer. Finally, Pat said that she had gone to Transylvania College in Lexington, Kentucky. Her answer didn't satisfy him as he asked what year she had graduated. She said that she had had to withdraw from the college due to a financial hardship at the time and then went on to say that she felt humbled to be in the presence of so many PhDs.

My friend promptly responded, "Look at who is sitting at your feet trying to learn from you. We are humbled to be in your presence."

Well, that about summed it up. We had found someone with a gift we did not understand, but we could not deny the results of the gift.

After meeting with our group a few more times, Pat suggested that she could channel Flemon, her guide, at our next meeting. That made me uneasy all over again. I had just gotten comfortable accepting that some people clearly have what is commonly called psychic abilities. I could accept that, although I didn't announce it to the general world. I still didn't feel comfortable imagining having everyone who knew me discuss what I was exploring and having them question my emotional stability. Now, I was actually going to attend a séance. It seemed to me that normal people could not seriously entertain the idea that a séance could produce something worthy of belief. Such events could only be fraud or the product of someone's imagination. However, I was not going to let my prejudices interfere with my exploration for the truth. I was going to attend the channeling session.

Pat began the session by sitting cross-legged on the floor in the basement family room of her house. She said a prayer asking for God's guidance and then was quiet for a few seconds. Her two arms started to move as she held a finger to her thumb in each hand and began to move her arms in a synchronized pattern.

"I, Flemon of the Seventh Blue Green Ray, salute you," began the session. Flemon then went on to explain that he was using Pat's body to speak to us. She would not remember what he said through her. He thanked her for her willingness to be his channel. Rather than providing us with a lot of specific predictions about the future, he spoke in a more philosophical nature about spirit, psychic phenomena, and its role in demonstrating that we are more than three-dimensional beings. Much of what he said was compatible with the Edgar Cayce material I had read.

At the end of his self-called "soap box presentation," he said that he would take questions from anyone as long as they were not of a personal nature. Personal questions would be addressed through an individual reading Pat would give to those who wanted one. The Flemon sessions became a monthly evening event. Word spread that Pat was channeling Flemon every second Thursday night of each month. Sometimes as many as thirty or forty people would show up for a Flemon session. The Flemon sessions have continued up to the present time. Most of those sessions were recorded.

I was a persistent questioner at the end of those sessions. If Flemon were real, I wasn't about to miss a chance of learning from him. If Flemon were an extension of Pat's sub-conscious or some other connection with her psychic abilities, I still wanted to hear what was said. The questioning session at the end of Flemon's discourse eventually evolved into his asking me if I had a question. I always did. The question would be of a philosophical nature relating to his comments during that session. After responding to my question, he would provide the group with a blessing and Pat would be herself once again.

The only time I can remember that Flemon addressed a

specific personal issue for someone in one of the channeling sessions occurred around the early 1980's. He had said that he had gotten "off of his soap box" and addressed a question or two about some developing world situation and was clearly at the closing point of the session when he addressed me directly.

"Jerry, your colleague who is in the hospital is in an emergency medical crisis right now. You are not to worry about this crisis. At noon tomorrow the crisis will resolve itself. She will be fine and released from the hospital without any lingering problems." With that pronouncement, Flemon ended the session.

I was stunned. I knew exactly whom he was talking about. She was an original member of our psychic investigative group and was currently working with me as a school psychologist with the educational cooperative. She had told me that she was going to take that Thursday off to have some routine elective surgery. She would be back to work shortly after the surgery as it was such a routine process. There was no need to try to see her at the hospital or make a big deal about her surgery. It was all very routine. I had accepted her explanation and was not concerned. Actually, until Flemon's comment, I had forgotten about it.

It was already too late that evening to call the hospital to confirm what Flemon had said. I determined that I would call my colleague's close friend, Sylvia, first thing in the morning to confirm Flemon's statement. If what he said was true and I could be of any assistance, I planned to take off from work to be at the hospital.

Around 8:30 the next morning I reached Sylvia by phone and asked her how our friend was doing. The news was devastating and puzzling. Sylvia said that the initial surgery had gone well. The surgeon had opened her abdomen and completed the surgery without the slightest difficulty. That was in the morning. Early in the afternoon she began losing a lot of blood. She needed several blood transfusions. They didn't know where the source of the bleeding was. Her loss of blood was massive. It seemed that the transfusions just went through her system almost as fast as they entered it. They decided to open her up again even though the surgery was considered risky because of her weakened condition. A large quantity of blood had collected in her abdominal cavity, but they could not find the source of the bleeding. In the hope that the blood loss was the result of multiple seepages around all of the stitches, they decided to re-stitch everything.

Late in the afternoon of the surgery she was still losing blood and receiving transfusions. The re-stitching had not stemmed the blood loss. At that point, Sylvia said, they were afraid to re-operate, given her weakened condition. She might die on the operating table. As of that morning, Friday morning, she continued to need blood transfusions because of the continued loss of blood. If the blood loss did not stop by noon, they were going to open her up again despite her weakened condition as her life was on the line.

I was stunned. First of all, I was deeply concerned for my friend. This was so unexpected. I was also astounded that Flemon would know about the situation. How could this be possible? Since he was right about the medical emergency, I hoped that he was also correct about her sudden recovery at noon. After Sylvia told me that there was nothing I could do to help the situation except to pray, I agreed not to go to the hospital. I told Sylvia that I would call her shortly after noon to get an update on our friend's condition.

It was about 12:20 p.m. when I reached Sylvia by phone.

"It's the most amazing thing. They had decided to operate on her at 1:00 p.m. even though she could die as a result. They made that decision about 11:00 this morning. They had no choice. When they checked her right at noon, right at 12:00, all the bleeding had stopped. They are not going to operate. They think she may be able to fully recover. No one can explain what happened. It's like a miracle happened."

I was astounded. The entire event had unfolded as Flemon had stated it would.

When Pat gave someone a reading, it lasted for about half an hour. She would have the person requesting the reading shuffle a deck of Tarot Cards and then make six stacks with them. Each stack represented a month, thus providing the seeker with a six-month reading into the future. The reading was recorded on a cassette tape recorder, and the recipient of the reading would be given the tape. During informal talks at Flemon sessions some of the respondents reported remarkable statements from Pat about concerns in their lives and hopeful predictions about how those issues would be resolved. Over time, many recipients of Pat's readings reported that her predictions had been accurate.

In my continued readings about Edgar Cayce, I was surprised to discover that he charged for his readings. Before he became heavily involved in providing people with readings, he was a professional photographer. It was explained that as requests for his readings continued to grow, he had to cut back on spending time working as a photographer. He had a family to support, which forced him to charge a fee for the time he spent giving readings. Eventually, he discontinued his photographic career to spend his working hours meeting the ever-increasing requests for psychic readings. I doubt that he ever turned down a request for a reading simply because someone could not afford to pay the fee. I shared this information with Pat and urged her to start charging for her readings. At that time, the readings were taking up a lot of her family time. She agreed and eventually provided readings and other related activities on a full-time basis.

Often, people who had received readings from Pat attended the Flemon sessions. Before the session would start and after it had finished, they would share some of the remarkable predictions that Pat had made for them that had come true. Among those accurate predictions were the following: a woman would become pregnant after having had extensive and unsuccessful assistance medically in that regard; a woman was told she would find the man she would marry shortly, and they would be happily married for two years (the man died after they had been married for two years) and a person was told she was about to change jobs unexpectedly and the new position would be highly lucrative. The list of her accurate predictions over the years is quite extensive.

Pat's readings for me over the years have been accurate on many fronts; however, not all of her predictions seemed to come true for me. Some of her predictions did not take place within the time span that she had stated. Other predictions were misinterpreted at the time they were given. Not until time had passed and I reviewed the audiotape of her reading did I see a connection between what she had said and what had actually happened. Some predictions just have not come true as far as I can tell. All of that acknowledged, there is no denying that Pat's readings have a consistent record of being remarkably accurate when there is no logical, straight-line scientific explanation for that accuracy.

In addition to providing readings, Pat began receiving requests for such psychic activities as contacting loved ones who had died, conducting past life readings, and finding lost objects as well as a host of other related activities. I think that some of the activities were an exploratory effort on Pat's part to learn more about the many areas of psychic phenomena. She was as much a student of psychic issues and discoveries as any other seriously interested party would be.

The results of one interesting attempt of a son to contact his recently departed father was verified as being unexplainable in strict scientific terms. In this case, the son was a member of our informal psychic investigative group. At the time of this event, I had considered the individual to retain a reasonable degree of skepticism concerning psychic phenomena. He was highly valued and effective as a psychologist. We all trusted his judgment and his truthfulness. When he went to Pat for her attempt to contact his deceased father, another member of our informal study group went with him. Both individuals have confirmed what happened then.

After going into a meditative state, Pat began speaking in Yiddish to the man requesting her to attempt to make contact with his father. The father was Jewish as was his son. The son knew what the father was saying. The son's friend did not understand a word of what was said. Therefore, the son requested that his father speak in English. In response to the request, Pat, speaking as the father, spoke his words in English although the father continued to use the Yiddish nickname that he had called his son when he was alive. The son asked his father several questions, which were answered.

After this channeling of the son's father, the son reported that no one knew that his father used the Yiddish nickname he called his son except the son. The father used the nickname only when the two of them were alone talking to each other. The son also reported that when the father spoke in both Yiddish and English, he related information to the son that only the father could have known.

For example, Pat, speaking as the father, told the son that his father was very disappointed that after the father's death, the father's best friend had lied about some joint business dealings they had together. His friend had lied and been very deceitful. In relating this information, Pat named the father's friend. She used the nickname the father had always used in identifying the business partner and friend. Later, the son related that only he, his brother and his mother knew of the deceitfulness and lies of the father's friend. They had never discussed that situation with others.

Pat confirmed that she did not know the Yiddish language. There is no logical explanation for her being able to speak fluent Yiddish during that session. Nor was there a way that Pat could have known about the son's nickname, the deceitful behavior of the father's friend, the friend's nickname, or the other factual information she related while in communication with his deceased father. The son concluded that he had actually communicated with his father.

Pat's ability to assist someone in finding lost items has been a source of amazement to many. Two quick stories that I can confirm as happening relate to my personal requests for assistance. Our children's hamster had escaped its cage. This was very upsetting to the two children. After searching the house for several days without success, we decided to call Pat and ask her if she was picking up on anything relating to the pet. We feared it had gotten outside or died in the house. She said that it was still in the house, and we would find it. She said that several months would pass before the hamster was found, but it would be in excellent health. Her prediction was both encouraging and disappointing.

As a few months passed, we forgot the missing hamster. One day my wife opened the drawer immediately under the oven in the stove. We stored nothing in that drawer except the stove's broiler pan, which we did not use. There was the hamster nest with the hamster inside. The creature had gathered dried kernels of corn from the ears of Indian corn we had sitting in a shallow decorative bowl on the floor in the living room. I had noticed recently that kernels of corn were missing from the cob at an increasing rate but assumed that the children had had something to do with that process. We concluded that the hamster had gotten its water from the defrost drip pan underneath the refrigerator. Pat was right.

Another time, we had lost a book from the university library. It was an older edition that had some relevant information for a major project my wife was working on. If we didn't find the book, we would have to pay the library for it. That would be expensive. My wife had taken it with us to study on our way down to Atlanta for a visit with our daughter and her young family. When we returned home, we realized that we could not find the book. After a thorough search of the car, our house and our daughter's house, we had not located it and feared the small-sized book had fallen unnoticed from the car at one of our rest stops.

After our fruitless searches, we called Pat. Pat said that we would find the book. She saw it on a bookshelf by a door. We looked at all of the bookshelves we had, including storage bookshelves in the garage and around all of our doors. When we didn't find it, we looked again and again. We just could not find it. The conclusion was that this was clearly one time when Pat was wrong. We decided to go online to a rare bookstore and purchase it. When the book became due, we would just inform the university library of the loss and give them the newly bought book. In the meantime, my wife had the book for her studies.

Several months later, our daughter called from Atlanta. She had found the book. Apparently, we had left the book in our youngest granddaughter's room. The book had been placed on the bookshelf located in her room. The entrance door to the room opens into the inside of the room. The bookshelf remained hidden until the door was closed. As a result, it was not constantly in view. We had not thought to look behind that door.

As the years passed, our investigative group dispersed across the country as careers continued to develop. We were not trying to convince the world that Pat was accurate; that she knew things that no "normal" person could know. She constantly demonstrated that psychic phenomena were real. Many of the people who came to the monthly Flemon sessions had received readings or other assistance from Pat and reported on her accuracy. The explanations for psychic occurrences were dependent upon a person's personal belief system.

We also knew that many con artists were taking advantage of others with their claims, predictions, and charges for their services. You could not accept someone as being "psychic" just because they said they were. Another important point we realized was that we had not found a psychic who was one hundred per cent accurate all of the time. You could not give up your sound decision-making abilities just because a psychic who was sometimes accurate was telling you to do something that you just didn't feel was right for you.

One of the patterns of Pat's gift that I have learned over the years is that she often gets correct information to pass on to those seeking it but not all of the information that one might need for a quick understanding of a prediction or location of something. I don't know why that is the case. Like everyone else, I am just trying to understand the phenomena.

Pat has become a life-long friend. Over the years I have come to the realization that she is seeking understanding of her gifts while she is confronted with the normal problems that we all encounter as human beings raising families, making a living, and finding joy in life. As our parallel search for a greater understanding of psychic phenomena has evolved, my understanding of spiritual values has grown as well. Along with that growth has come a series of hard-to-understand events.

CHAPTER TWENTY-FOUR

Aunt Bess

Pat Sisson was having her regular Flemon channeling session for the month. She had expressed a degree of concern about this event. Some of her elderly relatives were coming down from Kentucky to attend the session. One of her aunts was reported to be hostile to the entire concept of psychic phenomena, and Pat was not sure what some of the others thought. She hoped that the Flemon session would not be disturbing to any of them.

Early in the day I had gotten out of sorts with someone I highly valued. We had seriously disagreed about an issue. It really upset me. At this point in time, I have no idea what the disagreement was about. I just remember that when we arrived at Pat's I was not in a pleasant mood. My dis-ease remained with me through Pat's channeling of Flemon. With Pat's Kentucky relatives there, Pat's house was unusually crowded with attendees. My wife and I wanted to leave as soon as Flemon had finished his message for the group.

Once Pat had risen from the seated position on the floor that she always took while channeling Flemon, several people approached her. Wanting to ask her questions, they formed an almost impenetrable circle around her. I joined the back of the encircling group, waiting for a chance to say my good-byes and apologize for leaving the gathering so early. I was hoping to get close enough to catch her eye, speak to her and then leave.

As I stood there, I saw a small but distinct purple light above an elderly woman's hand. It startled me. She was seated on a couch situated to my right and slightly behind me. The purple light was a small, tight circle between her little finger and her ring finger. The purple light seemed to hover just above the spot were the two fingers met. She had that hand, her left hand, resting on the arm of a couch that she had sat in through the Flemon session. The end of the couch where she sat was fairly close to where I was standing. It might have been six feet or so from my position.

Changing my focus from seeing the light in my peripheral vision to looking directly at it, I expected the purple light to disappear. That's what always happened when I tried to see my own aura in the bathroom mirror. However, the light was still there. It was as steady and bright as I had seen it in the margins of my sight. I leaned backward and then forward. I leaned to both sides while looking at the purple light to see if it might be some sort of optical illusion. It was not. The small circle of purple light stayed centered above the meeting place of her two fingers. The angle of looking at it had no effect on the fact that it was there. Then I tried looking away from her hand altogether and then looking back. The light was still there. It remained there. It was not going away. I was alarmed. I was frightened. I did not know what to do.

Well, the Edgar Cayce material had many references to the meaning of colors. However, like so much of the other Cayce material I had read, it was interesting but had no relevant meaning to me in my daily life. As a result, I did not remember what the colors meant. If this purple circle of light above the woman's hand meant something, I didn't have a clue as to what it was. Maybe it meant that something needed to be done about that spot. If that were the case, what would it be?

The crowd around Pat had thinned. It gave me the opportunity to get close enough to speak in a soft voice to her. "Pat, that lady sitting at the end of the coach, see her left hand resting on the end? I see a purple light just above her last two fingers."

"She's my Aunt Bess. What do you think it means?"

"I don't know. Maybe it means that she needs to massage it between those two fingers, right at the spot where they join. I think you need to tell her that."

"No, you need to go to her and tell her."

"Yeah. I was afraid you'd say that. OK."

Oh, I dread this. This woman's going to think I'm a fool, seeing lights around her and telling her to massage her fingers. What if she's the aunt that's hostile to psychic stuff? Oh, I don't want to do this, but it is true that I see the purple circle of light. I see it even now. I can't deny the truth of what I see, no matter how I wish I didn't see it. I have to do this.

As I approached the couch, Aunt Bess looked up at me with an expectant smile. I knelt down beside the end of the couch so that we were at eye level, "Ma'am, forgive me for approaching you. I know you're going to think I'm crazy, but I keep seeing a purple circle of light between your little finger and your ring finger."

"No. No, I don't think you're crazy," she said with a beaming smile.

"What do you think it means?"

"Well, it gets weirder. I think it means you need to massage that connection, right there where the webbing is between the two fingers. I think you need to rub that area for a while."

"Please show me how to do it. Please do it for me."

With a sigh, I said, "OK, but I don't know what I'm doing."

"That's all right."

Oh, what a fool I am. Here I am seeing a purple light, rubbing this elderly lady's hand. I have just gone off the deep end. How do I get myself into these things?

Holding her left hand in my left hand, I began gently moving my index finger in the web of skin between the two fingers.

Immediately, the lady said, "That feels so good. It really does. You have no idea what is happening to my hand and arm. This is so wonderful."

Afraid that someone would stare at us, I stopped the rubbing of her hand.

"Oh, please don't stop. This is just so wonderful."

Her comments astonish me. I guess she is just trying to make me feel like less of a fool than I really am.

I resumed massaging her hand, and she continued to say that it was very pleasant and helpful as I continued not to know what I was doing.

After a few more minutes of continuing the massaging, I said, "I think I've done all I can do now. You can continue to massage it for a while. You might do that at home some, too, if you find it helpful."

"Thank you. This is wonderful. You don't realize what you have done for me."

What a gracious and kind lady, I thought, as I said good-bye and waved to Pat in parting.

Driving home my wife wanted to know why I was rubbing that lady's hand. I told her the entire story. We were both amazed and puzzled. My wife was reassuring. She said she didn't think I was crazy.

Two months later I finally got a chance to ask Pat if she ever got any feedback about Aunt Bess and what Aunt Bess thought about that purple light and all.

"Oh, that's right. You don't know. How could you know? When you did all that, the feeling returned to her arm and hand. She had lost the sense of feeling in her entire arm and hand years ago. She has been to all kinds of specialists. They could never fully explain why she lost the sense of feeling in her arm and everything they tried to do to bring it back failed. Now it's back. It's one hundred percent back. It came back when you massaged her hand."

Clearly, I did not know why I saw the purple circle of light above Aunt Bess's hand, nor did I know why I thought someone should massage her hand at the point where her two fingers came together. It was getting harder and harder to explain things like this within my old scientific frame of reference. I continued to remain off balance. My sense of being honest to the truth would not let me simply walk away from the whole issue. I continued to study the phenomena.

CHAPTER TWENTY-FIVE

The New York City Guru

The word on campus was that a guru was going to speak at the Catholic student center next Tuesday evening. I thought I might attend it. I had never heard a real guru speak about anything. Being a seeker, I wanted to learn if this was a direction of interest for me as I attempted to find the path for my own spiritual growth.

I had been exploring the world of psychic phenomena since around 1971. By the early 1980's, I had learned that a lot of different groups in town were exploring this topic as well. Many of them were certain that they had found the one true way. I was not as confident in the accuracy of their beliefs as they were. Maybe that was my personal curse, to be constantly seeking but never finding the one true way.

Madam Biopsic, or Madam someone, had her believers. She was a psychic around the early 1900's who had a large following. Apparently, she lost credibility when she was caught in a reportedly blatant hoax. Now, I'm not saying all of this is factual. It was just what I had picked up from some readings without researching the matter seriously. Anyway, a small group of seekers thought what had been recorded about her teachings was worthy of studying. It did not appear to be that way for me.

Other groups were focused on one teacher or another's thought system. There were the Hairy Coronas. You could be approached by one or two of them walking across campus. The guys usually had their hair tied in ponytails, and the girls wore their hair long and loose. Long flowing robes were the uniform of their sect. I must say they were attractive on the young women. The message of love they eagerly shared was accompanied by the music they played on simple instruments and a request for donations. Members of their group could often be found at airports. Somehow, they always appeared to be happy.

One group called itself Gallicards or something like that. They were heavy into a special kind of meditation. This group was somewhat secretive. I was told that there were different levels or orders within this group of meditators. You weren't told much about the higher levels until you had mastered the level just below the next one up. The whole process sounded pretty complicated to me. I didn't have the time to be trying to progress from one level of meditation to another. Although, I had read about research reporting on the physical and psychological benefits of meditation. It was rumored that the highest level had been reached by the locally acknowledged leader of this group. I was told that it was whispered by some of the inner circle members that they had observed him levitate a few inches off of the floor during his meditations. That was a little hard for me to accept. What did I know? I had not invested the time to go through all of the steps of meditation necessary to see if I could levitate. Anyway, why would I want to levitate?

The inner circle of the Gallicards was tight. They walked around campus as a collective group. The leader seemed constantly to be smiling as if he were working hard to send love to all he saw even if they were ignorantly rejecting that love through their lack of understanding the one true way. I kept my distance from this group. That is not to say that I wasn't interested in them. I just didn't want to become a part of it. Maybe I was just a fool. Who was I to say that one way or the other way was the one true way without first experiencing the one true way? All I knew was that I was trying to be an open-minded seeker who hadn't found a home in which to anchor a belief system as of yet.

A large gathering had filled the conference hall of the church for the guru's presentation. There may have been a hundred or more students and citizens from the community seated in the two large sections of folding chairs. A small table sat in front of the two rows, right in front of the aisle naturally created by the evenly divided sections. The crowd was in a buzz of anticipation. As I looked around, it became clear that many of the subgroups of seekers I have mentioned plus several others were in the audience. There were the Edgar Cayce people, the Madam people, a few semi-professional skeptics and the inner circle of the Gallicards. The Gallicards even had there levitating leader in their midst. *This guru must be something,* I thought.

In unison, the crowd seemed to know when to turn their heads to the back of the room. There he was. He was perfect. Well, he perfectly fit my concept of how a guru should look as he rushed down the aisle and climbed up on the low table to assume the standard guru sitting position. He was small in stature, had long, flowing black and gray hair that hung down below his shoulders, merging into his equally long full beard that was also generously peppered with gray. His skin was a smoky brown color with lots of wrinkles in his facial features. To top it all off, he was wearing a long, orange robe outfit that had artfully placed

244

folds in it. Now this had to be the real thing.

From his crossed leg position, he began speaking. His voice was high-pitched with a predominant nasal twang that produced words in a rapid-fire spray with a slight British accent. This guy had to be the real thing.

"How happy it is to be in your city. I am so very happy. I mean there are so many gurus sitting on the corners of busy streets in New York. With their prayer bowls in front of them, they send blessing to all they see, hoping for a few coins in the prayer bowl to sustain them for the next day. I mean, there I am, just one of many, many gurus on many street corners. Two people just walk up and ask me if I want to come to Knoxville. Knoxville, Tennessee. They will pay my way and be my travel companions. What a surprise! I don't know where your city is, but yes, I want to come. Here I am. This is so very wonderful!"

At this point I'm thinking, "Lad you've been had." It's ok. He is truly entertaining. Who knows what's coming next?

"I will give you the shortcut to reaching your God within. It is in your breath. How you breathe in. How you breathe out. See, like this." He began to take a deep breath and then slowly let it out. As the air escaped his mouth, he began to make a musical "Ohmmmmm" sound that increased in richness and intensity the longer the air passed through his lips. That was a long time. He could have been a champion free-water deep diver. It was impressive. It was relaxing. He did it again and then again several more times. I was captured by the gentle, calming sound.

Startled from my relaxed state by his voice, his rapid-fire speech, I heard him say, "There, you see, it is the vibrations of your entire body. They put you in harmony with your God's vibrations, your inner God. There you find the voice. There you can freely receive the guidance. The guidance of your inner God, which is the God of all. Your inner God is the true God. You don't need to waste time, hours and hours of meditation, of thoughts, of philosophical discussions. Just breathe properly. I will teach you."

From the mumbling of words within the Gallicard collection of followers, I sensed that they were rigorously rejecting these statements. The statements did not agree with the meditation process they were following.

The guru proceeded to direct the group to breathe in deeply, hold the breath for a few seconds and then to release the air slowly and make the "ohm" sound while releasing your mind to the vibrations. At first the "ohmmmms" were a ragged and rather feeble effort by the audience. The guru's bubbling enthusiasm never wavered. He instructed us on the best posture for breathing, how to hold our heads correctly along with other helpful hints. After four or five practice sessions, we began to sound pretty good. Actually, we began to become one voice under his happy coaching. It reminded me of the recordings of monastery chanting.

This was the first time that I had "ohmmed." I liked it. I was enjoying this. I was happy.

The hour presentation passed quickly. Remarkably fast. Having concluded the last practice session, he told us that when we did this each day we would find that reaching our God within was a simple process. Then he opened the session to questions from the audience.

At first no one raised a hand. He prompted the group, "Come, come. Don't hold back. This is important for your development, for your finding your God within."

Finally, one brave soul raised his hand. He wanted to know about the risk of passing out if you held your breath too long. Another person wanted to know about the musical qualities of the "ohm" sound. I think she was one of the music majors. There were a few more questions of this ilk.

During this questioning phase, I could see from the corner of my eye that there was a bubbling up of suppressed communications going on among the inner circle of the Gallicards.

A few seconds of silence passed after the guru had responded to the last question. Slowly, deliberately, the reported levitator, the leader of the Gallicards, raised his hand.

"Yes," responded the enthusiastic Guru.

"I was just wondering," the levitator said in a slow measured and possibly professionally trained, deep voice that contained a degree of sarcasm, "I was wondering--If you have met your God within--if so, --what was it like?"

The Guru sprang from his seated position on the table and hurried to the front of the section the Gallicards were sitting in waving his finger back and forth as he rapidly spit out, "Don't you worry about my God within. You worry about your God within. You have no business worrying about my God within. You have business worrying about your God within. Your only business is your God within. You have no business worrying about my God within."

Addressing the audience as a group, the Guru said, "Go, work on your breathing. Breathe in slowly and deeply. Then slowly release your breath with the ohm sound. You will find your God within."

With that pronouncement, he smiled at the audience, made a deep guruish bow, briskly walked down the center aisle and out the front door.

Even though the years have passed, from time to time, I find myself taking a deep breath and slowly exhaling as I make the "ohm" sound.

CHAPTER TWENTY-SIX

Embarrassed by the Truth

Now, I knew that there was something real to psychic phenomena. I still did not know why things happened, but things clearly did happen. They did not occur on a consistent level as I had encountered them, nor did I have any idea as to the range or limits of the phenomena. I began reading about psychic phenomena during every spare moment I could find. There were not all that many such moments with my working full-time and being a father to two children while also supporting my full-time working wife. However, I could manage an hour or so in the late evenings to devote to my pursuit.

My readings included requesting more and more copies of the original transcripts of the Edgar Cayce individual psychic readings. I purchased many paperback books on psychic phenomena as well. Some of those books proposed ideas that were just too impossible to believe. I remember reading one guru's book about meditation and connecting to God. That author stated that you did not need to do hours and hours of meditation each day, say mystic chants, make ohm sounds for hours, practice painful yoga positions and the like to make connection with the

Spirit of God. Halfway through the book, the author stated that all you needed to do was to get up each morning, face the rising sun, bend down and touch your toes and then rise up with your arms out-stretched over your head as you state to yourself that you are perfect. You are perfect because that was how God created you. Well, I knew that wasn't true. I knew I wasn't perfect. The concept was so outrageous to me that I closed the book. I had no intention of wasting my time on such silly concepts.

I continued attending the Pat Sisson and Flemon channeling sessions as well as attending other evening meetings that Pat would put together. Many of those meetings featured invited people with reported psychic abilities presenting on their areas of expertise. An Indian chief explained his belief in the power of the sound of an eagle's feather. Someone spoke on the work Elizabeth Kubler Ross had been doing on death and dying.

One woman came who was working with a nation-wide research project to determine some facts concerning past life regressions. She came to lead sessions in past life regressions for those who had volunteered to participate in the research. She began by leading the group of people who were in attendance at Pat's house in the standard relaxation activities. Her instructions included taking a very deep breath and then holding it for a few seconds, then very slowly exhaling. As you exhaled, you were to notice that your neck muscles were relaxing and then your shoulder muscles. Taking another deep breath and then slowly releasing it, you were to notice the deeper relaxation of your neck and shoulder muscles. The instructions continued until all of your large muscle groups were relaxed. Then she directed us to think of a specific time period in the ancient past. At this point, I don't remember the exact time periods, so I'll make some up for demonstration purposes.

"You will focus on the date 1200 A.D. Remaining very relaxed, you are focused on the date 1200 A.D. "

"Now you will look down at your feet. You will notice if you are wearing footwear. You will notice what type of footwear you have on or the condition of your feet."

All of a sudden, I saw some sort of sandals on my feet. My mind went wild. This could not be. I wasn't back in the 1200's. This was my imagination working. These thoughts brought me out of the relaxed state. The lady continued to give directions about what kind of clothes you were wearing, what you were doing and so forth. I tried to get back into the relaxed state that the relaxation exercises had put me in, but it never happened. I had lost the experience.

When the woman finished with her series of questions, she had the group slowly return to the present and be fully awake. Everyone was excited about his or her experiences. The director of the experiment told us not to discuss our experiences with each other until we had filled out a questionnaire that she was passing out. The questionnaire asked us to write down what we had on our feet, what we were wearing and other questions that paralleled the directions she had given us during the regression.

We would have two more regressions, she informed us. We would be given different time periods for each of the regressions, but the questions of those time periods would be the same. When we came out of each of the regressions, we would complete the same questionnaire.

For the next regression session, I decided to treat the instructions as a guided fantasy experience. This was a psychological technique I had been taught at the National Training Laboratory (NTL) sessions I had attended in Portland, Oregon, a few years earlier. I was not going to try to determine if the so-called regression experience was real or not. I would deal with that after the session had been completed. It worked. I stayed with the entire process of the regression and experienced a fantasy event with each specific instruction. When we had completed the questionnaire for this second experience, our leader led us through the third exercise. I experienced a complete fantasy encounter that fit the time period assigned and filled the questionnaire with my answers.

At the end of the third cycle, the woman thanked us for our participation and said we could discuss our experiences with each other if we wished. I knew almost none of the participants. The few I did know were simply those I had seen at one of Pat's Flemon sessions. The one connection we all had was that everyone knew Pat or had come to the session with someone who knew Pat.

Several people shared their regression experiences in the most convincing manner.

I was impressed with their accounts but not convinced that they had actually gone back to the specific time periods to relive that lifetime. When I was asked to describe one of my regressions, I chose to tell the one I knew could not be true. For the time frame we had been directed to go back to, I found myself wearing simple sandals and a flowing white tunic of some rough woven fabric that was a little heavy but comfortable. I lived in a cave-like house. The house had been partially built over an opening into the side of a hill. The structure was up high, overlooking the crashing sea below. The wind was blowing strongly from the sea. It was chilly. I had a garden I tended and some sheep I cared for. People would climb up the hill to talk to me from time to time. They were asking me for advice. My mind wanted my location to be in Greece somewhere on the coast, but it wouldn't accept that location. It seemed to be too cold for the Greek coast. My mind kept telling me that I was on the English coast. Well that simply could not be true, I told my fellow participants. As far as I knew, for that time period no one lived in houses built over cave entrances, making part of the cave an extension of the interior of the house; and I was an English major in college, I stated.

"Well, you are wrong," spoke up one man who had been pretty quiet through the various disclosures others had made of their regression experiences.

"I have a Ph.D. in English. I teach at the college. I have studied England in the time period you are discussing. There were such dwellings on the coast of England at that time. It would have been consistent for you to wear the clothing you described and to grow a garden and to tend sheep,"

That set me back. I was so confident that the regression was only a rich fantasy experience. If this fellow was correct, the regression could have been real. I could have been experiencing a past lifetime. Once again, I was stunned. It was becoming more and more difficult to know exactly what was and was not real concerning the realm of psychic issues. The Edgar Cayce material certainly made the case for past lives. Maybe they were real. I just did not know what to believe and wanted to discuss this and other issues with someone. I could not do that with the people at work. Many of the educators I worked with were born in the rural communities where they worked. Those communities were proudly Christian conservative. Most conservative Christians I knew were hostile to discussions of psychic phenomena. The potential for damaging my professional reputation was high if I openly disclosed that I thought there was some truth to psychic phenomena. In addition, the professional community of psychology in my state seemed to me to be a highly conservative body. I didn't want it to be widely known that I considered psychic phenomena to be real until I knew where the professional organization stood on the subject. I felt confident that they would not accept anything that was not scientifically proven. I know I would not.

Shortly after I was elected to be the regional representative to the state's psychological association's board of directors, the president of the state association called me. He invited me to ride with him to a board of directors meeting in Nashville. He lived in Johnson City and would be driving through Knoxville. We could meet at a truck stop he named. They would not mind my parking the car there for a few days, he noted. He also suggested that we share a motel room in Nashville to help reduce the expenses of the association. I agreed.

This was risky business. I desperately wanted to discuss all I had been learning and experiencing about psychic phenomena, but I could not reveal my interest to the president of the state association of psychologists. Since I considered them to be a highly conservative group, the president of that group would have to reflect those values or he would not have been elected as their association president, was my reasoning.

Our drive to Nashville was pleasant. My colleague talked about his work at the VA hospital and wanted to know more about the new area of practicing psychologists, school psychology. As the two days of meetings progressed in Nashville, I got to really like this man. He was open to people's suggestions on solving the problems the association was facing at that time. This psychologist simply had a gentle way of valuing various points of view on a topic while bringing those with different perspectives together. This enabled the group to agree upon a single strategy for solving the difficulties. I grew to admire and trust him.

Driving back to Knoxville was so much more pleasant than it

had been driving to Nashville now that I knew and trusted my companion. About an hour out of Knoxville he asked me something that prompted me to mention that I had been reading some of the Edgar Cayce material. I was guarded in what I said so as not to reveal that I was devouring the original Cayce readings. My new friend asked me what I had learned recently from my readings. I replied, as blandly as I could, with some small bit of information I had recently discovered in one of his readings.

The immediate response from my companion was that he knew about that too. He then provided me with another obscure fact about Edgar Cayce's readings that I had just discovered less than a week ago. There was no way this guy could have casually known that information. He had obtained information about Edgar Cayce that only in-depth students of the Cayce material would know.

I cautiously stated, "You seem to know a lot about the Edgar Cayce material."

"Oh yes, my wife and I have been to the Edgar Cayce Center in Virginia Beach many, many times over the years. We are long-time friends with Hugh Lynn Cayce, Edgar's son. We raised our children according to the Cayce materials. They regularly attended the Cayce Foundation's summer camps as they were growing up. We've raised them according to the principles in the Cayce material."

My God, I thought, *I have kept myself from learning from this man all of this time while I was bursting to talk to someone about this very topic.* How I had crippled myself with my fears and false assumptions! The remaining hour of our trip together just flew by. It was such a pleasure to discuss the Cayce material openly with a knowledgeable psychologist. He invited me to visit with him and his wife any time. I really wanted to do that. However, my busy schedule never let that happen. It was disappointing, but my searching and discoveries continued.

Pat's husband, Paul, recommended that I read something he had recently discovered. It was called *A Course in Miracles*. He thought I would find it interesting. After I had asked him what it was about, he went into a lengthy discussion of it. His explanation made me want to reject the thing without opening the first page. First of all, there was not an author listed for it. The author was a psychologist. She was apparently embarrassed to have her name associated with the contents of the book. Then, Paul stated that Jesus Christ dictated the book to her. I really respected Paul's opinions, but this was just simply too much. It sounded like one of those faith-healing revival tent things where the preacher pretended to be speaking directly with God or speaking in tongues, having God speak through him. God always spoke through the preacher just before the preacher asked you to be sure to put ten percent of your last paycheck in the donation plate.

Later, while reflecting on Paul's recommendation and how much I valued him, I decided to buy the book and read it. I could not criticize the material fairly without having read it. I owed Paul that much.

A Course in Miracles was actually three books. One book was called the *Text*. It seemed to be much like a college textbook on philosophy except it was so far outside of the realm of reality, as I understood reality to be, that I quickly put it aside.

The second book, a *Workbook for Students*, contained daily lessons. The lessons were set up something like an operant conditioning programmed textbook using operant conditioning you might encounter in learning algebra through a series of discrete but systematic lessons that built upon themselves. The first lesson in *A Course in Miracles* starts out with the statement:

"Nothing I see in this room (on this street, from this window, in this place) means anything." Then a series of exercises follow that reinforce this concept. The second lesson begins with the statement, "I have given everything in this room (on this street, from this window, in this place) all the meaning that it has for me." I liked this. It fit into my understanding of phenomenological psychology, the psychological theory that each of us invents our own reality. We form an opinion about what reality is and then interpret all the information we receive within our personal concept of reality. If we encounter something that does not fit into our concept of reality, we simply deny that it is true. It was from studying the concepts of phenomenological psychology that I understood more fully the maxim, "If you believe it, you have made it true for you."

The last book, the third book, of *A Course in Miracles*, was called a *Manual for Teachers*. It was clear that I was not a teacher of the *A Course in Miracles*. Thus, the obvious book for me to begin my study of A *Course in Miracles* was book two, a *Workbook for Students*. I started the daily lessons. While I tried to remember to do the recommended exercises throughout the day, I couldn't remember to do them during the recommended time intervals. My life was just too busy. Everything seemed to be going pretty well with the daily lessons until I'd gotten about a third of the way into the book. I don't mean that I accepted the ideas totally, but I at least considered them to be within the realm of believability. When the daily lessons shifted from telling me that I was not perceiving what was real to then telling me what the truth was, I had a problem. First of all, I didn't like anyone telling me what I should believe. All of the different communities and cultures I had grown up in had their own concepts of what was true. Those communities, those sub-cultures, were not about to let a new kid who had just moved into the neighborhood tell them that in the last place he had lived they didn't believe what these people believed, and everyone got along fine. The new community the child had just joined would want to punish the child for challenging that community's knowledge of truth. No, I was not ready for a book to tell me that my sense of the world was wrong and now it was going to tell me what the real truth was. This was where I would start to confront my friend Paul mentally about the merits of A *Course in Miracles.*

First, I had to read the material and understand it before I could formulate a reasonable set of arguments against the course and disprove its concepts. Some forty years later I am still studying the A *Course in Miracles.* Over time, I have come to accept the course's concepts but still am learning what they actually mean. I realize that this is a confusing statement, but it accurately reflects my state of mind.

Five years or so after I had begun to study A *Course in Miracles,* I had a chance encounter with another person who had read the material. At one of the monthly Flemon sessions, a youngish to middle-aged woman sat down beside me on the couch in Pat's living room. I hadn't seen her at any of the other Flemon sessions. I was still a little self-conscious about being at a channeling session. I thought too many people would condemn such behavior. They would consider the attendees to be part of a cult. I simply didn't want to have to defend myself to them. I was cautious about whom I let know of my interest in psychic phenomena.

Trying to be pleasant, I introduced myself as Jerry to the lady. We shook hands. She seemed pleasant enough to me. After sharing her name, she proceeded to tell me that she was an emergency room physician. She had seen many "miracles" in her medical practice and knew that there was a greater reality than what we could ever imagine with a paradigm limited by the three dimensions of our world. Unlike me, she was very open about her beliefs in psychic phenomena. I decided to risk revealing that I was more than a casual seeker of information about psychic phenomena. However, a degree of caution was still a part of me.

I stated, "I've found a set of books recently that have captured my interest. They are collectively called A *Course in Miracles*. Have you heard of them?"

"Oh yes, I read them in four days. I found them to be too elementary for where I am. I am into much more theoretical material."

"That's nice."

I didn't have much to add to her statement. I had a lot of inner thoughts about her comments but decided that it would be best to keep them to myself. Perhaps I am a slow learner. If that is the case, it is taking me a long time to integrate the principles of the course into my daily life. There is at least one positive thing I can say about my studies of this material over all those years. I am persistent.

Not long after this encounter with the emergency room physician, Pat Sisson informed me that she had been invited to speak about her work as a psychic on a local morning TV show. She was going to be interviewed on the live broadcast at 6:00 a.m.. Pat went on to say that she would like for me to be with her during the interview. She wanted me to be interviewed along with her. I could verify some of her remarkable stories. Pat was my friend. She had true psychic abilities. I did not want to be known to the general public as a believer, not because I lacked conviction in the truth of what Pat had done as a psychic, but because I feared that the rural communities and school systems in which I worked would misperceive what Pat and I would be trying to communicate. My appearing on the TV show could hurt the educational cooperative as an organization. I was also concerned about being identified as a licensed psychologist. What if the state's psychological association challenged me as representing that the field of professional psychology supported psychics?

I was immediately confronted with a host of conflicting issues within myself. Was I going to stand up and support what I had learned to be true about the reality of psychic phenomena or was I going to yield to social pressure, abandon my friend and stay silent rather than support the truth? I agreed to appear on the TV show.

As the morning of the show approached, my anxiety grew. I imagined all of the negative consequences that could happen to me and my family as a result of supporting this controversial truth. I had to stand for truth. I had to support my friend and speak up for the truth. That was all there was to it.

Clearly, Pat was the focus during the TV interview. I was simply introduced as a friend who had attended the Flemon sessions and had observed some of Pat's predictions to come true. That was about it. I was never described as being a psychologist. Towards the end of the interview, the interviewer asked me if Pat's stories were accurate. I said they were, simply because they were. That was all there was to it.

I was relieved that my involvement in the TV interview was so brief and that I didn't have to worry about being a licensed psychologist. All I had to worry about was the potential of negative reactions from the school personnel I worked with in my rural communities. A full day's work lay ahead of me after the early morning TV interview. I would be traveling to several of those school systems. If there was going to be reaction to my being on the TV show, it would come quickly.

Just about the entire workday had passed without one teacher, principal, supervisor of special education or superintendent acknowledging that I had been on the TV show, much less criticizing me for supporting the truth of some psychic phenomena. I was relieved.

The last school system I had to visit for the day was about forty miles out from Knoxville. I needed to meet with that system's supervisor of special education. She was a very kind person who had been born and raised in the community. Above all the people I knew in that part of the state, she was the most representative of that culture. She was approaching retirement age and had observed many changes in her community. I liked her and trusted her judgment.

As I walked into her office, she looked up at me and said, "I saw you on TV. We had the TV on this morning, as we were getting ready to go to work. I heard them mention your name. I called to my husband to get in here quick. He needed to hear what you had to say. I told him you always told the truth no matter how hard it was to tell the truth sometimes. If you were going to comment on this psychic stuff it would be the truth. We heard you say it was true. I think you're right. Now let's get to work on planning for this disabled child."

How foolish I was to worry as I did. I felt like Grover, the main character in the Sesame Street children's book, *There's a Monster at the End of this Book.* Through all of the pages of the book except the last page, Grover pleads with the reader not to turn the next page because "There's a monster at the end of the book." Once you get to the end of the book, the reader discovers that Grover is on the last page. He's the monster. Grover confesses to the reader, "I am so embarrassed." Well, I can only say, me too.

CHAPTER TWENTY-SEVEN

"How'm I Doing?"

About twenty years ago I picked up one of my last hitchhikers. Before this adventure, I'd been picking them up on and off for about fifteen years. I'd have to travel from Knoxville to Nashville fairly often for education-related meetings during that period. It was a nice way to pass the four-hour trip. The hitchhiker would tell you his story and you would tell him yours. When you were finished you were there. Often the hitchhiker was continuing further west. We'd part ways wishing each other luck.

My wife was worried about my picking people up. She would go through the dangers of it and all the things that could happen. She was right. I still kept doing it. The people were so interesting and nice. Besides, I learned a lot about how others in less fortunate situations than mine coped with life. Still, I was trying to curb my behavior and was picking them up less frequently by the time of this story.

I guess I was near Kingston when I stopped for him that spring morning. He was a young man, fairly fit and well dressed in casual clothing. The car stopped about twenty feet from where he stood on the side of the interstate. Picking up a satchel, he ran up to the passenger side window as I rolled it down.

"I'm going to Memphis," he said, slightly puffing from the run.

"I'm only going to Nashville, but I can take you that far."

"Great," he said as he opened the back door and put his bag on the floor before getting into the front seat.

We shook hands as I started the car down the interstate. I made a mental note on how dilated his eyes seemed to be. We exchanged first names. Then he began telling his story in a rush.

He had been in a hospital for some time in Maryland, but his relatives had not come to visit him. He decided to leave the hospital and hitchhike out to see them. The way he expressed it, he was angry with them and was going to tell them that they should have come to see him.

As his story unfolded, it became clear that he was in the Navy. He was a patient at the Bethesda Naval Hospital. As he talked further about his hospital, I began to suspect that he was in what we used to call "the section eight ward," the psychiatric ward. It also became apparent that he was probably AWOL, absent without leave, by leaving the hospital without permission.

He talked constantly with only perfunctory comments from me such as "oh," "hum" and "ahha." Occasionally I asked questions like, "What do you think about that?" "How did they react to that?" or "How did that make you feel?" Rarely would he look at me as he spoke. Most of the time he kept his eyes looking straight ahead out the front window.

At one point he explained that he had been up for about thirty hours on the road. That was why he was a little hyper and his eyes were dilated. He was ok, he reassured me. I didn't need to worry about that. Whatever "that" was, did have me a little worried.

As he told his story his speech became more rapid and his voice seemed to change pitch a lot. However, he maintained his straight-ahead-stare out the windshield through the long course of his monologue.

We were almost to the Lebanon exit before he asked me the traditional question, "What do you do?"

Always in the past, when I'm asked this rule-of-the road question, I tell the hitchhiker that I work with disabled children. This evokes sympathetic responses and triggers more conversation. Everyone has a relative or friend with a disabled child. We get into the strategies that are used to help the child they know about and explore my knowledge for any better ideas in understanding how to be of assistance to the child and family. Usually, I don't get into my professional training or its generalized category. I decided that this time I would simply state what I was.

"I'm a psychologist."

Snapping his head from looking out the windshield to staring straight at me, he asked, "How'm I doing?"

"You're doing well. You're really holding it together well."

"Thanks," he said snapping his head back to looking straight out to the road.

He returned to his monologue without asking me another question. About forty-five minutes later we arrived at the exit that would take me from the interstate. We shook hands. He exited the car, waved good-bye, and walked to the rear of the car. As I pulled away, he stuck his thumb out in the hopes of catching his next ride. In the rearview mirror I saw a car stop for him.

CHAPTER TWENTY-EIGHT

Misery

"Now, honey, please don't pick up any hitchhikers on this trip," my caring wife cautioned.

With reluctance, and in the middle of the final packing, I replied, "OK."

"You won't even be driving our car. It's a rental. What happens if you pick up a hitchhiker and something happens to the car?"

"Ok, Ok."

"I worry about what could happen, that's all. We love you too much. Please promise not to pick someone up."

Embracing her in a hug and giving her a kiss, I promised.

This was my first big-time presentation. I was actually being paid as a presenter to a group of students on working with gifted children at Cape Girardeau University. It would be an all-day presentation. They were paying all of my expenses plus a nice little fee. The pre-arrangements had been made by phone and covered by our one credit card. This was a good thing. We were still a week from the end of the month. That was a week from payday. Cash was really tight in our household budget. My loving wife always wanted me to have enough money on my trips. I assured her that ten dollars would cover my two evening meals with a dollar or two left over for unexpected expenses. In 1977 five dollars got you an acceptable meal almost anywhere.

Cape Girardeau, Missouri, would be a new experience for me. When I was about two years old, my family had lived in East St. Louis. It was right at the end of the Second World War. My dad had just gotten home and so had Uncle Jim. We didn't live there long as the family found a rental house across the river in Granite City, Illinois.

I'd fly from Knoxville, Tennessee, to Memphis and then to St. Louis. In St. Louis I'd rent a car at the airport. Arrangements had been made for me to stay that Friday night at a motel near it. I'd get up early Saturday morning. I'd get up really early to drive the three hours to Cape Girardeau and arrive by 9:00 a.m. to start the presentation. Saturday evening I'd drive the three hours or so back to the hotel at the airport. Then it was an early wakeup to be able to catch a 5:00 a.m. flight back to Knoxville. The hotel provided a free continental breakfast. It wasn't likely they'd be serving at 4:00 a.m. My wakeup call for the return trip was scheduled for 3:30 that morning to insure I had time to dress, brush my teeth, return the car and get to the boarding gate on time.

Of course, it was dark most of the drive to the university. I couldn't see much of the land I was passing through. From the look of things, once you got out of St. Louis, it was a no man's land. There weren't any lights on for houses, farms or small towns. Well, maybe it was just that everyone was sleeping. That late, cold January pre-dawn morning was really cold. What made matters worse was the constant, biting wind. It just pushed the cold into any break in your clothing. I hadn't expected it to be this cold. It was miserable. My sports jacket provided little protection. I was just plain cold.

The presentation went well until about two or three in the afternoon. One of the participants started it off.

"Have you noticed that the gifted children seem to be drawn toward psychic phenomena?"

"Well, yes and no."

"Just what do you mean?"

Laughing, I said, "I'm not sure what I mean. I've had the topic raised by one high school student. He reported a feeling, a kind of experience he would have from time to time. He said that he finally decided that he was having an out-of-body experience. He wanted to know if it could be true or if maybe there was something wrong with him. I was quick to explain that I was not a physician. He might want to discuss this with his doctor. There were physiological conditions that might explain what was causing the feelings. He went on to explain why he thought it was an out-of-body experience. He cited being in other rooms in his house looking down on family members as they discussed certain topics. The next morning he would ask one of those family members if they had said whatever it was that he heard them say during the out-of-body observation of them. He said they were astounded that he would know what they had discussed in such detail. He had gotten several confirmations that he was somehow gaining information in some mysterious manner."

"What did you tell him?"

"I told him I could not confirm or deny the reality of his experience. There were a lot of books on the subject in the popular literature. I told him what I knew that Elisabeth Kubler Ross and the Edgar Cayce material said on the topic. I also provided the various scientific explanations I was aware of that might provide an account of the phenomenon in a more conventional manner."

I really felt uncomfortable with the direction the questions were going. In my own mind I still hadn't worked out a solid place for myself concerning psychic phenomena. While I had spent a lot of spare time exploring the topic, I didn't want to tell them that. There was no doubt that I had encountered some things that I could not begin to explain using what I knew about the scientific realities as to how the world works on a three-dimensional plan. I didn't want to tell these people that, but I also wanted to be truthful with them in answering their questions. I just wanted these kinds of questions to stop. My comfort level had been seriously disturbed.

"What's something that has happened with children that you could not explain that seemed to be psychically unusual?"

Damn, wouldn't you know it, just what I didn't want to happen was now happening.

"Will, I did have one unusual situation take place that I can share."

"Go on, we want to hear it," the aggressive questioner stated as several of the other fifteen or so attendees nodded in agreement.

"I was co-teaching a fifth grade Sunday school class at a Unitarian Church. The kids attending it appeared to be pretty bright. I'm sure some of them had been identified as gifted, but I wouldn't know who they were. Anyway, it was a year-long class on different belief systems people have throughout the world. My co-teacher was absent that Sunday. He was and is a famous scientist. I would probably have been hesitant to bring this topic up if he had been there, but he wasn't. I told the kids that some people believed that they could see colors around other people, particularly around their heads. Recently, I told them, I had read about a way you could see those colors or auras as they were sometimes called. Of course, the kids wanted to know how to do it. I explained that I didn't know if the technique would actually work for them. When I tried the procedure, sometimes I saw something like colors around people's heads. It could simply be the result of eyestrain or some other logical explanation, I reflected. Again, I cautioned them to try to keep a balance between tricks of the mind and sound scientific principles.

"Of course, they wanted to try it. I explained the technique. You have someone stand or sit in front of a white background like a wall or sheet or something like that. Then you focus your eyes about two or three feet above the person's head and keep staring at that imaginary spot. After a minute or so you will begin seeing the person's aura in your peripheral vision. If you switch the focus of your eyes to the colors around the person's head, you will probably not see the aura. You have to keep your eyes focused just above the person's head and catch the colors in your peripheral vision.

"Well, they definitely wanted to try it. They pulled a table over against the one white wall in the room. A boy volunteered to sit on the table with his back resting against the wall. The other seven or eight or so children and I sat on the floor in front of the table and looked at the boy sitting on it.

"I focused my eyes just above his head. All of a sudden, I saw this big, long purple streak of light coming from the upper left side of the kid near the ceiling going all the way down to the child's head. I was really surprised by the brightness of the purple light and its overall clarity. This shaft of purple light was so dominant that I decided to look directly at it. It was still there. I leaned forward and turned my head slightly to the side. It was still there. I was stunned. I thought, *How am I going to explain what*

I see to these children?

"At that moment, one of them sitting on the floor spontaneously said, 'Wow, do you see that purple light slanting into his head?' Several of the other children said yes, they see it too. One child said he doesn't. One of the 'seers' explained where it is, which was exactly where I saw it. 'Oh, yeah, now I see it,' said the questioner. Since the time had about arrived for the children's parents to come pick them up, I brought the thing to a close. The children and I all agreed that we really don't know how to explain what we have just witnessed. I cautioned them to remember how the mind can play tricks on all of us and urge them to explore a variety of explanations for this experience before reaching a final conclusion. They all agreed to do just that."

Several questions about the details of this story were asked of me. I really wanted to change the subject and get back to the science around working with gifted students.

"Let's try to see our auras," one of the participants said. The other participants all thought it was a great idea. Someone stood against a whitish colored wall and the others looked. The results were mixed. Some saw a color or a distortion of light and some saw nothing. Different ones of them took turns being observed standing in front of the wall. Disagreement abounded as to who saw what. All of the participants seemed happy and to be enjoying the experience. I was not.

"Well, I think we can end our session now unless you have some other questions about the studies I have cited and our results from the research we did through the federal grant."

"No, no, no, let's not stop now. Let's explore this psychic stuff more."

"Yes, tell us what else you know about the psychic things. Clearly, you've been exploring that."

"No, if you don't have questions on the research related to the interaction with the gifted child in the school environment, we'll end it now."

"But we still have 45 minutes to go. Let's keep going."

"No, we are ending a little early. You get a break. Thank you all for coming." And with that I started to pack up my brief case with the leftover materials I had used during the presentation.

The audience seemed confused that I would stop early. They were clearly not pleased. I felt so uncomfortable talking about the psychic stuff. I was off-balance. It was one thing to read about it and quite another to have encountered things that you could not explain, things that just knocked you off balance. My anchor to reality had been recently shaken. Badly shaken. I couldn't talk about it to an open group of strangers. It was just too threatening to me.

Damn, it was cold getting into the car. I felt miserable. I was clearly out of sorts about the ending of the session with the educators. I knew that I hadn't handled the situation well at all. The weather served to accentuate that misery. The wind even pushed the cold inside the car. I sat shivering in it for several miles. The engine finally warmed up enough to send heated air into the compartment.

Lord, this land was desolate. It was just open land with no house for long stretches of miles. I thought there would be gas stations and fast food restaurants at the many exits that would be between Cape Girardeau and St Louis. There didn't seem to be any exits anywhere. What little snow that lay on the ground kept getting resettled by the strong gusts of wind that overwhelmed the constant, ever-present background rush of wind.

At least my wife wouldn't have to worry about my picking up a hitchhiker. There weren't any cars on the road, let alone someone walking alongside of the highway. No one could survive long in this weather unless he was an arctic explorer. It was simply brutal.

As I drove on in this uninhabited land, the late afternoon light began to take on the darker hue of approaching evening. This trip seemed to be lasting forever. I was hungry and thirsty. It didn't matter. There wasn't an exit to use. Even if there were one, it was clear that there would not be a gas station. There simply weren't any commercial developments along this unending stretch of road.

I began climbing a long hill that was pinned in on both sides by two large stone cliffs. The evidence of drill holes cut into the rock was visible where sticks of dynamite were placed to blast away the passage for the road. The detonation had blown away the center of this solid rock hill. It created the cut-through for this highway. *God, this would be a horrible place for the car to break down.*

You'd be trapped in this artificially created valley. The road rose as far as the eye could see to the distant crest of hill. At the top the full blast of the wind would touch you with its stinging cold. How far could you go walking in weather like this? Not far enough, that was for certain. This would be a place where people died. It gave me the shivers just thinking about it.

At fifty-five miles an hour, I crested the hill. Half-way down the other side of it someone was walking. Someone was walking down the hill. I couldn't believe it. What was someone doing out here, at this time of day, walking on this road? There's nothing here. There's nothing anywhere. He or she must be a local. They must know something about this area that I don't. That's the only thing that makes sense about someone being out here in this cold.

At least he wasn't holding out his thumb. He wasn't hitchhiking. He was just hunched over, bent into the wind, taking one plodding step in front of the other. I stayed in the slow lane hoping to catch a look at the person in the side view mirror. I wanted to see what someone who had the grit to face this weather looked like. He had my curiosity. What a relief it was to know that I wouldn't be tempted to offer him a ride. My promise not to pick up hitchhikers remained unchallenged.

I whizzed by him at the fifty-five miles per hour speed limit. I caught just a brief glimpse of his face in the passenger side view mirror. I was stunned by what I saw. It was the saddest, most miserable face I had ever seen. He never turned his head to look at the car. He just kept staring ahead, slowly putting one foot in front of the other. His hands were stuck inside his coat pocket. His back was hunched forward, and his shoulders were pulled into his chest as if he wanted to wrap himself into them.

Promise or not, I could not leave this person out here, alone in this cold. I couldn't do it. As I slowed to a stop, I pulled onto the side of the road. A lot of road had passed between the two of us. Slowing a car moving at fifty-five miles an hour to a stop takes up a lot of distance. He was a considerable way behind me. Usually, when I would pull over for a hitchhiker, there would be a distance between the car and the hitchhiker. Of course, you knew you were going to stop for the hitchhiker before you had passed him so there wasn't as great a distance between him and your car as was the case with this stranger. In any event, the hitchhiker you had passed would pick up his tote bag or backpack or whatever and start running to where the car was.

This stranger along the road did not increase his pace. He did not even seem to look ahead to the car. He just kept slowly putting one foot in front of the other, plodding on as before.

I put the car in reverse and began backing up towards him expecting him to start running or at least walking faster to get to the car. The stranger did none of these things. He just kept moving with his plodding pace. As he approached the rear of the car, I rolled down the passenger side window. When he was abreast of it, he leaned his fully bearded face towards the open space.

With no expression in his face or in his voice, he said, "What do you want?"

Taken aback by the question, I meekly stated, "It's cold. I thought I could give you a ride."

He just stared at me.

"I can give you a ride. It's warm in here."

Blandly, looking me straight in the face he said, "OK."

I began opening the door from my leaning position while keeping one hand on the steering wheel. He grasped the edge of the door. Slowly, he fully opened the door and seated himself.

Usually, when the hitchhiker first gets in the car, he profusely thanks you for picking him up and asks you how far you are going. This guy just sat there. He didn't say anything. He just sat there as I headed down the road.

After we had traveled several miles down the road, not being able to stand the continued silence, I stated, "I'm going as far as St. Louis."

"That's Ok," he said with the same bland projection of personality he seemed to have mastered long before I had seen him.

Gradually, he began talking. I would ask a few leading questions that extended his story. He was an artist of some fame in Florida. He had grown up in north central Ohio. He had won several art contests in high school. He decided to go to Florida after high school. He didn't want to go to college. His parents were willing to pay for him to go. He wanted to go live in an artist

273

colony in Florida. He wanted to study under one particular artist there. Well, that artist had moved on by the time my traveling companion had arrived. That was all right though. The guy stayed there and started selling some of his work to locals and tourists. After a while, he wanted to leave the Florida scene. He wanted to go back home to Ohio and maybe study art at Ohio State or somewhere like that.

My companion said that he had saved up some money for the trip but decided to hitchhike up to Ohio for the adventure of it. Hitchhiking would also allow him to have some cash when he arrived.

Two nights ago, he landed in a truck stop. He decided to sleep in a storage room behind the main truck stop. After eating supper, he took his bedroll and his backpack to the storage room and fell asleep. In the middle of the night, a couple of guys began beating on him. He woke up with these guys pounding on him. There was no way he could protect himself. They kicked and punched. They emptied his pockets, took his wallet and all his loose change, his backpack and even dragged out his bedroll. When they left, all he wanted to do was hunker down and sleep. He couldn't really sleep. He hurt everywhere. When dawn finally broke, he went to the front office and told them what had happened. Since he couldn't identify his attackers and he had no ID, they told him there was nothing they could do for him. They didn't even offer him breakfast.

He just started walking north. That's all he knew to do. He'd been walking for two days. He got some water by holding ice in his mouth that he'd picked up from the drainage ditches alongside the road. That was it. No food and no relief from the cold. He had just decided to commit suicide minutes before I came along. He was actually looking for a place to lie down that would conceal his body from cars passing by when I stopped, he said.

Damn, it was a hard story. I believed him. There was no doubt in my mind that he was telling the truth. Now, mind you, I knew there were some blanks in his story. There were gaps in time that weren't accounted for. Nonetheless, I believed him.

"I'm getting hungry," I stated to him. "If we find an exit that has a place to eat, I'll pull over. I'll treat you to a meal if that's agreeable."

"Thanks, I'd appreciate that."

About twenty minutes later there was an exit. A lone local diner sat on the corner. I pulled in. There were no other cars in front of it, but lights were on inside. We got out. Stuck on one of the windowpanes of the two front doors was a hand-written sign, No Credit Cards.

"Wait a minute. Let's get back in the car," I said to my companion. He looked puzzled but followed my lead.

"They won't take credit cards. I don't have much cash."

He just looked at me.

I pulled out my billfold and searched my pockets. Four dollars and eighty-three cents. That's all I had.

"Should we try to find another place?" I asked.

"It's your call."

"Well, I don't think we're going to find another place before we get to the outskirts of St. Louis. That's going to be another good hour or more. I could get what this will buy. We can share it, if that's OK?"

"Yeah, if that's what you want to do."

"It's decided. Let's go in and see what we can get for $4.83."

After being seated at a table, the waitress gave us the menu. We were the only customers in the restaurant. The menu said we could get a meat loaf dinner for five dollars. That was the cheapest meal listed.

When the waitress returned for our order, I told her we wanted just one meal and two plates. We wanted the meat loaf dinner but we had a problem since they didn't take credit cards. All we had was four dollars and eighty-three cents in cash. We'd like to get as much of the meat loaf dinner as our four dollars and eighty-three cents could buy. She smiled and said she would see what she could do.

A few minutes later she returned with a pot of coffee. She wanted to know if we wanted some. She said it was on the house. We did. We warmly thanked her.

When she brought the meat loaf dinner out on the one plate, there were two big slices of meat loaf, a big pile of mashed potatoes with gravy in the center, two rolls and a few green beans filling up the little space left for them to fit on the plate. She had a spare plate in hand.

During the meal I asked a lot of questions about my companion's artwork. His responses became more detailed as the meal progressed. I liked the guy. Towards the end of our feast, I offered to have him stay in my hotel room for the night. It had two beds in it. I'd have to leave around 4:00 a.m., but he could sleep in. You didn't have to leave the room until 11:00 a.m. He could sleep in. They had a free continental breakfast. When we got there, I'd tell the front desk that he was with me and would be staying after I left. Since the room had already been paid for, he didn't have to worry about checkout or anything.

He was reluctant to agree and said he'd think about it. That seemed strange to me. There were no other options for him that I could see. He had made it clear earlier that he planned on continuing going to Ohio. He thought the hitchhiking into Ohio wouldn't be all that bad from St. Louis on north. He had been in

St. Louis when he lived in Ohio and was familiar with the roads. He thought he could make it. He might even find some paper and do some artwork and sell it, if that were necessary. Once he got near Indiana, there were friends he could contact that would help him out. He'd make it just fine from St. Louis.

As we drove into the suburbs, he agreed to stay in the hotel room with me. He didn't sound very enthusiastic about it. He did thank me.

We entered the hotel lobby together. I explained to the night clerk that he was staying with me in the room. The room was registered in my name. I'd be leaving the room at 4:00 a.m. He would be staying in it until around check-out time. I didn't want anyone to get confused about his being in the room after I was gone, I told him. The clerk looked as if he didn't like what he was hearing, but he agreed to what I said. He took my companion's name as an additional guest in the room. He gave me the key and agreed to give me a wake-up call at 3:30 a.m.

When we got to the room, I opened my suitcase to get out my toothbrush and other gear. I stated that I wanted to take a shower. He could take one before I did or afterward. It was his choice. As I was speaking, I noticed that he stayed about as far away from me as the room would comfortably allow. Even from that distance, I noticed that he had a body odor.

No, he said, he didn't want to take a shower, and he wasn't going to sleep in the other bed. He was going to take the blanket off of it and sleep on the floor. I said that was fine with me.

In the shower, I reflected on the guy's behavior. I wondered if he thought I might be gay. He might think he risked being attacked by me. If that was the case, I understood. I would be sure to give him his space.

The ringing phone woke me at 3:30 a.m. as promised. I went

into the bathroom to shave, comb my hair and dress, hoping not to disturb my sleeping guest. When I emerged from the bathroom he was up. He'd slept in his clothes.

As I was gathering my coat and suitcase getting ready to leave the room, he said that he was going to take a shower after I left. I said that was fine. We shook hands. He thanked me. He said that someday we would meet again. When we did, he'd give me one of his paintings.

Thanking him, I left.

CHAPTER TWENTY-NINE

It Continues

A dear friend of ours called us one afternoon. She was checking to see if it would be all right to spend the night with us. The next morning, she had to have a cyst of some kind removed from her abdomen. The operation was to take place in a Knoxville hospital. It was an early morning appointment. She lived thirty some miles away. Leaving from our house rather than hers would make the trip easier for her. Of course, that was fine with us. She was to explain her condition to us when she arrived.

It was always good to visit with this dear friend. We had all known each other since our graduate school days. It was common for us to spend an overnighter at the other's house. We had the downstairs bed all set up and ready for unexpected guests. Like our other very close friends, she was aware of my interest in psychic phenomena but did not have much more than a courtesy level of interest in it herself. At least, that was the way I had interpreted her responses to my comments about it. As a result, I just didn't bring up that topic when we were all visiting.

This visit was unusual. She had a medical condition that appeared to need rather sudden surgery. We anxiously awaited

279

her arrival.

When we settled into our comfortable visiting that early evening, she explained her condition. She had some kind of a cyst that had grown to about the size of a large grapefruit in her abdominal cavity. It had been growing larger over the last few months. The doctors had performed numerous tests on the cyst. They thought it wasn't cancerous, she reported. Since the cyst had continued to grow and was causing her considerable discomfort, arrangements had been made for tomorrow morning's surgery. Our friend had left her doctor's office and come straight to our house, she said. That final examination late that afternoon was to confirm the exact dimensions and location of the cyst for the morning's surgery. There was no doubt as to the cyst's location and size. She said her physician stated that it might have grown some since the last time it had been examined

Of course, we were supportive and expressed our concern. The whole process would be pretty routine, she stated. At this point, she did not know how long she would be in the hospital. It all depended on the surgery and what they learned about the cyst.

That night, after we all went to bed, I said a brief prayer for her. It was not a long, drawn out one with dread and foreboding. I thought the whole process would be as our friend had described it, pretty routine. If I had suspected that it might be something truly serious, I might not have been so casual in my concern or in my prayer.

In the morning, I had to leave for work earlier than my wife and our friend would leave. I was about to go out the front door when our friend came up from downstairs. Giving my wife a hug and our friend a quick wave goodbye, I said, "I'm sure everything will be fine."

We planned to visit her in the hospital that evening. Just as I walked into the house that afternoon, the phone rang. I answered it. Our friend said it was all so amazing. They did not perform the operation.

"You prayed for me last night, didn't you?"

Well, yes. Just a little one."

"I knew it. When I got to the hospital, they wanted to do one more test on me just to be sure they knew exactly where the cyst was and how big it was. It was gone. Now yesterday, just before I left for your house, my doctors examined me. It was there. They have the records to prove it. Then this morning it was gone. They did find a little thing the size of a small pea. They said that didn't warrant the surgery. No one can explain what happened. That couldn't have happened, but it did. Thank you."

"There's nothing to thank me for. We loved your company. Let's get together again soon. When Anna gets home, she will be so excited about this good news. We are so happy for you."

Maybe I should have denied having anything to do with the inexplicable disappearance of her cyst more vigorously. It was really just a fleeting prayer. I felt a little guilty that I hadn't taken her condition much more seriously than I did.

A few years after the mystery of the cyst occurred, our children were eager to have a summer vacation at the beach. All of their friends seemed to be having family vacations at the beach, and our kids thought it was only fair that we have a vacation at the beach as well. My wife and I yielded to their desires by making a compromise. We would go to the beach in Virginia Beach, Virginia. That way, the kids could go to the beach during the day, and my wife and I could attend the various sessions being held at the Association for Research and Enlightenment (ARE), the Edgar Cayce Center, there. In the afternoons and evenings, we would be with the children. Both of the kids were old enough to be responsible for themselves during the day. Besides, we reasoned, the ARE Center was close to the beach and our motel. We would be able to periodically check on the kids, and they knew how to reach us at any time.

We all had a good time. Anna and I attended a few ARE seminars together as well as splitting up when there were simultaneous sessions going on that we wished to attend separately.

That was the case when the training session on developing your own psychic abilities conflicted with the prayer group presentation in which some of those at the ARE Center who prayed for others were presenting. The ARE received and continues to receive many requests for prayers to be made for specific individuals. The prayer group regularly met and prayed for those individuals. It still conducts these prayer sessions.

My session began with the instructor explaining that everyone is psychic, but most of us deny that fact. He was going to demonstrate to us that we were, in fact, psychic through an exercise in which he was about to lead us. Before he could start the demonstration, he needed us to find a partner. He directed our group of twenty-six or so people to pull all of the chairs in which we had been sitting out of the center of the room and push them against the walls. Once that was done, he told us to start walking around the open space in a random manner until we were directed to stop. After a minute or two of this meandering, he shouted, "Stop." We did. Then he directed us to identify the person closest to each of us so that we knew who our partner would be for the exercise. My partner was a woman of about thirty, plus or minus a few years.

We were directed to get two chairs and sit facing our partner.

One of the partners would be the subject and the other the psychic. After completing the exercise in that relationship, we would switch roles and repeat the exercise. My partner was a little self-conscious and wanted me to play the role of psychic first. I would rather have been the subject but yielded to her request.

The next set of instructions was for the psychic simply to look at the subject and let his imagination go on what he was thinking about the person. No restrictions should be put on any wild or absurd thoughts that came into our heads. After a few minutes of our doing this silent imagining, the instructor would announce that it was time to stop. Then the participant being the psychic would tell the subject what he had imagined during the quiet time. The subject was not to interrupt the psychic as he told her what he had imagined. Once the psychic had finished, the subject would give her reaction to what the psychic had said.

When it was time to tell my partner what I had imagined, I began by apologizing to the woman because my thoughts were so strange and bizarre. They did not make any sense. At least, we would both get a good laugh from what my imagination had produced, I told her as a way of apologizing for what I was about to relate.

With an embarrassed smile, I began, "You are riding some sort of a train, but it's not exactly a train. The sound of the wheels on the track keeps trying to establish a rhythm-like clickety-clack-clickety-clack, but the rhythm keeps getting interrupted. It is both humorous and irritating to you and the other passengers. The train seems to go in and out of tunnels, but the interior lights of the car are out of synchronicity with the tunnels. They don't always go on when the train goes into a tunnel, and they don't always go off when it enters the sunlight. People just laugh and shake their heads when this happens. Then you suddenly get hungry. You have to eat. You walk through a few cars, trying to find the dining car. Finally, you find it. It is full. You are about to leave when the maître de comes forward and escorts you to the one open seat. Three businessmen are sitting at the table. You don't know them. You take the remaining chair. The maître de hands you the menu, but you can't read it. It's like it's in a foreign language or something like that. You're embarrassed that you can't read it. In your embarrassment, you just point at something on the menu and say you want that. The maître de is taken aback by your choice and asks if you are sure that is what you wish to order. Your embarrassment is very high as you insist that is exactly what you want. Reluctantly the maître de accepts your order and walks away. The sound of the wheels on the track continues out of sync and the car goes dark in the tunnels as usual. You and the businessmen laugh. There is a big commotion at the back of the dining car. People turn to see what is going on. The maître de is leading a llama down the center isle with the assistance of a few others. He stops at your table and hands you the reins, telling you that this is the llama you have ordered."

I expected the lady to laugh at my outrageous, imaginative story. She did not. She just stared at me.

Then she said, "I live in New York City. I have to ride the subway to work and back every day. The cars and tracks are old. The wheels of the subway make the very sound you described. They are always just out of rhythm at the most annoying times. Sometimes we just laugh about it. At other times it does irritate. And the lights of the subway are just as you said. They are out of sync with coming on when it enters a tunnel and going off when it exits. We all laugh when it happens and just shake our heads. I am hypoglycemic. When I get an urge to eat, I have to eat right then. I can't help it. I have to eat or I'm in trouble, and I am always embarrassed in restaurants. I am dyslectic. I can't make sense out of the menus. In my embarrassment, I do just point at something and say that's what I want without knowing what I'm ordering. I have no idea what the llama means. Do you think I'm going on a trip or something?"

"I have no idea as to its meaning. I thought the whole story was just made up. I thought you'd find the whole thing funny. I'm amazed that so much of it fits."

"Yes, this is strange."

The instructions came for me to be the subject and the lady to be the psychic. When it came time for her to tell me what came into her mind as she silently looked at me, she told me what she was thinking. As far as I could tell there was nothing in her story that fit me, nor did it appear to be an accurate prediction of any future events. We were both disappointed. I tried to help her feel better about what she had told me. At this point, I can't remember anything that she said about me.

As time passed, it seems that several psychologists in the area knew of my interest in psychic phenomena. No one outside of my close circle of friends ever discussed the topic of psychic phenomena with me. The way that I learned that others knew of my interest came through an unexpected phone call.

The caller identified himself as Ben Berger. He said that he was a cancer patient who had just moved to Knoxville from Connecticut so that he could receive some alternative cancer treatment. He had been searching for someone with formal training in psychology who had also explored both psychic phenomena and alternative belief systems. My name kept being mentioned to him as a person who could relate to him effectively on those topics. He would like to meet with me. I could come to the apartment where he and his wife lived since it was a little difficult for him to get out. His cancer was in an advanced stage of development.

We set a time for us to meet. At that meeting, Ben explained his condition and what he hoped to gain from conversations with me. Ben was a highly successful attorney in Connecticut. He and his wife had two grown sons. When he came down with cancer in his lymphatic system, he did not want to undergo all of the chemotherapy the doctors recommended nor all of the pain medication they had prescribed. He did not want to poison his body or lose his full awareness of his thoughts and feelings. That was why he had sought out alternative therapies. Much thought and time went into his search. He was very careful about what he ate, making sure that everything was organic with no man-made chemicals in it. If he couldn't find those things, he just would not accept the alternatives. He got enough pure, healthy food to maintain his nutritional needs, he thought. A physician in California had written about having cancer and how he cured himself of it through a carefully controlled diet and the consumption of various supplements. That physician then advised other cancer patients on his newly developed treatment method; and, reportedly, they were cured as well. Unfortunately, that physician's strategies had not been scientifically researched. He was banned from practicing this kind of medicine. Sometime after that, the physician died, Ben reported.

Fortunately, Ben related he had found one of the cancer patients who had been cured under the direction of the now deceased doctor. That recovered patient lived in Knoxville and was a practicing physician. The Knoxville doctor had told him that he was not qualified as an oncologist and could not be his attending physician for his cancer treatment. However, he could work with Ben on some other related medical issues that were taking place as a result of Ben's cancer. Ben decided that he would move to Knoxville so that he could be near this recovered cancer patient. He hoped to gain from the insights the former cancer patient and physician had acquired while being treated by the California doctor.

Ben stated that he was in a considerable amount of constant pain. The pain was so great that he could not sleep except for a few minutes at a time. Despite the pain and its results, Ben was committed to following the treatment path he had set for himself. At this point, Ben assured me, his health was not failing as fast as his Connecticut doctors had predicted that it would.

Ben wanted to meet with me on a regularly scheduled basis to discuss what I thought was real about psychic phenomena and what it meant both during one's lifetime and after death. He offered to pay me for my time. I explained that I had not been formally trained in death and dying issues. Therefore, I could not accept payment for visiting with him. However, I would actually like to meet with him and discuss the whole issue of psychic phenomena and its meaning. I was still trying to understand the phenomena myself. I was aware of the power of personal belief systems and the difficulty involved in changing those belief systems. Perhaps the two of us could explore the topic together as equal partners. Ben agreed, and we began meeting together on a regular basis for approximately a year and a half.

From the first of our meetings, Ben claimed that when I was with him his pain left him. I did not know what to make of that. Often during our meetings Ben would sleep. Sometimes he would sleep as long as half an hour while I sat with him. He said that he just felt so relaxed when we were together that he just fell asleep. He reported that he could not sleep for that length of time during any other part of the day. Again, I didn't know how to respond to that statement other than to say it was fine with me if he slept the whole time that we were scheduled to be together.

As it turned out, Ben was well aware of the Cayce material and many of other writings that were new to me. He was a vigorous student of a wide variety of religions. His family had left Germany for New York City shortly before the start of the Second World War. From the best I could determine, Ben was about ten years old when the family relocated to New York. His father was a world-renowned scholar of the Jewish Kabala. Ben explained that the Kabala concerned Jewish mysticism. People from all over the world would come to his family's apartment just to talk to his father about the Kabala.

A few months into our regularly scheduled discussion sessions, Ben related that when he was about twelve years old, he had approached his father and asked him to teach him about the Kabala. His father had refused to do it. As Ben related the story, his father told him that he shouldn't spend his time studying the Kabala. Instead, he should be like his uncle and become a lawyer and make a lot of money. His father's refusal to share his knowledge about the Kabala with him was clearly upsetting to Ben. He wanted me to explore with him the reasons his father would not want to share his life's study with him. Ben and I discussed his father's life situation during that time. The family was poor. His uncle was probably helping them pay their bills. My speculations seemed to help Ben come to a degree of peace with his father over his refusal to teach him about this.

The big bulges of cancer cells on Ben's neck and in other places identified with the location of lymph nodes continued to grow as time progressed. It was clear that Ben's health was beginning to deteriorate as our meetings continued month after month. However, Ben wanted to continue the discussion sessions. We became friends. He talked about his sons and his hopes for their futures. He was proud of them. He loved his wife. He wondered what would happen to these family members after he had died. Those decisions always led back to explorations of belief systems and spirituality. Ben both challenged my own thoughts on the topics and provided me with support for my continuing explorations. He also continued to sleep during some portion of our time together and claimed to remain pain-free while I was there. I never did understand those claims.

Towards the end of his life, Ben had to be hospitalized. His condition rapidly worsened. Ben's wife kept me informed of his situation. Just before my last visit with Ben in his hospital room, his wife had informed me that Ben was very weak. He needed assistance in getting out of bed to go to the bathroom. The end was near.

When I walked into Ben's hospital room for that last visit, I was shocked to see how weak and frail he had become since I had visited with him two weeks before. I sat close to his side as we talked. We weren't speaking about anything particularly disturbing when Ben unexpectedly started crying.

Between his sobs and with anger in his voice he came close to shouting, "Why wouldn't my father teach me about the Kabala?"

I was stunned. I thought this issue had been resolved when he had brought the topic up about a year ago. This was still a burning issue with Ben. Here was this highly successful and respected attorney who had acquired many honors over the decades of his professional life still disturbed about an incident with his father that had occurred when he was twelve years old. Ben was on the verge of death; yet he was consumed with anger, sadness, and grief over this one incident. I had to do something.

"OK, Ben," I began, "I want you and me to go back to that time when you were twelve, the time when you asked your father to teach you about the Kabala. This time I am going to be you and you are going to be your father. I am going to ask your question of your father, and you are going to answer me as your father. You have two grown sons. You know how a father thinks. You know why your father answered you as he did. You will answer my questions as your father would."

Ben agreed. I proceeded to speak to Ben as he played the role of his father, and I played the role being his twelve-year-old son. I even tried to sound like a twelve-year-old as I asked, "Father, I want you to teach me about the Kabala."

Speaking as his father, Ben denied my request and told me to study and become an attorney and become rich like my uncle. I persisted, asking why he did not want to teach me since he was teaching so many others. Ben, staying in the role his father, responded to my question. I continued with a series of follow-up questions. Ben answered all of them. As his father, he explained that he was embarrassed to be so poor all of a sudden. He did not speak good English and lacked the education to be financially successful in America. Ben needed to get a good American education so that his family would not have to depend on everyone else to take care of their basic human needs, as was the case with their family. His uncle had been able to do just that. His uncle was a better example for Ben to follow in the United States than his father was. Ben would be better served to study in the New York City Schools and be successful in that system than spending his time studying the Kabala right then. As an adult, Ben could study the Kabala all he wanted. Now was not the time to be studying the Kabala. Now was the time to be studying how to succeed as an American citizen, Ben, speaking as his father, explained.

With that, Ben and I became ourselves again. We stopped role-playing. Ben was no longer crying. He had a peaceful smile. We hugged each other and said our goodbyes.

Ben's wife later reported that after I had left and she returned to his hospital room, Ben looked totally different. He had regained his natural color in his face and had renewed energy. That evening Ben got dressed and the two of them went out to a nearby restaurant and ate a regular meal. Every evening for the next several evenings or so, they left the hospital to eat their evening meal at a restaurant. Ben was able to sit up, go to the bathroom and move about his room without need of assistance. They continued to eat out for supper. At Ben's funeral reception, his wife told me that he was energetic and joyous right up to the afternoon that he quietly died while taking a nap.

Among other things, Ben taught me the importance of coming to peace with one's past. It doesn't make any difference how old you are; you are oppressed by hurtful memories until you can come to an understanding of them that gives you peace.

CHAPTER THIRTY

The Wreck

It was a brisk spring afternoon that day in 1979. The drive into Knoxville, Tennessee, was pleasant. Traveling east, the traffic was light, not jammed up the way it always was on the two lanes going west every morning. This afternoon the traffic was light in both the east and westbound lanes on I-75/40 although the westbound side of the interstate was starting to pick-up. I appreciated driving east into Knoxville at this time of day.

I wasn't paying attention to my speed. Maybe I was doing sixty. While I was in the fast lane, there really weren't any cars to pass in the right one. I simply wasn't thinking about driving. I just was. My thoughts were on how pleasant the afternoon was. I needed to meet some faculty members at the university. They were old friends. We had arranged the meeting about two weeks ago. It's always hard to match up with busy people. I was going to arrive a little early. Then it was seven miles to home. I'd get home a little early today. That's always nice.

Looking ahead, it wasn't right. What I saw wasn't right. About four miles ahead in the westbound lane there was a cloud of smoke. It was right at the end of the Paper Mill Road overpass bridge. The smoke was bluish white. Instinctively, I began to slow down. There was a car across the grass median going west. After that, there were no westbound cars. There seemed to be a traffic jam behind the blue smoke. The cars were moving, but they were behind the smoke. No one passed the smoke. There was this big space between the car that just passed my left side going west and the smoke. I slowed even more trying to make sense of it.

A car sped past me on the right. It just went on by. Glancing into the rearview mirror, I saw that the few cars behind me were slowing too. The blue smoke moved beyond the bridge. As it did, a tracker-trailer truck moved with it. The eighteen-wheeler was moving fast. Traffic behind it slowed. The traffic jam was thick.

Why doesn't anyone pass the truck?

It was in the fast lane. The lane to the right and in front of the truck was clear. Why didn't they pass? My eyes saw it all. My mind couldn't make sense of it.

I continued to slow down as the mass came towards me. The blue smoke was in front of the eighteen-wheeler.

My God!

There's a car pinned against the front of the tractor-trailer. The blue-white smoke is from his tires. The car's tires are sliding across the road, burning with the friction of being erased. Maybe some of the smoke is coming from the tires of the semi. I can't tell. They are moving fast towards me.

I am barely moving. If the driver of the car allows his front wheels to turn just the slightest, he's going to roll. He's dead. He has to hold those wheels steady. If the trucker puts too much pressure on his brakes and ends up bumping the car, the car will roll. Both drivers have to do this perfectly or the passenger car driver is dead. If a tire blows, there is death. The mass is slowing ever so slowly. Perfection or death. There is no other option.

I'm about at a stop when it hits me. If the car rolls, it will go into the grass median, down its little dip and then right up the slope into my lane. I will be part of the wreck. This thought brings my car to a stop. I stop right there. Right there in the fast lane on the interstate going east to downtown. I come to a complete stop.

The side-ways car sandwiched to the front of the eighteen-wheeler is coming towards me.

God, I can see it's a black man.

A black man is driving the car. The trucker has to be white. There has been trouble here. Racial trouble carrying over from the late sixties is still here. A decade has gone by, yet it could reappear with little or no provocation. The black man is frozen. Both hands are on the wheel. He is fighting to keep the wheels steady as they slide sideways in perfect formation. They parallel the front of the semi. His tires are being erased. They could blow at any second. He will roll.

Oh Lord, please help!

I see a woman in the front passenger side. Her mouth is open. She is screaming. Her hands are pressed against the window as if to hold the grill of the semi from pushing through.

Death rides in the air.

I am frozen in place. These people are so close to death. The mass of metal is slowing to a stop.

It gently stops. We are stopped beside each other.

The black man instantly throws open the driver's side door. He runs to the rear of the car and towards the cab of the semi.

At the same moment, the white trucker is opening his door, climbing down the steps of the truck, and jumping onto the asphalt. Then he's running towards the driver.

Oh no, I don't want a confrontation.

This could be a disaster on top of a miracle.

The two men rush towards each other.
They collide into each other's arms.
They embrace each other.
They rock in each other's arms.
Wiping tears from my face, I drive by them.
There's a meeting to attend.

CHAPTER THIRTY-ONE

Reunion

It had been five years since the last Washington High School reunion. This one was particularly special. Fifty years is a long time. The classmates came from all over the country even though the majority of them still lived in the old borough just outside the Pittsburgh city limits. Last night's banquet was primarily for our 1960 class of graduates and their spouses. There were around one hundred members of the class. About fifty-five of those graduates were in attendance. Today's picnic included members from other classes before and after ours.

My dear wife, Anna, and I arrived at the picnic right on time. Small groups had already formed with sodas or beers in hand. They were laughing and becoming reacquainted through friendly greetings and sideward glances at name tags. After getting our identification tags, which, thankfully, included the year of graduation, we mingled. Following the first few awkward conversations primarily oriented to establish the ID of the persons in the group, I excused myself to visit the restroom. It is an excellent strategy for withdrawing from the pressure of talking to strangers. At my age, I had gotten fairly comfortable with acknowledging that I needed to use the bathroom.

The vast majority of the former high school students were strangers to me. They all knew each other well. Most of them had been in school together since kindergarten or first grade. My family had moved into the community at the start of the second semester of my sophomore year. That group of young people had been especially nice to me. They quickly embraced me into their social subgroups. I made life-long friendships even though my family moved to the Texas coast the year after graduation.

However, outside of that close circle of friends, I did not interact with very many others from the classes before or after ours. There was one exception to that. It was the football team. I had been a contributor. This allowed me contact with older and younger players. Being on the football team had definitely given me a degree of status then and now.

It was time to leave the men's room and return to the gathering. Picking up a diet soda, I walked across the grass to the registration table where Anna was talking to a group of five, six, seven or so women. I knew two or three of them. After receiving quick hellos from the women I knew, and bright smiles from the ones I didn't, I stood beside sweet Anna. She was being her bubbly self, engaging the women in conversation through her artful questioning.

"You're Jerry. You're Jerry," the lady immediately to my front said to me in an excited voice. It took me and the others by surprise. It was definitely a conversation stopper. I had no idea as to who she was. "I came here specifically to see you. I did. I came specifically to apologize. I need to apologize to you."

I was stunned. My mind raced. Who was she? What was she talking about? Is this a joke? No, she is flushed in the face and agitated. What had happened between us fifty years or so ago?

"You don't know who I am, do you?" she exclaimed as she stepped up holding her blouse out for me to get a better look at her nametag.

"Well, no, I, uh," I muttered straining to read her nametag. Betty Sue something and Hampton at the bottom, with the class of '58. She was a senior when I was a sophomore. No bells ringing, as I stammered and stuttered backing slightly as she pushed her name tag closer. Looking at her face and then back at her name tag and then back at her serious stare, then, "Hampton, Hampton, you're with Russell," I shouted.

"Yes, yes, you remember!"

It flooded back into my thoughts. For a fraction of a second, I relived the moment. I hadn't been at the school much more than a month. I had stayed late after school that day for some reason. The day was dark, cold, and miserable. Immediately, I remembered it with all of the details. No one was outside the school. The cold had quickly driven everyone indoors. I was walking on the opposite side of the street from the football field hunkered down inside my heavy winter coat. The duplex we lived in was just off the end of the field on the street to the right. My name was being shouted out. Stopping, I turned to see Russell running to catch up to me. He was rapidly approaching me while displaying a big grin. Maybe he was going to say he understood, and it was over. I waited. Panting, he ran right up to me. I was smiling back at him. He ran right up to me so that his thin coat was pressing mine. I sensed the uppercut rushing to connect with my chin and pulled back as it lightly brushed the cold skin of my face.

I knew exactly what she meant. She saw the recognition in my eyes. Smiling as I recovered from my momentary loss of composure, I mumbled something like, "Oh, there is no need...you are so sweet. Thank you but..."

"No, no. I've waited all this time. I needed to tell you."

"Did you marry him?"

"Yes, we had three children."

"How is he?"

"He died of melanoma 14 years ago."

"I'm sorry..."

Moving away from the group of women who were silently puzzled by this brief but intense exchange, Betty Sue explained, "I was shocked when they asked me if I had heard about the fight behind the football field. I didn't know it would..."

We had moved far enough from the others to have a degree of privacy as she continued, "He was always getting into trouble. The classic hood. He beat people up. Almost flunked out. We dated on and off. After the Marines, that changed. He came back from Viet Nam different. He completed college in two and a half years. The Marines. Something happened to him. He was different. He became an auto body teacher at the vocational school. He did it for years."

"That's wonderful," I stated in support of her enthusiasm. "Did he have brothers or sisters?"

"There were a pack of kids at his house. None of them were treated right. They were poor. It was a bad home life."

The conversation continued, but I was having trouble following it. The memories and related emotions were flooding my consciousness. It was remarkable that she knew what she had done. She had carried it with her all this time.

At one point, I heard her say, "Having two boys fighting over me was," and then my mind raced on. This event had been with me all these years. Anna and I had discussed it several times during our married years. I had thought it was an old story long forgotten when it was smashed into my face during the thirtieth

299

reunion gathering. Anna hadn't come with me to that one.

"Well, you've stayed as lovely as you were then," I said with such skill that she blushed again. This time even her ears turned red.

As Anna and I excused ourselves from the group and were walking away, I whispered to her, "She really owed me that apology."

"Not now, we'll talk later," she said as we approached another clutch of old-timers laughing and waving their cold drinks in the air as greatness was discussed with glee.

The reunion organizers—always the same group of class members for the most part--had thought I'd been killed in Viet Nam back in the late 60s and given up trying to reach me after several failed attempts to contact me for earlier gatherings. They did get an address from my undergraduate school for the twenty-fifth gathering. That was the first one I attended. The thirtieth was the second.

At the thirtieth reunion several of us were riding in a car going out for a late-night meal at one of those all-night-breakfast-served-24 hours-a-day restaurants. Four old friends crowded in the car after finishing the evening hours in the local pub. I liked these guys. We all agreed this thirtieth reunion was the best. I was riding shotgun. My good friend, Sam, the reunion organization hub, was driving. Our class's leader, Tom, a class member beloved and admired by all, was in the back seat with Joe. I didn't know Joe all that well. He was on the fringes of our close-knit group. He never came to Tom's house on Saturday nights after we had dropped our dates off to play hearts or poker. He was just a little on the "hood" side. Now don't get me wrong. He was OK. It was just that I didn't know him as well as the other two did. They had gone all the way through elementary school into high school together. Sam and Joe had remained in the Pittsburgh area after graduation. Tom and I lived many states away.

The conversation was flowing and prompting spontaneous laughter as we tooled down the road remembering landmarks. It was good to be with old friends. Then the bombshell hit.

There was a pause in the conversation. Abruptly, Joe filled it.

"I had a beer the other night with Russell Hampton. He was in the Marines for Viet Nam."

God Almighty, that name. Those memories flooded back.

Specifically addressing me, Joe said, "Russell said he won that fight. He said he had you pinned to the ground. He was straddling you with your arms pinned to the ground. He said that he was holding you down until that storeowner came out and said he was calling the cops. Is that true?"

A question seared through my mind. Why was a guy forty-seven years old still bringing up a fight he had his senior year of high school with a sophomore? This was bad. Why was this being kept alive? Why was he keeping it fresh this late in his life? Russell's mentioning this incident at this point had to be part of a larger drama in his life.

"Yes," came my muted reply as I looked out the passenger side window. There was so much more to tell. The details told a more complicated story.

"Well, why did you let us all believe that you had won it? Why did you say you had won it?"

I stared out the window as the car passed the houses on either side of the street. My mind raced with thought. Seconds of silence that lasted for years passed with each rhythmic bump of the tires on the road. How could I answer? What would be a simple enough explanation? Every part of me was tense. Russell lived here. His ego was tied up in this. I would leave the state the next day. This was Russell's home. For some reason he needed to be known as the victor of the fight. He needed to justify himself. This was how he defined himself. These friends of mine would think I deceived them. I never said I won the fight. I told whoever would listen the details of it. I was truthful. The details told the truth. I had him, and he knew it. He knows it. If I tell it now, will he seek me out and attack? Would I have to pit my Army training against his as a marine? He would lose. I knew the basic training given Marines. It was not a match for the advanced training I had received. If the fight came, it would be desperate. My friends will think I'm a liar and a coward if I don't get the truth out. This is really important to Russell. Can I let him have his victory even though he knows it's not real? They don't know the manipulations done by the girl. They only know that he said he won. He said he had me pinned, and I lied. Could I endure my friends' thinking I was less than I was? All these thoughts raced through my mind during this long period of unspoken words.

From the back seat, Tom broke the silence, "I think it's time to change the subject."

We got to the restaurant. After ordering breakfast two or three hours before the sun would rise, we told funny stories. We laughed a while and then we all went our separate ways. Joe's question and the related issues were never brought up. I guess we all carefully avoided it for reasons only known to each of our private selves.

Over the years I would reflect on the possibility of clearing my name with these guys. I never brought it up again nor did they. I had thought about it at strange times as the years slipped by. What if I had told the story? How would it have changed Russell's life? There is no doubt his life would have changed. I could let

302

him live in his community with those he valued thinking he was---what? He knew what he was. I did not. I could never violate his need to be honored and respected as he wanted to be respected. If my friends thought less of me with this untruth in the air, then it was the way it was.

As the years passed, this moment would flicker in and out of my thoughts. The four of us in the car, the question, the long silence and then, "Time to change the subject." I doubted that he ever saw the girl after high school. He probably had a laborer's job and his marine experiences to keep him company at the beer joints he frequented. If I did tell the story, would he seek me out? Would I really be able to defend myself? My combat training did teach me one thing. You would survive because you knew what had to be done and you knew that you would do it.

Betty Sue's need to apologize at this moment, at the fiftieth reunion, triggered all these thoughts and answered my fantasy questions. He did see the girl after high school. When he got out of the Marines, he was a changed man. He was driven to make something of his life. He was successful. He married the girl, completed college, was a secondary school teacher for years and raised three children. He had been dead for fourteen years. I knew little of the truth about the man. What I had thought was the truth about the kind of life he led after high school was simply my fantasy, and in the process, I was doing him a great injustice just to feed my ego.

I was free to tell the story. Tom and Sam were here at the reunion. I could clear my name. The old British black and white movie, *Four Feathers*, suddenly popped into my head. The accused coward, the main character in the movie, was a soldier fighting in the desert with his friends. I knew how the principal character must have felt as he sent a feather back to each of the four friends as a symbol of his honor. Each of them had rejected him as a coward through sending him a feather. As I remembered the film, after the war each accuser received the feather he had given to the alleged coward. As each of them looked at the returned feather, he recalled being saved by a "native" who was the disgraced hero in disguise. Our hero knew he had been redeemed.

Well, I wasn't totally freed. If I told either of them the true story, I'd want to do it in such a way as to not embarrass Betty Sue. I particularly wanted to tell Tom.

As the picnic wore on, I found myself seeking quiet spots and reflecting on that winter day fifty-three years ago.

It began in the gym. The mixed-grade gym class was over. We were standing outside the locker room waiting for the bell to ring. Then we would go upstairs to our last class of the morning. I really didn't know many of the guys. You couldn't have expected me to know many of them. I had been attending the school a little less than a month. There were a few seniors in the class. A couple of them were representative of the stereotypical hoodlum "bad" group. You know, ducktail hair, shirtsleeves rolled up, developed arm muscles being flexed and an attitude that said, "I might stomp you if you look at me in just the wrong way." They weren't the kind of guys a skinny sophomore wanted to "irritate" unless he wanted trouble. I had left a community in South Milwaukee, Wisconsin, that was dominated by these guys. I had managed to hold my own there. I didn't want to return to that way of life. It tended to be more violent than was my nature.

BAM, two hands slammed into my chest. My back crashed into the wall. I was pinned. The fists held my shirt tight at the neck and pressed me to the wall. The worst of the senior hoods had me in his grip. Everyone was stunned.

"You been messing with my girl. Don't you talk to her again.

304

Don't you even look at her or I'll get you. I'll beat the shit out of you," he hissed into my face.

I was mad. I was scared. He was so much stronger than I was. I'm not going to let him bully me. If he thinks he can get by with this, my life is hell. I know the drill. If we go at it now, I'll get kicked out of school. Just who in hell is his GIRL? WHAT IS HE TALKING ABOUT?

Raising my arm and pointing my finger in his face while still pinned, I fixed my best Gregory Peck stare on him. With great anger but in a quietly controlled voice, I stated, "I'll talk to anyone I want. I don't know who your girl is, and I don't care. Mess with me again, and you'll pay."

Unfortunately, my eyes always tear up when I'm really angry. I was really angry. He saw my eyes watering up. The smile on his face told me he thought that I was crying, I was afraid. He thought he had me. This made me madder. This meant that he would be bolder.

"What's going on here? You boys break it up. The bell has rung. Go to your classes," the elderly gym teacher ordered. Just as quickly as I was grabbed, I was released. We dispersed rapidly.

Word spread quickly through the small high school of five hundred ninth through twelfth grade students. Russell Hampton had cornered the new kid, me. I asked some of my newfound friends who his girlfriend was. She was Betty Sue Brown, a senior too. They discreetly pointed her out to me. I had never seen her before. There was no reason for me to notice her. We clearly did not have any classes together. She was not overly attractive to me even though there was reason to understand why she might be to someone else.

I could not allow myself to be intimidated by him nor could I allow him to think that he had done so. That would be a living hell. I had seen it too many times in too many schools as my family moved across the Midwest. It was better to stand and fight and get the crap kicked out of you and then to fight again and lose again rather than become the easy prey of the bully. I hated being in this position once again. It just repeated itself over and over in every new school. One good thing had come out of it; I had acquired seasoned fighting skills. My early boxing lessons had become invaluable in these situations. Sadly, my body did not openly communicate these skills. I was wiry in body build. At a casual glance, you might even call me skinny. More heavily muscled boys my age would be amazed that they could not beat me at arm wrestling. On top of that, I did try to use various social strategies to solve a conflict rather than immediately fighting my way out of it. However, at least one good fight was forced on me at every new school. So far, I'd never lost one. If it came to fighting Russell, I risked ruining my perfect record. He was clearly much stronger than me and he had a truly mean look in his eye. Damn, I wish my eyes hadn't watered up in that confrontation.

A few days after identifying Betty Sue, I decided to speak to her. I needed to understand what was really going on. Besides, I reasoned, I had a right to speak to anyone I wanted. I was not going to be intimidated even though 1 was. I needed to establish the fact that I had not been intimidated.

My chance came at the foot of the school stairwell. We were passing each other. I spoke to her. She smiled and faced me. When I asked her if she was Russell's girlfriend she said no. They had dated a little, but she wasn't going out with him now. Anyway, she reported, he was just all talk. I shouldn't believe anything he said about her. She suggested that I talk with her at the next night's home basketball game. She would be sitting on the lefthand side of the bleachers as you walked into the basketball court. I said that I might be attending the game. If I did, I would talk with her a little more about this.

Right off, I knew that this would be trouble. I did not want to have anything to do with Peggy Sue or Betty Sue or whatever her name was. Well, yes, it was flattering to have a senior girl express interest in you, but it would infuriate Russell unless she had actually broken up with him.

It wasn't until the night of the game that I decided to go. The point was to demonstrate that I was not intimidated. I really did not want to have anything to do with the girl. She might just be using me. My desire not to be intimidated overcame my good judgment.

I saw her in the bleachers and sat beside her for about five minutes. She gave me no new information about her relationship with Russell. I left the building and went home.

The next day greeted me with great apprehension. Was this the day I got my clock cleaned? No, it wasn't. The day passed without an encounter; then the next week came and went. Russell never showed his face. The same was true for the next week, too. Apparently, the incident was over. It was a relief. I was starting to fit in. My classmates were very nice and inviting. We all seemed to enjoy each other's company. This was far better than being just outside of South Milwaukee living in Racine County, Wisconsin.

For some reason the following week I had stayed late after the school day had ended. It was probably about one of the extra-curricular activities I had signed up for. There were so many fun things to do at this school. All the kids seemed to be glad to have me join them. I liked being here.

I was just about to the end of the street beside the football field. At the corner I'd turn right. In the middle of that block was our duplex. I walked fast to get out of the cold. Even with my heavy winter coat zipped up to the neck, I was still cold.

Right in front of the little radio and TV repair shop on the corner I heard someone call my name. Turning, I looked back towards the high school. Russell was running towards me.

"Wait up, wait," he shouted as he ran towards me with enough speed to slightly billow out his light jacket.

He was smiling. For a brief moment I puzzled as to why he was calling out to me. His smile told me it was not going to be a confrontation. He may well have learned the truth. I really had nothing to do with his girlfriend and was not interested in her. His smile grew bigger as he came closer. Yes, my interpretation was correct. He was coming to apologize.

I returned his smile as he slowed his running. He ran right up to me and stopped really close to me too quickly for me to step back.

"Hi," he said with his face almost touching mine. His right fist was traveling straight up my torso. Instinctively, I turned my head to the right and slightly arched my back away from the fast rising-uppercut. As the knuckles of his fist lightly brushed my cheek in its rush to the sky, I wrapped my arms around him, trapping his left arm to his side while leaving his right arm extended above his head.

I was in a rage. He tried to deceive me to deliver a sucker punch that would have knocked me out, or worse. In our mutual rage, we wrestled in a tight embrace, quickly falling to the ground. All I could think about was hurting him as badly as I could. I was not working on a fighting strategy. I made no attempt to keep him from hurting me. I just wanted to hurt him as badly as I could. There was no thought of protecting myself from his fists. Hurt him. Hurt him. Hurt him was all the thought my mind could register.

At one point in the desperate struggle of our prone bodies on the sidewalk, my left arm became free. His face was parallel with mine as they both hovered a few inches above the concrete. My fist shot in several times to connect to the side of his nose. I popped it three, four times, maybe more. There was just enough room for me to draw my fist back two or three inches to deliver each blow. They came faster than he could turn his head to the side. Immediately, his nose gushed blood. My heavy winter jacket was seriously restricting my freedom to move. I wanted to hit him with the full force of my fury.

We twisted and turned with each trying to gain an advantage to land a blow. So far, he hadn't been able to free his arms enough to throw a punch.

Suddenly, he was on top of me. He struggled to contain my arms as I continued to try to hurt him in any way that I could. Hurt him. Hurt him. Make him hurt was my only goal, my intense reason for existing. I had to hurt him.

I was pinned. Both my arms were slightly above my shoulders as he held them by the wrists in a death-like grip while straddling my chest with his legs. His nose was bleeding in a massive stream. The blood was striking my forehead just above the hairline and flowing down through it onto the sidewalk.

Trying to raise my arms against the downward pressure of his hands and his body was too much. Instantaneously my strength drained from me. All I could do was provide enough resistance to his hands with upward pressure so that he dare not release his hold on my wrists.

He smiled at me and moved his head to direct the flow of his blood to the center of my forehead. I began to think. This rest was really helping me. My strength was coming back. In a minute or so I knew I would be strong enough to throw him off. Then I would really, really hurt him. Go ahead, let your blood flow onto my head, I thought as I smiled back. You are getting weaker as I am getting stronger. I've got you. You're mine.

"I could just punch you out now that you're pinned."

"Go ahead and try. As soon as you release my arm to pull back for a punch, I've got you! You're mine now!"

He stopped smiling. I did not. My strength came rushing back.

"Hey what's going on here?" shouted the man in the doorway of the store from the top of its landing.

We both turned our heads towards this intrusion into our intensely isolated world. The man looked down at my head and exclaimed in horror, "My God, you're killing him. All that blood. Oh my God. I'm calling the cops," he stated as he ran back inside the door.

Russell sprang to his feet and took off running down the road. I jumped up and ran down the side street to my home.

It was over.

The next morning the word was already out at school by the time I arrived. Russell and I had fought behind the football field. It seemed that everyone wanted to know the details. I told them as factually as I could. I told them that he had me pinned and his nose was spilling blood all over my head and onto the sidewalk. I told them about our conversation at the end and then the storeowner saying he was calling the police. I am not sure, but I probably told them that I knew I had him beat and would have beaten him if the man had not intervened. I never lied about it. I never exaggerated the telling of it.

For the rest of the school year, I never saw Russell. The large dark stain of his blood on the sidewalk was a daily reminder of the conflict. It remained etched into the concrete well into the summer. It was as if Russell had disappeared. I had no fear of seeing him or fighting him. I knew I could take him anytime I wanted to. I never saw Russell again or the girl until this encounter at the fiftieth reunion.

That was the first time and the last time I was ever involved in a fight in which I lost my reasoning. I was in a rage. Who knows how badly I could have hurt him if I had gotten free? I am grateful to the storeowner for having stepped in. Without him, my life would have been changed. I don't know how, but it would have been different. I must remember him in my prayers.

The reunion picnic was winding down by late afternoon. People were becoming tired from all the talking and a little listening. Anna was in the park pavilion sitting near the food tables talking to the husband of a kindly classmate of mine. When I caught her eye, I intended to signal that I was ready to leave anytime she was.

Betty Sue came walking towards me with a camera in her hand trailed by a female friend of hers. "Is it ok if Carol takes our picture together?" she asked with a bright smile, handing the camera to her.

What can I say but yes? I can't say no because I don't know what's going on here. *Why would you want your picture taken with me? What's going on?*

"Sure, that will be fine," was my pleasant response as she sidled up beside me. The flash flashed, we smiled at each other as we said goodbye and went our separate ways.

Shortly afterwards Anna joined me. "What was the picture taking all about?"

"She asked to have our picture taken. Now what could I do? Say no?"

"She had asked to take my picture earlier," Anna said in reply. "I was pleasant about it, and she was too."

"Good. At least I'm free to tell Tom the story. With Russell dead, I won't be betraying his myth."

"Be careful. You don't want to hurt the woman."

"You're right. If I can catch Tom by himself, I'll tell him, otherwise I tell him some other time. I'd really like him to know the truth about me and the fight. All he probably remembers is that conversation in the car. I want him to know that I never lied about it. I couldn't go into the details of it in the car and undermine Russell on his home turf."

Changing the topic, I went on. "I saw Tom and Joan drive off a little while ago. Let's hang around for a few minutes and see if they come back. Besides Jim wants us to see his racing video. It's about ten minutes long. If they're not back soon we'll just say our goodbyes. It's waited this long, a little longer won't make any difference."

It was agreed. We went to see Jim's video. He wanted several of his good ol' high school buddies to watch it. This was clearly his thing. The camera had been placed somewhere on the dashboard of his car as he raced around the track. He was proud of the fact that he had started out in forty-fourth place in finished in fourteenth. When the video had finished, Anna and I began the ritual of saying goodbye. We had a ten-hour drive the next day to get home. We needed to have our rest.

As we walked out of the pavilion with the last goodbyes said, I saw Tom standing in the lawn a few yards from us talking to a couple of guys. Everyone always wants to talk to Tom. We looked up to him in high school, and we value him now.

"I'll talk to him another time," I whispered to Anna as we started towards the parking lot.

The two guys talking to Tom walked away from him. He turned and looked up to see Anna and me. A big smile crossed his face as he strode over to greet us.

"You're not leaving already?" he asked, reading our intentions.

"Yes, we need to get an early start tomorrow."

"Hasn't it been great!!" he beamed.

"Yes, it has," both Anna and I affirmed.

"A strange thing happened earlier today."

"Oh, do tell," Tom blurted out, with his signature smile.

I explained about this woman from the class two years before ours saying she had come to this reunion specifically to apologize to me. He didn't recognize her name but immediately recognized Russell Hampton's last name.

"So, what did she want to apologize about?" came his more serious words.

"You remember that fight that he and I had right after I arrived our sophomore year?

"Ya?"

"And then the time of the thirtieth reunion when Sam, Joe, you, and I were driving that night after the beer bust to get a late-night breakfast, and Joe said that he talked to Russell, and Russell said that he had me pinned and won the fight until the storeowner chased us off. Joe asked why I let everyone think I'd won the fight?" I spilled out in too rapid a speech pattern.

Tom, looking puzzled replied, "No, no, I don't remember that at all. Did that really happen?"

I tried to rush through a brief version of the story. All of the drama was out of my narration except for my rapid speech pattern making for bland conversation. Tom was polite but clearly not interested as he constantly commented, "I just don't remember this at all. Did that really happen?"

During the conversation Joan, his wife, joined us. "What did I just miss?" she shot in.

"Ah," I replied, "Earlier today someone gave me a great lead-in to a short story I might write someday. It's too long to repeat now. I'll have to send you a copy of it once it's written."

We all said our goodbyes.

I was free.

CHAPTER THIRTY-TWO

Synchronicity Times Three

Synchronicity One

I remember that I couldn't get her out of my mind. It began while I was driving to work. I remember feeling that she wasn't very supportive when we worked together way back in 1969. This was about 1992, so that was twenty-three years ago. Why would I be thinking of her now?

It was my first job after leaving the Army in June of 1969. I was to be the school psychologist serving several schools in Pinellas County, Florida. When I reported for work in the middle of August, they assigned the schools to me: seven all black inner-city schools being integrated for the first time in St. Petersburg, Florida. The first year of the integration plan was to have white school staff work in the all-black schools. I assume some of the black professional educators were being sent to some of the all-white schools, but I didn't know it as a fact. The school system's plan for the second year of integration was to bus out some of the black students to the all-white schools and some of the white students to the formerly all-black schools.

I didn't have a problem working with white or black people. My experience working with black soldiers during my three years in the Army enhanced my understanding of the sameness of all races. If anything, I thought the black Army officers I worked with were equal to if not superior to their white counterparts.

The woman that I kept thinking about was an elementary principal at one of the five elementary feeder schools to the Sixteenth Street Junior High School I served, which was one of the two junior high schools that fed into Gibbs High School. There was no way I was going to remember her name. Everyone who knows me is well aware of the fact that I don't remember names very well. Remembering this elementary school principal's name would be about as impossible as remembering the name of her elementary school. There were five elementary schools, but I can only remember interactions with three other elementary school principals. The main reason I can recall the junior high and high school names is that so many dramatic things happened at those schools. Also, Sixteenth Street Junior High School had some truly outstanding guidance counselors. They were dedicated to helping children.

All day long I kept thinking about this woman. In my office at the Little Tennessee Valley Educational Cooperative, I was as busy as I could be. There were so many phone calls to make and respond to that you would think my focus could not have handled even one distraction. Yet there it was. As I would hang up the phone, there she was in my mind. As I wrote another memo to be sent to the staff, there she was. Even as I reviewed possible grant applications for needed funding of one of the cooperative's programs, this principal popped into my mind.

OK, I had to think about her. Davis, that was her last name. It just came to me. It was just there, Sallie Davis. This was remarkable! I could call her. No, that wouldn't work. There would be too many Sallie Davises living in the St. Petersburg area. I don't have the time to try to track that down. Besides, what would I say? Anyway, she probably retired years ago. Why, she might even have died. She didn't really talk to me much. Oh, she wanted to know what I was doing with her teachers when they had a classroom behavior problem, particularly when I was going to videotape the classroom situation. But she never reviewed the tapes with me or seem to want to know how it all worked out. At least, she never asked me. However, she seemed to know what was going on. From time to time I would notice her observing a classroom I was working in. She did want me to explain how I was going to implement positive reinforcement activities in general but not for a specific situation.

Now that I had twenty plus years of working with teachers, principals, and administrators, I had a little different perspective of Mrs. Davis. There was no doubt that she knew what I was doing in every classroom and with every strategy I was trying to implement to assist a troubled child. She may not have totally approved of those strategies, but she allowed me to implement them. She had to have been supporting me when some educator had objected to something I was doing. There are always those who object to any new strategy in education. They want everything to stay as it is. While "as it is" may not be working well, there is comfort in knowing that you know how to implement what is not working. It is frightening to have to try something you're not sure you can learn how to do.

Anyway, I could call Mrs. Davis and thank her for her quiet and gentle support of me and my efforts to assist her staff and students. Sure, that's what I could tell her if she were alive and if I

317

could find her. Maybe if I called St. Petersburg telephone information and asked for the number of Melrose Elementary School, I could find out how to reach her.

Wait a minute, where did I come up with the name, "Melrose Elementary School?" It just came into my head. I think that's the name of the school, but it may not be. I'm just not sure. Another hour of work passed before Mrs. Davis invaded my mind again!

Well, it's 3:00 p.m. The school secretary will be there. Oh, those elementary telephone lines are always busy this time of day. I'll never get through. There may not be a Melrose Elementary School in St. Petersburg and if there is they may never have heard of a Mrs. Sallie Davis.

At 3:15 I dialed information. They gave me the phone number for the school.

"Melrose Elementary School. May I help you?"

"Yes, this is Jerry Morton. I'm calling for a Mrs. Sallie Davis who may have been a principal at your school way back in 1969. I was a young school psychologist for the school then."

"Mrs. Davis isn't here. She left about a half hour ago for home. I can give you her home phone number."

"Sure, that would be fine."

She gave me a school principal's home phone number. This is most unusual. School staff just doesn't do that. I was just a voice on the phone. This receptionist doesn't really know who I am. A principal's home phone number is a classified bit of information to the general public. Angry parents, strange people with even stranger points of view can't have unlimited access to a principal's home phone number. This was highly unusual. What was going on?

With a great deal of hesitancy, I dialed Mrs. Davis's home phone number.

"Hello," the slightly harassed voice at the other end of the line stated.

"Mrs. Sallie Davis."

"Yes."

"This is Jerry Morton. I was your school psychologist back in 1969."

"Yes, I remember you."

Now, that was remarkable in itself, I thought.

"You have been on my mind all day. I've been thinking about you and how you quietly supported me. I wanted to thank you."

"They put you up to this, didn't they?" she stated in a matter-of-fact tone.

"No, no. I don't understand. No one put me up to calling. It's just that I have been constantly thinking about you all day. Why do you say that?"

"Come on, they put you up to this!"

"Mrs. Davis, it is just as I have said. I just wanted to call you and thank you for all you did to help me grow as a professional. That's all."

"Really? Are you sure?"

"I'm positive. I just wanted to say thank you."

"Oh, that is so nice. Thank you! You see, the reason I thought they put you up to calling is that I left the school early to get dressed for my retirement banquet tonight."

"That is so wonderful! Congratulations! I truly did not know. I am so glad I called."

"I am too. Thank you."

We said our goodbyes, and that was all there was to it.

Synchronicity Two

For years I had wanted to spend the night on top of Mt. LeConte in their camping facilities. It was the highlight of any Smoky Mountain hiker's adventure, in my opinion. The problem was that you needed to make reservations far in advance or their limited space at the highest point in the Smoky Mountains would be full. Some people had told me that you needed to make your reservations more than a year in advance. Food for the daily three meals was provided. The accommodations were reported to be somewhat primitive. The hike up the mountain was not easy. Many who started out hiking to the top decided to turn back before reaching their goal. I had only made it to the top of Mt. LeConte on one occasion. Fortunately, on that occasion, I had been in acceptable shape to make the climb without over-straining myself despite the fact that my two companions were highly regarded mountain climbers both in the Smokies and elsewhere. My companions were also in a hurry. One of the women was hosting a dinner party later that Saturday afternoon. She wanted to get to the top and back to the parked cars in near record time. We made it.

When my good friend called to say he had an extra ticket available for a guided hike and overnight stay at Mt. LeConte the coming weekend. Did I want to go? I immediately said yes. This was a wonderful opportunity to fulfill my long-held goal. I would get to do it with an accomplished backpacker who had brought me into his annual fall backpacking group twenty years or so before. Those fall hiking trips were a true highlight of adventure, fun and fellowship.

The guide would be the director of a Smoky Mountain

research project documenting the diverse plant and wildlife in the mountains. He and some staff members would take a group up to Mt. LeConte. On the way up the mountainside, the guide would point out animal signs and unusual plants. We would have supper in the Mt. LeConte dining hall, sleep overnight in one of their cabins, eat breakfast and receive a picnic type lunch for our hike down the mountain if we wanted it. John thought there would be about ten people joining the hike. He was right.

We all met at the designated parking area at the trailhead of the path we would be taking up the mountain. The appearance of various members of the group was a telling sign of their mountain experiences. Some of the participants had state-of–the-art packs ready to be mounted on their shoulders. The packs contained sipping tubes that were connected to hidden bottles of water inside them. Regardless of the quality of their packs, hiking sticks or their sweat-wicking pants and shirts, the real measure of each participant's hiking skills resided in their footwear. Most of the group's footwear was adequate with a few exceptions. One significantly overweight man was in regular shoes, the kind of leather shoe you would see worn in the shopping mall. Surely, I thought, he wouldn't be going on this hike. First of all, he was badly out of shape. I doubted he would be able to make it to the top. If he did, he would be far behind the group. The guide for the trip would have to assign a staff member just to hang back with this fellow in case he had a medical emergency. His wife was with him. Her footwear was not much better, but she appeared thin enough to make it up the mountain.

Almost everyone making the hike was with a companion. There were some married couples, a few same gender friends such as John and me, as well as one-middle aged woman who was making the hike alone.

The hike up the mountain was slow with many stops taken by our guide to show uncommon plant life along the sides of the trail. He was very knowledgeable and an easy conversationalist. As the morning moved into afternoon, we stopped for lunch.

Everyone had over-packed their individual lunches, which allowed for a lot of sharing. The sharing of food was the final icebreaker for all of the hikers to socialize. By the time we had reached the top of Mt. LeConte, we had learned a great deal about each other. This was the second time the overweight man had climbed to the top. Three days before he and his wife had made the trip with our guide. He explained that he decided that he was going to lose the weight after his doctors made it clear that his life probably depended on it. The fact that he could have a heart attack climbing up the mountain this day was a risk he was willing to take. In my mind I questioned that but had to admire his grit. He had to be in great discomfort going up the steep mountainside, but he did it. I just hoped I wouldn't have to help carry his body back down the mountain if he died.

Once at the top of Mt. LeConte we were assigned to cabins. Our cabin had two large sleeping rooms and one bedroom with a single bed. The large common area of the cabin was open with benches around a table and a few chairs scattered about. Nice rocking chairs were on the porch. It was comforting to rock in them overlooking the wide expanse of unending mountaintops below us. The large bedrooms were a surprise. The beds were primitive wooden structures with two levels that spread out close to the three walls they were not attached to. Thin mattresses covered them. They were unusually wide. Since four of us men were assigned to the room, it was obvious that there would be two people sleeping together at each level. A large woolen blanket spread over the mattress would need to be shared by the bed companions. The other big bedroom was for the two married couples with the single bedroom going to the woman hiking without a partner.

Supper was served in a large dining hall. All ten long tables were full of hungry hikers. I ended up eating at a table full of hikers from other groups. They were from several different states with two guys from England. You just had to ask a few questions to stimulate interesting discussions. It seemed everyone had some interesting experiences in their hiking adventures to share. It provided a comfortable environment in which strangers quickly became friends. The food was basic country fare and good.

After getting up before dawn the next morning to catch the morning sun rising above the mountain peaks a half mile from the cabins, John and I decided that we would start back down the mountain after breakfast. We didn't feel rushed, but we didn't want to hang around just to eat lunch on top of the mountain.

At the breakfast table the woman staying in the single room of our cabin asked if she could join us in the trek down the mountain. That was fine. About mid-morning we started down. We made good time. It's hard on your legs going down a steep mountain for hours at a time. While you don't sweat as much going down as you do going up the mountain, it's still a strain on your system. We took several rest stops. The woman began sharing her story with us.

She stated that she was between jobs at the moment. As a high-level corporate executive, she was not going to take just anything that opened up for her. She wanted to work with a company that was doing something good for society, had a strong sense of ethics and a pleasant work environment. The firm she was working for had been bought out by a larger one. She just didn't like the corporate culture the new firm represented. So, she accepted a mini-golden parachute offer, which gave her a nice financial cushion while she searched for the perfect employment.

Reflecting on her past, she wished that she could rejoin a firm she had worked for several years ago. What made that job so nice was the supervisor. He was such a considerate person. He always seemed to approach a problem in a calm, rational manner that was supportive of all the staff. With him, you just felt that the solution to the difficulty would be found, and everyone involved in finding it would be honored for his or her contribution. She was sorry she allowed herself to be lured away from that position. Maybe it was so that she could realize how important it was to have someone as competent and kind as that supervisor to work with.

As the hike down the mountain approached the lowlands, the afternoon sunlight was partially blocked by the tree leaves. This brought a pleasant coolness to our perspiring skin as well as a picturesque display of moving shadows and patches of sunlight on everything below the canopy of the trees. It was time to rest.

We approached a beautiful stream of water beside a level stretch of trail. There were ferns near the edge of the creek and wonderfully green moss on both sides of the worn trail. A welcoming log provided seating for one person with rounded rocks nearby for others to sit on. It was definitely time to stop and rest.

As the three of us approached this special spot in the Smokies, the woman concluded her account of wanting to work with the supervisor she had so admired. She finished by saying that she had tried to locate him but failed. He had left their former operation. The staff their did not know where he went from there. She tried calling all of the old phone numbers he had without success. It was as if he had just disappeared. She finished by quietly stating that she guessed she would never find him. With that she simply sat down on the log and watched the water bubble over rocks in the stream.

"Hey, what's this?" she said as she started pulling something up from a large crack located on the backside of the log.

Looking at a black, palm-sized book or pocket calendar, she held it up for John and me to see as she flipped through some pages and then declared, "It's a small *Bible. The New Testament.*"

John and I came closer to her as she looked at the first page. It had writing on it.

"It's his! It's his!" she shouted. "It's my supervisor's. It's got his name and address and phone number right here," she excitedly exclaimed.

"I know it's his new address. It's in the state his former firm thought he'd moved to. I can contact him. I know I can."

She was so excited. The short walk for our resting station to the parked cars was filled with exclamations from the woman about the unbelievable coincidence of her find. At the cars John and I gave her hearty hugs of goodbye and wished her success in contacting her former friend and supervisor.

Synchronicity Three

"Don, it's great to see you! How are you doing?" I asked my old friend in this chance meeting. It had been years since we were able to communicate although I had kept track of his activities since he left his Tennessee State Department position. We had both been highly involved in obtaining funding for services and providing services to children with disabilities over the years.

"Well! How about you?" he replied with enthusiasm.

"I've been writing and have started a podcast," I quickly replied.

"I've been writing, too. As a matter of fact, I've got a book signing this Saturday morning at the Coffee House in Maryville. Please stop by if you have a chance."

I'll make a point to do just that. We can get caught up on all of our life adventures then!"

"Until Saturday."

We waved goodbye and continued our separate journeys for the day.

As promised, there was Don with his wife in the Maryville Coffee Shop the following Saturday morning. They had a book-signing table set up on a small performance stage in the main section of the coffee shop. Don was selling one of the copies of his book to someone as we approached the signing table.

When he finished the transaction and his conversation with the buyer, he turned to me and gave me a big hug, which I warmly returned. Don had been a true advocate for children. When he retired, he continued his work by starting a foundation that advocated for children's services in his area of expertise. I had continued working with the educational cooperative and the internship consortium for several years after his retirement. Our paths during those years did not bring us together often. However, we maintained a high degree of mutual respect for the commitment each of us had in obtaining quality services for children.

Don explained the focus of his writings. They related his insights into his spiritual understanding of the world and the journey each of us has in expanding our own insights into our spirituality.

"So, tell me about your writings, Jerry. I bet they're about the many situations you found yourself in working at the cooperative," Don stated.

"Well, actually I really haven't written about my professional work and encounters during those developing years. I guess I need to get to that someday. I don't want to hurt anyone that I'd had conflict with during those times. There was a lot of conflict during those years. Implementing those new special education laws in the schools met a lot of unexpected resistance. They were good people who just didn't understand. I don't want to hurt them or make them appear to be bad. They just didn't understand, but the law had to be followed. You remember those struggles all too well," I laughingly stated.

"Yes, we had to overcome a lot of resistance. It was a struggle for them and for us."

"There is one story from those early years I have been thinking about over the last few weeks. It happened around 1980. In fact, I've been kind of obsessed with thinking about it. This one school system we both know well asked me about a junior-high-school-aged student whose mother wanted him to leave the Tennessee School for the Blind in Nashville to attend the regular junior high school in the system, the junior high school he would naturally attend if he were not a student with a disability. The school officials said he was small in stature. The system didn't think it would be appropriate to allow him to attend one of their schools. I thought the law required them to serve the child unless they could prove otherwise. They didn't like my opinion."

"You need to tell that story."

"Well, I'm reluctant to do that. Since I tested the child, I'd need his permission. I can't risk violating his confidentiality."

"Was the child really short?"

"Well, I guess you could say that."

"He was gifted, too. I'm pretty sure I know him. He's a friend of mine. I'm sure he would give you his permission. He graduated from college and did some graduate work towards a masters in psychology. Give me your email address and phone number. I will talk with him and get his permission for you to contact him. I'm certain he will want that story told."

A few days later, Don gave me the man's phone number. I contacted him. He was the person I tested back then. We reviewed what happened when I tested him. He remembered my testing him and gave his permission for me to tell the story. I told him that I would have him review the account of my interaction with him and the educators involved from that time before I made the story public. He agreed to review it to ensure its accuracy. We had already realized that the background information the school system had given me was a little inaccurate as to the facts of his situation at that time. For example, I had the name of the junior high school wrong, but its location was accurate. He provided me with insights that I did not have at that time. Here is the story as I experienced it back then.

The school system's supervisor of special education and a more senior supervisor asked me to meet them in the system's central office. This was an unusual request. Most of the system's requests of the educational cooperative came from the supervisor of special education and were most often in written form. As supervisor of the cooperative's school psychology services to the member school systems, I often found myself in stressful situations when it came to the services provided by the school psychologists and other special education service providers to the member school systems. The resistance to the new special education laws at that time was significant. The laws were making fundamental changes in how the school systems were providing education to all of their students, not just the new services to children with verified disabilities as defined by the law.

Since I had been specifically trained in the law, was a doctoral level school psychologist, had created the school psychological services delivery model for the cooperative's school systems, had trained all of the cooperative's service providers in implementation issues of the law, was the supervisor of those service providers, was the executive director of the cooperative and a due process hearing officer for the Tennessee Department of Education in adjudicating special education law in cases between school systems and parents of special needs students, I often found myself advising the cooperative's school systems to provide special education services that they did not particularly want to provide. In fact, several member school systems were so irritated with those recommendations that they were considering withdrawing from membership in the educational cooperative. The system that had just called had been in the process of internally debating the termination of its membership for several months. The principal of the junior high school the child in question would be attending was one of the leaders in the movement for his school system to cut all ties with the cooperative.

The supervisors stated that they had a mother of a blind dwarf who was insisting that her child return from the Tennessee School for the Blind in Nashville and attend regular junior high school. The mother said that her son complained that he already knew everything they were teaching in his classes at the school for the blind. He was bored. He wanted to come home and go to school at the junior high school he would normally attend. That was it. She was bringing him home and the junior high school would have to take him. They told her she would have to wait for them to work out the details. She said there was no need to wait. He was coming home. What did I think they should do?

I knew the unquestionable reality of the state and federal special education laws was that the school system would have to evaluate the child to determine if he qualified as a special needs child that could not receive an appropriate education without educational assistance. The school system and this principal would not like my recommendations to them. I was correct. They were certain that a normal educational setting, a regular junior high school, was not the proper place for this child. I explained that if the mother wanted to bring a due process hearing against the school system for refusing to evaluate the child and to develop an appropriate educational plan for the child, they would lose the case. It was that simple. No matter what the system did to avoid evaluating the child and developing an educational plan to meet the child's needs, in the end, the system would have to do it.

OK, the system agreed. They wanted one of the cooperative's school psychologists or a school psychology doctoral intern at the cooperative to do an intellectual evaluation of the child. I was unsure that the cooperative had anyone who was trained to test a blind child's intellectual abilities. I asked them for a day's time to see if we had an appropriately trained professional to conduct the evaluation. The next day I met with the supervisors to report that the educational cooperative did not have a school psychologist who had been trained to conduct such an evaluation.

"Well, what should we do?" they asked.

My suggestion was that I could do the verbal portion of an individual intelligence test as a screening measure to see how he scored on individual subtests in the verbal section as well as to obtain a composite score in verbal IQ. Naturally, I could not administer the performance half of the intelligence test, as he could not see what he was to do on that section. That section required him to respond visually to the testing tasks. The results of the verbal testing might give the school system some clues as to the intellectual functioning of the child, providing guidance for developing strategies in how to proceed in this case. They agreed. The testing date was established.

After I had tested the child, I made my report to the school system. This child, this blind child of very short stature, produced test results that found the child to have a verbal IQ in the highly gifted range as defined by the Tennessee Department of Education's Rules and Regulations for identifying gifted students.

I explained to the school system that without the performance portion of the intelligence test being administered to a child, they could not use my test results to declare the child intellectually gifted. However, it was clear to me that they would be in legal jeopardy if they did not determine to place the child in the junior high school as the mother had requested. They would have to continue their professional efforts to determine how the child's disabilities would interfere with the child's ability to receive a normal public-school education and make the appropriate adjustments. I went on to report that during the testing process the child was highly articulate and eager to please me. He was very courteous and pleasant to interact with. I thought he had the social skills to interact well with other children and adults.

The supervisors were not overly pleased with my results. The junior high school principal's body language indicated that he was "agitated" by my comments. The officials thanked me for the recommendations, indicating that they would handle the situation from then on.

That was it. I was never informed as to what was decided about the child. I did not know if an individualized educational plan had been developed for the child or if he had been allowed to attend his home junior high school.

Several months after providing the school system with my oral and written report, I was attending a regional conference for school principals and supervisors. Walking into one small session group a little late, I was surprised to see the junior high school principal who was considering admitting the blind child into his school. He was commenting to the group about a blind dwarf child.

"He was such a delight to have him in my school. I was so worried about his being in the school with all of the students. When classes would change, in all of that rushing chaos, I was afraid he would be knocked down and hurt. We assigned a football player to be with him at all times during the out-of-classroom time to protect him. The boy was so appreciative of everything anyone did for him that everyone came to like him. The football players quickly adopted him. They let it be known that he was under their protection. Our school adopted him. We all look out for him; students, teachers, staff, all of us. He is such an addition to our school. And the teachers said he knew all of the classroom material. He was up to date in every class. They agreed that he was gifted. The only problem that came up was that the boy sometimes became dehydrated towards the end of the day. He was too short to get a drink from the water fountains. He didn't want to cause anyone any kind of inconvenience, so he never asked for help getting up to the waterspout for a drink. Well, as soon as we found out about that, I had the woodworking shop make steps for every water fountain in the school. We weren't going to let this continue. This boy is such a nice person. Admitting this child into our school was the best thing we could have done."

That junior high school principal became one of the educational cooperative's strongest supporters. A few years later he was elected to a public office in his county and appointed to the cooperative's board of directors.

ABOUT THE AUTHOR

Jerry grew up in a Coast Guard family. He lived in many diverse subcultures from Northern Minnesota to the Gulf Coast of Texas. He quickly learned that strongly held social norms of one community were not believed to be valid in others. However, each community's certainty of the correctness of their interpretation of the truth did not allow for outsiders to deviate from those norms. This early awareness on Jerry's part sensitized him to look beyond the way others express themselves within their culture and focus upon the intent that motivates the observable behavior.

As time passed and Jerry continued to learn about the underlying issues that produce the behaviors in a culture, he reached the conclusion that people perceive their actions towards others to be right. They see themselves as the heroes of their scripts. From their perspective, they are justified in whatever behavior they display. Could a hero, one who is noble, just and right behave in any other way? Over time, Jerry learned to react more and more to the hero behind inappropriate behavior in finding ways to obtain his social objectives.

This developing perspective naturally led Jerry into the field of psychology. His graduate studies were interrupted by the draft system during the Viet Nam era. Fortunately, he was able to complete a master's degree in school psychology before beginning basic training. After graduating from infantry officer candidate's school, he was assigned to the Special Warfare Center to be an instructor at its psychological warfare school. The Army allowed him to study how people in various cultures processed information and communicated their thoughts and feelings through their behavior. What Jerry learned served to reinforce the idea that people see themselves as the heroes of their stories. They see their behavior as honorable and justified because they know that they are good, caring individuals. Once you understand their perspective, you can see how they can interpret their actions in this way. If their behavior produces negative consequences with others, it is due to their own misinterpretation of other people's behavior or their lack of learning more appropriate strategies to implement.

Upon leaving the Army, Jerry's first job was as a school psychologist serving seven inner-city schools being integrated for the first time. His frame-of-reference in interaction with students and school staff proved to be effective as he continued to learn.

After two years in the public schools, he returned to graduate school to obtain his doctorate in psychology, specializing in school psychology. What he learned in the Army and in the public schools enabled him to complete his program in two years.

He was then employed as the director of psychological and

special education services for a newly created educational cooperative serving school systems in East Tennessee. He began that role just as the state began implementing its new special education laws.

Jerry's experiences helped him to be an effective change agent as the cooperative's school systems struggled to understand and implement the requirements of the law for children with special needs. It also allowed him to share what he had learned with the doctoral students in school psychology under his supervision.

In the winter of 1975, the director of the cooperative died. Continuing in his role of director of psychological and special education services, Jerry also became the cooperative's director. He continued in that role until his retirement in 2014. While fulfilling those duties, at various times Jerry took on additional roles.

For example, he was a due-process-hearing officer in special education law over a ten-year period. He redesigned and directed an alternative school for five years and was the director of a consortium for a doctoral internship program in school psychology over fifteen years.

The stories in this book take you on a trip through Jerry's memories from early childhood into his adult years with events that help shape the way he learned his way of interacting with others. As time passes, he continues to learn.

Other writings of Jerry's include, *Reluctant Lieutenant: From Basic to OCS in the Sixties,* Texas A & M University Press *and A School for Healing: Alternative Strategies for Teaching At-Risk Students,* co-authored with Rosa Kennedy and published by Peter Lang Publishing.

Made in the USA
Columbia, SC
18 April 2023

15107303R10189